Bureaucracy

in

Higher

Education

Bureaucracy

in

Higher

Education

By Herbert Stroup

DEAN OF STUDENTS,
BROOKLYN COLLEGE
OF THE CITY UNIVERSITY OF NEW YORK

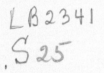

THE FREE PRESS, New York
COLLIER-MACMILLAN LIMITED, London

Collier-Macmillan Canada, Ltd., Toronto, Ontario

Library of Congress Catalog Card Number: 66–15500

FIRST PRINTING

TO

Grace,

Trudi,

and

Timothy

Cras ingens iterabimus aequor.

Horace, *Odes*, I, vii, 32

Preface

Many people consider bureaucracy as a modern, secularized Juggernaut. Like the Juggernaut, it is a mixed symbol and social form. Bureaucracy to the "enlightened" person is a term of opprobrium, while to the believer it is a source of much human good.

In this book, higher education is analyzed as a bureaucracy. The analysis, however, is not meant to praise or blame bureaucracy. Bureaucracy is society's most important social form in that much of individual and group life currently tends to take place within one or another of the bureaucracies. Large-scale organizations are the most common and obvious fact of modern social life. The college, from the standpoint of social analysis, is simply one bureaucracy among many others. It may be a god or devil to others; for the present purposes it is simply a fact of social life.

The literature on bureaucracy is relatively scant, but is growing. No effort is made in this book to debate or refine the generally established descriptions of bureaucracy. Of course, they do not all agree with each other. But the final harmonization of the variations in theory is not the basis of the present effort. Hopefully, that task can be assigned to others.

The careful reader will charge possibly that some "ideal type" of bureaucracy lurks between the lines of this book. He will be right, of course, although the creation of such a type has not been the primary concern nor is a careful delineation and defense of such a type necessary for the purposes of the book. It is hoped, however, that there are no major discrepancies in the general perspective on bureaucracy which is both assumed and at many points made explicit.

The reader, furthermore, must be warned that this book is not an exercise exclusively in sociology, anthropology, political science, education, or some other discipline. Obviously the subject of bureaucracy may be approached and has been approached from the viewpoints of many of the disciplines. An eclectic interest predominates in this book.

In this book, moreover, it is the structure and function of higher education as a bureaucracy which is deemed to be impor tant. The various chapters aim to do little more than to establish certain principles of bureaucracy as they pertain to the college and to make available certain illustrations not only from the experience of the colleges, but from other bureaucracies as well. There is no intention to describe the college in bureaucratic terms which are inapplicable to other large-scale organizations.

In analyzing higher education as a bureaucracy there is necessarily some stress upon the perplexing problems which persist in the organization of higher education. At various points some comments are given on these problems. Yet this book is not meant to be "practical." It has not taken as its objective the solution of any particular problem of the college. It should not be viewed as an administrator's handbook or as a series of earthy suggestions on how to nurture success in a difficult location. In this regard, illustrations of concrete situations, persons, and colleges have for the most part been carefully avoided. While this procedure may stifle curiosity, it may lead to the consideration of principles for their own sake.

Throughout the book, with certain unavoidable exceptions, reference is made mainly to the college as a bureaucracy. Obviously almost everything said about the college is true of the university. In fact, while the university presents a greater diversity of form, it also provides a richer variety of illustration. Perhaps the university stands out from the college on the basis of two principles: diversity and exaggeration.

The educational bureaucracy is not confined to the college and the university. It may be found in the whole of education, in the elementary school, the junior high school and the high school. Former Mayor Robert Wagner of the City of New York sought to explain the inadequacies of the public school system, operated by the Board of Education, when it came under extensive attack in 1961, by blaming "bureaucracy, red tape and excessive paper work for many of the problems of school administration." [1] Also, Martin Mayer, who spent thirty months visiting one thousand classrooms in one hundred fifty schools across the United States and Europe, notes that New York City alone has more school administrators than the whole of France, a condition which has lessened the independence of the teachers.[2]

No systematic bibliography has been provided at the close of this book. It is assumed, however, that the conscientious reader will discover enough leads in the footnotes to satisfy his inclination for further reading. Also an extensive bibliography on bureaucracy already is in existence.[3]

There is a personal factor, of course, involved in the writing of this book, but it is complex. Like every student, the author as a student has been a long-term observer of education, both higher and lower. He also has enjoyed more than twenty years of experience in higher education as a teacher (in all ranks) and as an administrator. As a professor of sociology and anthropology, moreover, he has had a continuous interest in the subject of bureaucracy. The writer's interest, however, has gone beyond the narrower confines of sociology and anthropology. Finally, the author has benefited over the years from short and extended visits to several dozens of colleges and universities throughout a large part of the United States and indeed the world. There is no substitute, too, for reading.

No assumption is made in this volume of completeness or finality. The study of higher education as a bureaucracy is only beginning. Studies involving a variety of methodologies are greatly needed. Later findings will undoubtedly modify some of the elements of the present study. This is as it should be. The present effort is tentative, preliminary, exploratory. For this reason considerable reliance has been placed upon the views of others.

For several years I have served the Danforth Foundation in several capacities. This book gives some expression to the nature of that relationship, especially to my being a Consultant on the Personalization of Education. I am indebted especially to Merrimon Cuninggim, Robert Rankin and David Zimmerman of the Foundation. Also, I have enjoyed a number of years of helpful association with the Department of Higher Education of the National Council of Churches and the Department's leaders, particularly Hubert Noble and William Lovell. Many of the ideas in this book also found expression within the Thornfield group to whom I am grateful in many ways.

I am appreciative of the help of many in the preparation of this volume. Mrs. Trudi Katzer and Miss Margaret Susan Scott have checked many technical details. Miss Thelma Aronson prepared the index. Mr. Maurice Eastmond has kindly read the entire manuscript and has offered valuable suggestions on both style and content. Mrs. Sylvia Mass, my secretary, her co-workers and the faculty members of the Department of Student Services by their devotion to regular duties have enabled me to read, think, and write. I owe a principal debt to President Harry D. Gideonse of Brooklyn College who through many years has been my mentor and friend. The author is deeply appreciative of these contributions, but is quite willing to bear the burden of any errors or misjudgments to be found in the present volume.

HERBERT STROUP

Contents

1

Bureaucracy

in

Modern

Society

*H*igher education is organizationally big. It is getting bigger. How big, then, is higher education and all education in the United States? The Office of Education has reported the facts. Detailed figures for higher education are not as precise as those for elementary and secondary education. But it was claimed that the 1964–1965 budgets for public and private institutions topped $26.9 billion. In addition to this sum, the colleges spent about $12.1 billion on buildings.

About 6.3 per cent of the Gross National Product was spent during 1964–1965 for public elementary, secondary, and higher education. This amounted to approximately $39 billion. This sum was spent for current operation, capital outlay for such things as land, buildings, and equipment, and for debt interest. This amounts to $588 for each student in daily attendance. For public elementary and secondary education in 1964–1965, localities provided 56.9 per cent, states provided 38.7 per cent, and the federal government contributed 4.3 per cent.

Education, on all levels, not only takes vast sums of money, it also embraces vast numbers of students. For fall 1965 the enrollment in schools and colleges in the continental United States was 54,200,000 as against 53,400,000 for the previous year. The total enrollment in higher education institutions in the fall of 1965 was 5,477,000 as against 2,116,440 in 1951. About 3,500,000 of the 1965 total were in publicly-controlled institutions. The contrast of the present with the more distant past makes for even more striking conclusions. The proportion of students enrolled in resident colleges at the turn of the century was about 4 per cent of the total population between eighteen and twenty-one years of age. In the fall of 1961, however, the last date for which accurate figures are available, the percentage leaped to 36.37. Education, and especially higher education, is claiming the time and talent of an increasingly larger proportion of the American population. This modern behemoth is one of the major factors in American life.

The expenditure of billions of dollars on the education of young people inevitably results in enormously large and complex organizational machinery. Ideally this machinery is intended for the purpose of aiding the educational process. It is the gears by which the educational transport moves students from ignorance to wisdom. It exists to support and enhance the life of the mind. Yet, according to a variety of critics, the organization of education frequently has little or nothing to do with true education, runs parallel to it in ignorant unconcern, or actually and maliciously thwarts the finer purposes of learning. Educational organization which does not positively maintain and enrich the educational objectives has been called many names, some unprintable. But one of the current and widespread terms of disapprobation employed in this connection is "bureaucracy." Subsumed under bureaucracy are such critical appellations as: red tape, conferencitis, reports, overbearing administration, specialization, gross institutional size, and so forth.

An illustration may inform. John Q. Academesis, the *nom de guerre* of a professor who spent years in leading universities, complains about "a lush undergrowth of nonteaching administrators" which "is choking the groves of Academe." His particular attack, of course, is upon the growth of administrative personnel within higher education—one phase of the general charge of bureaucracy. The title of his article is "A.B.—Academic Bureaucracy." [1] The professor draws a bead on his target in the first paragraph of his article:

The most striking change in American higher education during the past generation has been not the increase in the proportion of young people going to college (although this seems little short of miraculous), nor the increased number of imposing buildings and other physical facilities (even though some of them are breathtaking), nor the proliferation of courses (difficult as this may be to justify in view of the goal of a well-rounded education to develop the individual potential). Towering over all has been the phenomenal growth of administrative personnel. This largely nonteaching bureaucracy, which has shot up like a child with abnormal glands, today equals, at some institutions, the number and cost of the teaching staff.

The pseudonymous professor provides his own examples:

Consider University X. Twenty-five years ago, one definite part of its administrative work was done by one person, aided by a secretary. Ten years later, with no change in the size of the job, there were a director, an assistant, a receptionist, and two secretaries. Today, still with no basic change, there are a director, an associate director, an assistant to the director, a receptionist, and three secretaries. Or take Division K in an another university, which has had a fixed enrollment for many years. Twenty years ago, the administrative force of the division consisted of a dean and a secretary-assistant. Today, besides a dean, there are two associate deans, two vice-deans, and a battery of secretaries and assistants.

Professor Louis M. Hacker, formerly Dean of the School of General Studies of Columbia University (not hiding behind anonymity), in his final report to the University in 1958, prior to his resignation and return to teaching, established a number of recommendations. Among them, in conformity to the ideas of John Q. Academesis, was the following: dispense with "a number of nonacademic services (we have piled assistant deans and assistants to the dean, man on top of man, until this structure has reached mountainous proportions)." Shades of horrendous bureaucracy!

The attack upon bureaucratic overextension is only one type of criticism currently leveled at large-scale educational organization. Later other alleged malignancies will be analyzed in relation to the phenomenon of bureaucracy in education. For introductory purposes, however, it is clear that the term "bureaucracy" is today employed by some as an instrument of severe criticism of the existing system of education and particularly of higher education. The college, it is said scornfully, is a bureaucracy.

The truth of the matter is that if the college is a bureaucracy in these latter times, so are a number of other functions in society, such as business, the military, labor unions, the churches, and the government. Our time is characterized by organized hugeness in almost every aspect of life.[2] Hugeness is a basic condition of bureaucratic organization. In fact, bureaucracy can scarcely exist where there is not a marked degree of size in the establishment itself. It is size itself, among other conditions, which calls for the definition of the meaning and scope of a social system, its hierarchical personnel relations, the reliance upon well-circumscribed authority, the assimilation of recruits through plans of career development, the creation of group cohesiveness, the elaboration of methods of communication and restriction, and similar features of bureaucracy.

Bureaucracies are called into being whenever there are tremendously large social functions to be performed. The intermeshing of a complex economic order with features of freedom and control calls for bureaucratic arrangements.[3] The organization of national defense in a world of threat and lawlessness constitutes a challenge so great in size that bureaucratic organization is necessary.[4] Similarly, government itself, whether local, state, or federal, being a multi-billion dollar enterprise annually, must depend basically upon bureaucratic organization.[5]

As distasteful as it may seem at first glance, it appears that even crime in the United States possesses a bureaucratic structure. In the so-called old days, individually perpetrated crimes predominated, although group organized offenses also existed. But the bureaucratization of crime followed the First World War. Especially did it characterize the 1920's. Arnold Rothstein epitomized the organizing executive of that period. Leo Katcher, in summarizing Rothstein's contributions to society, says:

What was it that Rothstein did?

Basically, he transformed the world of crime from an anarchic into an authoritarian state. He gathered the loose, single strands of crime and wove them into a tapestry. He took the various elements that were needed to change crime from petty larceny into big business and fused them. The end result was a machine that runs smoothly today.[6]

In bureaucratizing crime in his time, Rothstein, as leader, necessarily was more than an individualistic criminal; he became an executive criminal, the leader of a complex social organization which reached into almost every corner of the community. He became, in Katcher's language, a "gambler, fixer, corrupter, politician, businessman, and pawnbroker." He was never convicted of breaking the law, yet he was the bureaucratic leader of crime in at least one locality. In these and other functions today, including that of education, bureaucracy has been called into existence.

Bureaucracy is not characteristic of the United States or of capitalistic countries alone. Communist societies also are bureaucratic. Commonly, they are well aware of the fact and at times speak out against it. For example, in June, 1959, former Premier Nikita Khrushchev spoke against the existence of frustrating red tape in the scientific work of the U.S.S.R. at a plenary meeting of the Central Committee of the Communist Party. In August of that year, Nikolai N. Semynonov, a vice president of the Soviet Academy of Sciences and co-winner of the Nobel Prize for Chemistry in 1956, criticized the bureaucratization of science in the country and made an appeal for a full-scale reorganization of the Academy and other scientific institutes in a full-page article in the government newspaper *Izvestia*. He claimed that he himself spent about one third of his official time on matters having no direct relation either to the sciences or to techniques.[7] Thus, in perhaps the most vaunted aspect of the Russian society there exists a degree of bureaucracy which impedes advancement. The fact is, moreover, that, despite the valiant words of its founders, communism historically has been characterized not by the absence of organization but by the superabundance of it.

In itself bureaucracy may present persistent and perplexing problems. Its critics may be justified in many of their diatribes. It may be possible, however, to overcome to a hitherto unrealized degree the inadequacies of bureaucracy. Improvement of bureaucracy without destroying it has been the aim of many critics. Marshall E. Dimock, has shown how expanding organizations can preserve the vitality of personal initiative, loyalty, and spontaneity (qualities which bureaucracy is said to threaten if not to squelch). Through the use of case histories he illustrates how industrial organizations have "successfully beaten off the stultifying effects of bureaucracy."[8]

But, whether bureaucracy can be improved or not, it will continue to exist. Its continuance is assured on the grounds that no other kind of social organization can take its place and do its work as effectively. With all its faults, it still is the one rational, dependable way of meeting big social functions, given the nature of our society. No responsible critic of bureaucracy would advocate its abolition as a social system. There may be some who long for a return to social forms appropriate to periods prior to the present, but, for the most part, these are nostalgic escapists. There is no more reason to work toward such an order than there is to build a water-tight fence to stop Niagara's flow at the brink of the falls. Bureaucratic society is a fact, not just a theory. It exists and will continue to exist. It will change, of course, as all social forms change, but its obliteration is too much to expect.

Higher education is both a reflection of the general society and a force in it. It tends to be bureaucratic in large part because the society in which it is nourished is so thoroughly bureaucratic. The similarity between the college and business, ecclesiastical bodies, the military, labor unions, and government, insofar as organization and procedures are concerned, is no idle happenstance. All are cut from the same social fabric.

Higher education also is a force in society—a bureaucratic force which tends to educate its members to an acceptance of bureaucracy. The student who learns about bureaucracy through the admissions process, the relations between departments, the requirements of the registrar's office, the student personnel program, the hierarchy of statuses in the faculty and administration, the codification of rational procedures in bulletins and other publications, becomes familiar with the anatomy of bureaucracy. The ways of doing things within the college become for him the intelligent ways of doing things generally in society, so far as social organization is concerned. They are putatively intelligent, since those who manage the college are by community definition the intelligentsia. Thus, the college is not simply an inert object influenced and molded by the social forces which are at play about it. It also is a social force in itself, shaping its own organization and educating the succeeding generations of leaders to the presumably workable and even ideal nature of organizational makeup.

The criticisms of bureaucracy have been made with deadening regularity and with emotional vehemence. Few are willing to admit as much as neutrality toward it. Yet, a strong advocacy is neither unacceptable nor undesirable. Although a long list of advantages to bureaucracy might be developed, the five which will be noted briefly here are illustrative of the total.

Bureaucracy can be efficient. The largest industrial organizations are bureaucratically-organized: General Motors, American Telephone and Telegraph, General Electric, Standard Oil of New Jersey, among others. It is too much to suppose, for example, that automobiles would be nearly as cheap, durable, and plentiful if it were not for the large automobile manufacturing companies. General Motors is the largest; its organizational and productive subdivisions sit astride the nation, geographically and economically. Yet despite its size and complex organization it is able to produce efficiently.

Of course, higher education is not General Motors in any way, shape, or form. Yet there are similarities. The large college may well be the efficient college. It is able to provide a larger faculty, with a greater number of departments and courses, and more student services than its opposite extreme. Costs, as Beardsley Ruml pointed out, may be lower.[9] In many other ways size and bureaucratic nature favor efficiency.

Bureaucracy is rational. It is unimaginable that reason would and should not be applied to the formidable challenges which our society presents: political, religious, economic, educational, etc. Bureaucracy is in large part the result of efforts in the past and present to form permanent answers to the challenges. The federal government, for example, must have some form which can be counted upon and which persists. The division of powers as formulated in the Constitution, the various laws enacted by Congress, the administrative agencies created to give effect to the decisions of Congress, and other features of the federal government constitute one part of the governmental bureaucracy. If the system were different it would still have to be a system, an arrangement which responds publicly to the orders of logic.

So, too, with higher education. Colleges have a particular organization, each having its own distinctive features. Like fingerprints, no two are alike. Yet in their more basic organizational aspects they bear a strikingly common relationship to each other. With a few exceptions, the ranks of the faculty are almost universally similar; so too, are the departmental divisions of the college. The relations between trustees, administrators, faculty, students, and others, are almost everywhere the same. And so it goes, insofar as organization is concerned. Higher education represents organizationally the rationality which generations of educators have brought to bear upon their problems of organizing education.

Bureaucracy offers opportunities. The common notion about bureaucracy is that it thwarts individuality. To some extent, as will be examined later (see Chapter 10), it does. But it also provides opportunities to those who constitute its personnel. Those who are employed by a bureaucracy often have larger work opportunities placed before them over a period of a lifetime than do those who work for themselves or in small-scale organizations. Those who enjoy the products of a bureaucracy often have a wider range of choice presented to them than otherwise.

The faculty member who teaches in a large department or college probably has more opportunities of teaching, promotion, and similar advantages than does his colleague in a smaller department or college. The larger and bureaucratically formed institution of higher learning also presents more opportunities to the student. He may find on the campus an extremely wide array of teachers, courses, services, and other benefits. The modern university consists of an almost limitless array of resources compared to the smallest colleges, both for faculty and students.

Bureaucracy offers security. The bureaucratic way of organizing a social function is to prescribe certain specialized activities as the province of particular specialists. Merit is sought for and recognized in a variety of ways; chief among these are: payment, rank, retirement, tenure. Tenure, for example, is the hallmark of bureaucracy, work in a sense being guaranteed to the worker. In fact, practically the whole range of the worker's relationship to the organization is regularized by rationally devised and written formulae.

Colleges usually offer uncommon benefits in security arrangements to their employees, especially the teaching staff. Instructors, it is claimed, in order to exercise their right of academic freedom, need particularly to be protected by the organization from incursions from the community. But, aside from such protection, colleges everywhere grant their faculties a growing number of "fringe" benefits as well as certain central features of life security. In this sense, but with some exceptions, they are similar to other bureaucratically organized enterprises. Of course, there are those within higher education, such as presidents, deans, business managers, and others, who as often as not are not granted the same degree of security as are the faculty.

Finally, bureaucracies share in competition. It might seem in the light of the literature on conformism in American life that the element of competition is no longer an existent or vital force. There are, however, few bureaucracies, if any, which are able to monopolize their fields. Under the American system of government, local, state, and federal bureaucracies stand in some measure of opposition as well as cooperation with each other. The significance of the antitrust legislation and its applications to business scarcely needs to be repeated here. General Motors still has Ford and Chrysler, as well as many other companies, here and abroad, to compete with. So too with all bureaucracies, they live by competition; even though at times and from certain perspectives they may seem to be inured to it.

Colleges also compete with each other. The liberal arts vie with the nonliberal arts, the private with the public, the Ivy League with the non-Ivy League, the denominational with the secular. Sometimes the closest rivalries are reserved for colleges within particular geographic regions, such as the state of Ohio or New England. They compete with each other in order, in business terms, to attract customers as well as to fulfill their own lofty objectives. Each claims to be distinctive.

There also is competition within the college. Faculty members compete with each other for promotion. Departments compete with each other for budgets, promotions, prestige, and in other ways. While the relations between persons and agencies within the college are regularized in rational and predictable ways, there also is a margin for upset in the arrangements, for "special cases," indeed for individuality itself.

The five proposed advantages of bureaucracy as listed and commented upon briefly here are not put forth in a spirit of contention and surely not without an awareness of the validity of some of the criticism of bureaucracy. Yet, even the Devil deserves his due. In fact, the Devil also has his uses, as Scripture and history seem amply to prove.

2

The

Nature

of

Bureaucracy

*P*eople have strong feelings about bureaucracy; seldom do they have a clear meaning of what it is in reality. They are for or against it, in whole or in part. But what it means precisely is not always made obvious.

For one thing, "bureaucracy" is an intellectual term. Not everyone uses it, since it is a long word and one which follows in a certain literary tradition. Also, it has mainly been confined to a particular segment of society—government. The so-called plain man may speak about "the organization," "the business," "the Army," "the colleges." "Bureaucracy" has a stilted aspect to it; sounding as though it were a technical word to be employed by those who are used to bandying meanings about in discussion.

The word has had a long association with "the administrative state," the agencies of government which consist of civil service employees who plan, coordinate, administer, and review the various activities of the government. In Europe, especially, bureaucracy is spoken of in quite unemotional terms as the body of government workers. In this sense, bureaucracy has no plus or minus meaning; it is simply a descriptive term.

So far as government is concerned, however, bureaucracy has taken on another meaning—government by bureaus. Bureaucracy, with this meaning attached, signifies the thwarting of democracy. It implies that the "master" of the government is not the people and their representatives in assembly. Rather, it is charged, the various bureaus of government control the decisions of government including those of the people and their representatives. "Administrative tyranny" is another way of putting it. Bureaucracy in this special sense implies, furthermore, that those who administer the government are consciously allied or even organized and that they have selfish aims in mind which are achieved by unethical and diabolic means. Bureaucracy, then, can mean the perversion of democracy. This connotation which has been tagged on to government is conveyed by some when they speak of bureaucracy in higher education.

To the extent to which the word is employed, therefore, "bureaucracy" may be said to be based on two presuppositions. One suggests that a critical purpose is being served; bureaucracy is that which is bad. The second suggests that an objective and emotionally guarded purpose is held in mind; bureaucracy is a descriptive term. In this book the effort will be made to discuss bureaucracy in higher education from a descriptive point of view. Admittedly this approach may be less satisfying to those who hold strong emotions at the mention of the word. The effort will call for the balancing to some degree of the pros and cons and the painstaking elucidation of the subject matter at hand.

It is not simple or self-evident, if one accepts the task of defining and describing bureaucracy objectively, to say exactly what it is. People differ in their conclusions even when they admit the same self-imposed methodological aim, so too with bureaucracy. Serious students of its descriptive nature differ among themselves, especially on details, as to what the phenomenon connotes. Therefore, it is desirable at this point to say how bureaucracy is conceived. Later the fundamental concept of it will be applied to higher education specifically.

For the present purposes, bureaucracy will be defined as a large-scale organization with a complex but definite social function. It consists, moreover, of a specialized personnel and is guided by a system of rules and procedures. In addition, a carefully contrived hierarchy of authority exists by which the social function of the bureaucracy is carried out impersonally.

This definition of bureaucracy is not entirely original. In fact, its main lines are borrowed from the German sociologist and historian, Max Weber. To some extent it also is shaped by the views of others, such as: Gaetano Mosca, Leonard White, Herman Finer, Robert Merton, Arnold Brecht, Peter Blau, Carl Friedrich. The principal indebtedness of practically all students of bureaucracy today, however, is owed to Max Weber (1864–1920).

Let us now break down the definition into its component parts.

A bureaucracy is a large-scale organization. In a period of history in which big organization seems to predominate, it may be difficult to conceive of a society in which other conditions have prevailed. On all sides there is the ready intrusion of bureaucratic organization. The trademarks on the commodities used daily in the home, the names of the sponsors of the most costly television shows, the most common reference of ordinary conversation, the subtle shades of perspective and value held by many, these and other hallmarks of bureaucracy exist in our time. Yet, obviously there have been periods in human history in which large-scale organizations did not predominate. Yet, although bureaucracy may not have predominated in prior periods, it has existed for a long time and has developed under a variety of cultural conditions. It existed during the Middle Ages and even as long ago as the heyday of Egyptian and Roman civilizations—at least in certain aspects.

But despite the encroachments of bureaucratic organization, there is much evidence in the modern period that nonbureaucratic organizations are thriving. This is perhaps most true in the United States where a plethora of voluntary agencies of one kind or another exist.[1] These small enterprises may have bureaucratic leanings. They may at points even ape the big organizations. But they exist not as large-scale and bureaucratic structures; they are small, voluntaristic, and confined setups. When one thinks of bureaucracy in social welfare, for example, one may consider preeminently the federal social security system. But, in contrast to it are the many small, voluntary agencies which exist in numerous instances only on a local basis. So it is with civic, educational, religious, philanthropic, and other activities within American society.

Even the predominately bureaucratic functions of government and business may prove deceptive. When bureaucratic government is mentioned, it may be the federal government which is called to mind. But there are, of course, the state governments following to some extent their own patterns of organization, each in a sense in competition with the others and with the federal government. In addition to the state governments, there are the hundreds of local governments. There is big government in the United States today. But it lives side by side with, relatively speaking, small and informally organized governments. The story is somewhat the same, although with different ingredients, in the case of business.

A bureaucracy seeks to fill a social function. It is organized very carefully in the distribution of its general function in society so that some definable and public gain is achieved. It does not exist in a conspiratorial guise to achieve purposes which are not openly declared. It is publicly accountable, whether by law, as it often is, or by public opinion.

A bureaucracy's function may be "materialistic" or "spiritualistic" or any combination of objectives. Standard Brands exists to further the production and distribution of food to satisfy human needs, but the National Council of the Churches of Christ in America exists to advance the Kingdom of God. The purposes within most bureaucracies, whether businesses or churches, are mixed. Most bureaucracies would not seek to exclude a socially acceptable aim for its claimed social function. A bureaucracy, however, may assert a hierarchy of goals. Thus, the foremost purpose of Standard Brands is not the Kingdom of God and the first aim of the National Council of Churches is not the production and distribution of food.

Commonly, bureaucracies have arisen to meet important social needs. Their objectives, to say it another way, are seldom trivial or base. They exist to create justice and social order (government), to protect the citizen from foreign enemies (the military), to channel the highest religious aspirations (ecclesiastical organizations), to meet the need for transportation (the various transport industries), to provide recreation (the baseball industry) and so forth. Not all significant social functions, even in our society, are fulfilled by bureaucracies. The family, for example, is a notable exception. Informal play groups similarly meet the needs of children, but lack a bureaucratic basis of formation.

A bureaucracy features specialization of personnel. The regular activities of a bureacracy are distributed to the personnel as fixed duties. The division of labor is clear-cut and considerably detailed. Each worker has a well-defined subfunction of the total function to perform. He knows what his work is. It is distinctively his own and he takes considerable pride in the knowledge that the entire organization rests to some degree on him for its efficiency. There may be others who perform the same task and with whom he feels a camaraderie. In fact, with them he may find his deeper personal satisfactions in work. They know best about his qualifications, his skill in performance, and even his aspirations.

On the other hand, while he stands in close association with them, he is also their competitor. When promotions are considered within the bureaucracy, he becomes competitively involved, and, as in other close associations, the pressures of prestige, preferment, and other benefits lead to rivalries. A modern definition of Hell is that condition of rivalry which exists in the same rank among the specialized personnel in a bureaucracy. Yet, both "togetherness" and rivalry are in many situations intertwined values.

Specialization in a bureaucracy provides for the recognition of gradations in competence. The person of lower status is presumedly (often not in his own eyes) less qualified by some stated standard than the person of higher rank. It may be that technical qualifications (degrees from academic institutions, service in the hinterland, relation of a personal nature to the bureaucracy's leadership, production rate, etc.) determine the nature and history of a person's status. But at its best, bureaucracy has stated standards by which persons qualify at the start and by which they proceed from lower to higher positions.

The worker in a bureaucracy is a participant in a career. He thinks of himself as fitting into a personnel system of achievement and promotion. This is the mark of the civil service, but it also is established in the nongovernmental bureaucracies. He tends to identify his interests with the success of the organization; therefore, he is willing to work hard at what he has been assigned. Because he expects to win a lifetime of recognition and emolument from the bureaucracy, he is willing to defend it against attack from the outside and under a variety of conditions also from the inside. Loyalty to the organization is a keynote of the successful bureaucrat.

The personnel in a bureaucracy think well of themselves. They are proud both on account of the loyalty which they bear to their organization and because of the nature of their specialized effort. The fact that they take part, however small the part, in a huge organization tends to magnify the importance of their positions. The idea that a chain is as strong as its weakest link can be inverted to become: a bureaucracy's reputation depends upon the expertness of every last member of its staff, or whatever qualitative distinction a bureaucracy may have is imputed to every one of its members.

The personnel also feel proud in their own knowledge and skill. The most anathematized status to a worker in a bureaucracy is that of the unskilled, for the unskilled person by definition has no genuine basis for acceptance in a highly ordered social structure. The skilled workman, on the other hand, is by definition recognized within the community as "belonging" or having an approved status simply by reason of his ability to perform a specific task successfully.

The bureaucratic organization provides an unusually higher degree of personal and familial security to its workers. Such organizations meet the career aspirations of their specialists by offering various provisions which encouarge long service. One aspect, termed tenure, provides for a lifetime of employment to the worker unless drastic and unforeseen situations arise, such as publicly indefensible immorality on the part of the worker or the failure of a legislative body to appropriate a budget for the bureau. Generous retirement systems, both in terms of early retirement and adequate income on retirement, are also features of the security arrangements. Graduated-vacation plans, health benefits, organization camps and clubs, special housing, expense accounts, and other means are a part of the bureaucracy's effort to regularize the security of its workers.

A bureaucracy is maintained by a system of rules and procedures. Those who think negatively about bureaucracy often term this feature "red tape." By this is meant the senseless employment of paper requirements for the conduct of the social function of the bureaucracy. Presumedly the required paper work is lacking in rationality. The function could be fulfilled without it.

"Red tape" also possesses the meaning of duplicativeness. By this idea is conveyed the over-requirement of paper activities, as though one copy of a request is reasonable, but three copies would be unwarranted by the situation. Unnecessary duplication and proliferation of forms constitute red tape.

At other times, red tape means over-restrictiveness. Red tape in this sense cuts down on spontaneity and creativity. Exceptions to the written-down policies are few and far between. Bureaucracy lives by the letter of the law. Creative ideas go by the board for the lack of flexibility within the organization by which policies and procedures are kept open-ended.

Of course, the use of the term "red tape" is prejudicial. It possesses the emotional bias of which objectivity also is critical. Actually, and more descriptively, what works against one's interests in a given moment, from the standpoint of organization policy and procedure, is called red tape. What works for one's interests very often is considered the expression of democracy. But, no matter how one may view rules and procedures, they are part and parcel of bureaucracy.

The activities of the bureaucracy are governed by abstract rules. These rules may be formulated by the owning, policy making, top authority person or group within the organization. They are generally not too precise or detailed. If they were so they would not be serviceable. They constitute, rather, so-called first principles, that body of generalization which establishes the ethos of the organization, its basic philosophy, the patina of "holiness" about it. These abstract rules may be expressed in the papers of incorporation, in bylaws, in policy statements by the founder, in systematic memoranda by the chief policy authority, or in other ways, singly or together. They delineate which social function the bureaucracy is seeking to fulfill and what means it will use to that end. It may prescribe the fundamental structure of the organization or set limits on its vision of its responsibilities. Without this "charter" the secondary rules and procedures lack meaningfulness.

Next to the abstract rules in depth stand the secondary rules. These are derived assumedly from the more primary principles. They may be direct and specific rationalizations of the primary principles. On the other hand, they may arise as middle-level generalizations taken from the application of the abstract rules to a variety of practical situations. Thus, there may be a kind of common-law inheritance which a bureaucracy possesses.

The purpose of this system of rules and procedures is that of providing consistency, rationality, and defensibility to the operations of a bureaucracy. By the rules every person on the staff of the organization, and even those who are not officially attached to it, know exactly what the bureaucracy is up to, what its limits are, what its established procedures are for meeting special cases, what the responsibilities are of individual workmen. The coordination of a large number of seemingly disparate and unconnected actions on the part of individual members of the bureaucracy is thereby obtained. Operation by rule is a keystone in the edifice of the large-scale organization.

Every one within a bureaucracy is bound by the regulations, from the top administrator to the lowliest worker. Theoretically, no one is able to make exceptions. Exceptions are the bane of bureaucracy. Bureaucracy is devoted to the application of law, even though some persons are unhappy and unwilling to accept such living under the law when applied to themselves. Bureaucracy behaves like justice itself—blind to individuality. Bureaucracy seeks the achievement of a certain kind of justice, one which eliminates arbitrariness and individualization.

The application of the abstract and secondary rules of an organization, however, does not in itself consist only of simple conduct. The clerk in the social security agency may be confronted only by simple decisions when it comes to filing applications. The agency's policy may dictate that alphabetical filing by name be followed. This results in a very simple act. Yet, the field worker in the same organization may find himself with considerably more responsibility and freedom to make decisions where the policy, both abstract and secondary, hardly applies in neat ways. Some latitude is allowed every worker in a bureaucracy. The degree of it, however, is less, probably much less, than in nonbureaucratic organizations.

A bureaucracy also is characterized by a hierarchy of authority. Previously it was noted that a status system prevails in a bureaucracy. This system places one person or group in a commonly well-defined position in relation to authority. Authority is graduated; each lower office is under the control of a higher one. Freedom to act is confined by the status position of the office. Each official is responsible for his own actions and those of his subordinates to the person who by definition is above him in the organization. Authority means in a bureaucracy that the higher rank has the right to issue directives and that the lower rank has the duty to obey.

All authority in a bureaucracy, however, is limited. It is limited formally by the authority which exists above it at a given point in the hierarchy. The authority above cannot be capricious. It must be responsible. It must follow the abstract and secondary rules which are binding on all. It must follow, furthermore, those aspects of the rules which are especially pertinent to the particular rank exercising the authority.

Informally, too, there are restraints upon the employment of authority. The higher order usually cannot fail to be aware of what it is able to get away with in the issuing of directives. The lower order may not debate the logic of the order, but may on other grounds feel unprepared to act upon it. Or in extreme cases there may be a disagreement between the higher and the lower orders as to the wisdom or efficiency of the directive. Higher authorities soon learn what directives they may and may not issue. Experience teaches them not what are their rights but what the lower order is willing to accept gracefully and effectively. Authority, then, paradoxically may be said to be the attitude of the lower toward the higher order; it resides in what will be accepted, both formally and informally, rather than on a quality or an ability on the part of the higher order.

It is clear that authority exercised by the higher rank is meaningful and effective only in relation to assigned responsibilities within the bureaucracy. The person showing authority is limited by the circumscribed tasks of the subordinate. The person cannot give orders regarding extra-organizational aspects of the subordinate's life, whether he will place his child in a public or private school, whether his wife will wear a hat in church or not, and so on. Authority is legitimate only in connection with the assigned duties within the rank.

Finally, a bureaucracy is governed by impersonality. The worker in a large-scale organization must of necessity remain detached from his subordinates and his clients. He cannot favor one person against another, for such partiality would play havoc with the general assumptions of bureaucracy, namely, that all decisions be made without reference to persons as such. The worker, therefore, tends to view those who work for him as equals to each other. His workers are quick to expect equal treatment. Any sign of partiality tends to work against morale. Bureaucracy calls for level-headedness and even-handedness among its workers. The official who is inclined to be overly lenient toward one subordinate or client runs the risk of having his decisions challenged (at least behind his back) in other situations in which he fails to show leniency.

The lack of emotional involvement on the part of the bureaucrat makes for certain advantages both to subordinates and clients. Each worker can be sure that he, at least, is not working at a personal disadvantage, so far as his superior is concerned. Equal opportunity, part of the American way of life, is therefore implemented in exact and detailed ways. The client may also benefit. He cannot accuse the bureaucrat objectively of bias. The worker is bound not by his feelings for the client but by the rules of the organization. He is remarkably detached as a person; therefore, it may be possible for him to provide a more objective decision. Clients, contrary to their feelings, should want an objective answer to their requests. The negative connotation of "discrimination" is removed from the procedures of a bureaucracy.

The various elements which compose a bureaucracy, as discussed in this chapter, should not be viewed as unconnected parts of a totality. They are in fact closely interwoven. Each bears a relation to the others and together they form the nature of a bureaucracy. One observer in a particular circumstance may be inclined to view a fact or event connected with a bureaucracy as fitting into one of the elements outlined above. Yet, another observer may claim that it more obviously is an illustration of another. Bureaucracy is not to be defined in terms of only one or even two of the elements that are present, although it may be said that an organization thereby has bureaucratic tendencies. In general, all of the elements are found in combination.

Again, the factors making up bureaucracy should be considered, in Max Weber's concept, as "ideal-types." By this term, Weber meant not the average of attributes of all existing bureaucracies, but a pure type. This pure type is secured by abstracting the most characteristic features of all known examples. Therefore, there may actually be exceptions in one detail or another, when the above-developed definition of bureaucracy is applied to specific cases. Just as one element does not comprise a bureaucracy, so the lack of one does not disqualify an organization from being classified as a bureaucracy.

Historical and sociological analysis shows that bureaucracies do not spring up as the result of rational decision. Certain conditions are necessary culturally for their emergence and development. One of the predisposing factors is size. So far as government is concerned, to use only one illustration, the rise of the national state and the interconnectedness between modern states brought bureaucratic government into being. It may have existed previously in the Middle Ages in some political jurisdictions, but it came into its most marked growth when localities became integrated into national systems of corporate life and government. The very development, historically, of the United States provides a most apt example of the centralization, growth, and elaboration of governmental organization. Size, sheer size, in the various social functions has lent itself to the creation and development of bureaucracy.

Probably a money economy also contributed. A money economy is part of the extreme rationaliation of life on which bureaucracy thrives. It enables persons to be paid fixed and carefully scaled sums for other work. The basis for achievement is transparently clear. Thus, the largest number of bureaucracies have come into being with the rise of the money economy.

Bureaucracies, furthermore, can scarcely exist under conditions of voluntary work or slavery. The voluntary worker does not look to his voluntary work as a career and career-mindedness is a prerequisite to the maintenance of a bureaucracy. He is inclined to be less loyal, especially in the pinch, to the organization. As for slaves, they are too dependent upon their masters to have that degree of individualized motivation on which the success of bureaucracy depends. The bureaucracy limits individual initiative, but it does not crush it. Initiative and self-interest play a strong role in large-scale organization.

Max Weber makes the claim that Protestantism has provided an ethos in which capitalism or large-scale economic enterprise has become possible.[2] According to this view, Calvinism taught that the existing social order is not God's doing, but is the result of man's corruption. Man, therefore, has the responsibility neither to adapt himself to his society nor to escape into some otherworld realm of spirituality; he is obligated to transform the world into the Kingdom of God, the divine realm. This burden, in Puritan consequences, led to the frowning upon pleasure and the praising of disciplined living, including hard work, as a significant virtue. These ideas, bolstered by the concept of double predestination, encouraged ever-expanding economic effort and achievement. Thus, the spiritual basis for the rise of modern capitalism was laid, according to Weber.

As capitalism developed, so runs the argument, it made firm and widely accepted the money economy. It also gave incentive to very large economic organizations. These, in turn, affected almost every part of life, since other segments of society were directly or indirectly forced to adapt to the economic. Government, for example, was called upon to be large and stable in order to provide the necessary political conditions upon which bureaucratic economic enterprises could flourish. The individual worker could not effectively bargain with his employer. He was forced to band together for his own protection. So, big labor unions resulted. In this view, bureaucracy was initiated in the modern period by spiritual forces, although other factors were broadly influential once the start had been made.

William H. Whyte, Jr., in contrast, believes that the Protestant ethic is no longer operative.[3] He thinks that Americans have given up the hopes and ambitions which previously characterized them. Having lost their transcendent and historical rootage they now look to the big organizations—corporation, government, university, charitable organization, or labor union—for their security. The present dominance of bureaucracy, in this view, is the result of the failure of the older and more vital perspectives and motivations and the substitution for them of the supreme value of bureaucracy itself. Bureaucracy becomes a controlling end in itself. Its support and justification no longer are based on a system of values from which it is derived. It is the top good.

But, whatever the effective causes and explanations of bureaucracy may be, it is a present fact. It is a towering fact in the experience of present-day persons. It is here to stay. Its molding and binding influence has been felt in all sectors of living, including that of education.

3

Intellect

Incorporated

A common impression today among those who criticize the bureaucratic nature or tendency of higher education is that colleges have been corrupted by business. The assumption is that business is the most fundamental of all bureaucracies and that its influence, therefore, carries over into every department of life.

This view seems to be well-founded when attention is focussed upon the governing boards of colleges. Thorstein Veblen, among others, took this stance. He spoke of the nature of the college, its business-dominated board and its business-like executive, the president, in these words:

Men dilate upon the high necessity of a business-like organization and control of the university, its equipment, personnel and routine. What is had in mind in this insistence on an efficient system is that these corporations of learning shall set their affairs in order after the pattern of a well-conducted business concern. In this view the university is conceived as a business house dealing in merchantable knowledge, placed under the governing hand of a captain of erudition, whose office it is to turn the means in hand to account in the largest feasible output. It is a corporation with large funds, and for men biased by their work-day training in business affairs it comes as a matter of course to rate the university in terms of investment and turnover. Hence the insistence on business capacity in the executive heads of the universities, and hence also the extensive range of business-like duties and powers that devolve upon them.[1]

William H. Whyte, Jr., extends Veblen's thesis. He claims, so far as higher education is concerned, that big business today dominates the thoughtways and many of the practices of the colleges. It is not just that the board of trustees and the president represent business interests and attitudes. Business in the recent decades, at the active invitation of the colleges, has taken a more direct, conscious and inclusive interest in the colleges. Says Whyte:

The union between the world of organization and the college has been so cemented that today's seniors can see a continuity between the college and the life thereafter . . . Come graduation, they do not go outside to a hostile world; they transfer. For the senior who is headed for the corporation it is almost as if it were part of one master scheme. The locale shifts; the training continues, for at the same time that the colleges have been changing their curriculum to suit the corporation, the corporation has responded by setting up its own campuses and classrooms. By now, the two have been so well molded that it's difficult to tell where one leaves off and the other begins.[2]

This observation is perhaps more true of the private than the public colleges. As private colleges feel the pinch of inflation, they eagerly look everywhere for more funds. They have systematically cultivated the alumni in ways which years ago would have been thought impossible and downright undignified. They have complaisantly taken government surplus equipment and research grants while loudly raising the cry of a theoretical danger of governmental influence. Some have urged the governments (local, state, and federal) actually to appropriate money, despite the influence disclaimer, for the subsidization of higher education. In these and other ways, colleges have appealed for money.

But one of their most effective promotions has taken place with the business community. As business becomes increasingly bureaucratic, it, too, becomes specialized in its personnel. Special-ized personnel calls for exact training. No longer is it possible for bureaucratic business to secure its workers from the ranks of the unskilled. A carefully organized, describable, and defensible sys-tem of preparation becomes indispensable to the staffing of busi-ness. Colleges are the places where this preparation is secured. So, business owes higher education an enormous and continuing debt. This indebtedness is paid the colleges by the development of a mutually beneficial relation. Business makes sizable contributions to the college; the college cooperates by selecting and training future business personnel. This, in brief, is the line of reasoning put forth by Mr. Whyte.

According to this viewpoint, bureaucratic business is a prime determiner of higher education. Whyte speaks of this influence in a chapter headed: "Business Influence on Education." The ex-tent to which this influence has pervaded the college reaches even to the point of selection for admission:

One Dean of Freshmen told me that in screening applicants from sec-ondary schools he felt it was only common sense to take into account not only what the college wanted but what, four years later, corpora-tions' recruiters would want. 'They like a pretty gregarious, active type,' he said. 'So we find that the best man is the one who's had an 80 or 85 average in school and plenty of extracurricular activity. We see little use for the "brilliant" introvert who might spend the rest of his life turning out essays on obscure portions of D. H. Lawrence's letters.' [3]

In such manner, Whyte's experience leads him to think that col-leges are, primarily, devoted service stations for the selection and training of bureaucratic personnel for business.

The case for the influence of business on colleges can be made even more strongly, if one has a mind to do it. For example, the notion that a college education is a sound economic investment for the student, and that therefore he would be willing to finance it like any other business venture has gained wide currency. This idea uproots the more traditional concept of the college as a place of learning without specific and repeated reference to its economic worth. The student studies Milton, the nature of primary groups, the makeup of the atom. What price tag should be placed upon each of these from a pragmatic, business standpoint? In the past they were presumedly studied because they were interesting in themselves and the objects of a curiosity that found its organized expression and satisfaction in higher education. But, today, the primarily economic value of a college education is judged in terms of financial return after graduation.

Naturally, this attitude may have a legitimacy for certain kinds of college students, such as those who clearly desire to rise socially and economically as a result of their education, business men and women, some professionals, and others. But for those, such as prospective teachers, the humanities scholar, the scientist, this argument scarcely is compelling in its logic. The general idea of the student financing his own education, as any other person would invest borrowed capital in a business, smacks of the influential presuppositions of business in higher education.

Similarly, cost accounting has allegedly been taken over from business by colleges. "Everything has its price" is the motto of those who seek to analyze the precise cost of every function on the campus. Should a course in Russian literature be introduced into the curriculum? What is its cost? How many students will enroll? Will it carry itself financially? Will its cost loss be offset by a new course in cosmetology? These concerns are not those merely of college administrators, who, it must be admitted, are most prone to think of them. They are also influential in shaping the thinking of the curriculum committees in a number of colleges. Needless to state, business managers of colleges are most keen in their criticisms of operations which are financially unanalyzed. There is no more reason, however, to assume that colleges should not attempt to understand themselves in terms of cost accounting than for them to be bound absolutely by what the findings might disclose. Colleges are not businesses, although they can benefit from some business methods. Yet, the extent to which they feel beholden to business practices confirms the view that business does bureaucratically influence the colleges. The same conclusions may by drawn from other business-like concerns of colleges: staff schedules, use of buildings and facilities, the curriculum, and salary arrangements.

In addition to these arguments, it may be said that the influence of business on higher education is expressed through the use of student loans as a "remedy for poverty" rather than a reward for excellence, through offering educational programs in industry, the enlarging staffs of business offices, the sprawling invasion of income-producing activities (student unions, dormitories, educational institutes, endowment management), faculty internships in industry and in other ways. By such means the "house of intellect" has been converted into a stable for the training of the prancing horses of business.

In the face of the evidence it would seem that business does exert a tremendous influence upon higher education. The colleges at times seem like spineless creatures willing to wiggle in any direction which pays off. Business holds its form of green lettuce before the nose of faithful old alma mater, who trots down the road to blissful complacency.

The whole truth, however, is seldom conveyed by those who argue for the influence of business on education. They take their stand within one of society's bureaucracies and interpret everything else in its terms. One sees whatever one's glasses permit.

The fact is that colleges are a far cry from businesses in many of their aspects. Business exists for profit as well as service, but surely no one seriously argues that higher education exists for profits. If anyone does so argue, the contrary facts stare at him boldly. The colleges have been saying for as long as they have existed that they need more money. They need more money than they have been getting just in order to break even. They also want more money to expand; their ideas always outstrip their pocketbooks. But they do not seek money for its own sake; money is desired to initiate and develop educational programs. Few businesses would long continue with the financial management characteristic of most colleges.

Again, there are complaints that the colleges are thoroughly unbusiness-like in their activities. "Bad as the quality of the liberal college curriculum is," says Beardsley Ruml, "its efficiency is even worse." [4] Colleges by and large only play with the business-derived ideas of cost accounting, plant utilization, balanced budgets, and so forth. To a degree the college is the success it is when it bucks notions taken whole cloth from business. The laboratory scientist who gives untold hours to his project, far beyond what he or anyone imagines the college pays for, is not motivated by cost accounting. To the extent that his counterpart exists in business, business is less like its stereotype. Colleges have their own ground rules for efficiency and often they are dissimilar to those which hold in business.

Business is primarily consumer conscious. It lives from the acceptance it receives of its products. Colleges are in a somewhat parallel position, except that they scarcely can be said to be business-like in their concern. Colleges may extol their special brands of education. Their catalogues are replete with self-adulating descriptions. But, from a business standpoint they do not operate efficiently. When David Riesman was asked how "consumer research" might be accomplished in higher education, he replied:

It requires a respectable group with large foundation support to be that courageous. It is fantastic that decisions which are relatively trivial are protected by law. We have consumer research when the dimensions of decision are minute—research about cars, about housewives and their preference for one or another shape of soap, about teen-agers and the bottle shapes they prefer for Coca-cola. Far more critical decisions about college choice are made by chance, by convention, by high school guidance counselors, and by all kinds of high prestige factors which operate to subordinate the youngster to the interests of the high school. I don't know the answer to the question of how such research could be done, but I think it is the most important single thing which could be done. For instance, just to publish the College Board scores or the Graduate Record Area Examination scores of colleges would be salutary.[5]

Far from operating on a business basis, so far as the investigation of their program and its fitness to the students (both actual and potential), the colleges are most unbusiness-like.

The lack of true business principles in the colleges has another feature. With few exceptions, the colleges do not produce anything for sale. Instead of taking the second and third steps whereby initiated ideas might flourish in concrete products of a marketable nature, colleges stop short. They are the creators of new ideas; not factories. They are institutions of education and their marketable product is the educated.

Thus, it appears true that business has a marked influence upon higher education, but hardly a complete and controlling one. Certain aspects of the college, as described, have come under the influence of business methods, but others have resisted. At some points the college has both been influenced and has resisted, as in cost accounting. The intermeshing influence of business upon education would in itself bear an extensive analysis before any conclusive statements could rightfully be made. But this is known: the colleges are not adjuncts to business, Veblen, Whyte, and others notwithstanding.

An elementary understanding of comparative bureaucracies in our society would indicate that the same claim can and is being made for other institutions as for business. The influences upon higher education are manifold—as wide as society itself. Some colleges are managed as extensions of ecclesiastical organizations. In the garb of the faculty, the nature of the curriculum, the composition of the sponsoring board, the language employed in bulletins and in the chapel, and in other ways, these colleges are shadows of a larger and more churchly organization.

A case could be made, moreover, for the existence of a more indirect influence of the churches upon the colleges. The subject matter of liberal arts colleges, even to this day, shows the prestige of categories of knowledge found useful to a former society in which the churches played a key role. The physical organization of many colleges, with the chapel at their center, is expressive of churchly influence. So, too, with some of the titles employed: Dean, Rector, Chancellor, Chaplain. There probably are as many divinity schools attached to private, major universities as schools of business. Harvard, for instance, in the presidency of Nathan Pusey, has given a strengthened position to its divinity school, not simply as a means for the training of parish clergymen but also for the purpose of aiding in the integration of the university through a somewhat traditional hierarchization of subject matter.

A sober view of churches and colleges, however, indicates that neither is the adjunct of the other. Harvard may have gained a new interest in religion; it scarcely is the handservant of any ecclesiastical organization. Denominational colleges may recognize a distant and vague loyalty to a churchly organization; they in most instances are highly autonomous. Religiously-derived categories may have informed higher education historically, but they seldom are to be found on the lips of curriculum committees today. The colleges of America are secularized to an amazing degree. They reflect, so far as the churches are concerned, the general society in which they have been established.

Lest anyone think that religiously-sponsored education always fails to express the pure and lofty motives and organization of the churches at their best, it must be pointed out that bureaucracy apparently is less evident among some of them. Father Joseph Fichter, then head of the Department of Sociology at Loyola University of the South in New Orleans, made an empirical study of the Roman Catholic schools in Indiana. He reported first that the public schools in the state possess the "essence of a highly bureaucratic system." He concluded that the public school had been hampered by "a rigid, stratified, complex organization" and that control "from above" had taken "decision-making for the most part out of the hands of teachers and principals." He noted "numerous" city and state regulations. "Red tape" appears necessary in the public school system, according to Professor Fichter.

"In contrast to these superimposed and restrictive practices, the parochial school seems like an island of freedom with a relaxed and informal atmosphere." "The teacher," states Father Fichter, "can make decisions on the spot and, what is more significant, she can permit some freedom of choice to her pupils." [6] In these and other ways the parochial schools in Indiana apparently have been able to resist or frustrate the influence of bureaucracy as compared with the public schools. Possibly the same conditions are to be found in some religiously sponsored colleges. If they are so found, they constitute exceptions to the general rule among colleges. Colleges, it would seem, like other institutions which fulfill social functions in our era, are notably bureaucratic. Their bureaucracy, however, can hardly be laid at the door of religious influence.

The same kind of charge can be and has been made regarding the influence of government upon higher education as has been made concerning business and religion. At the present time, somewhat more than half of the nation's students attend colleges and universities sponsored by one government (local, state, or federal) or more. Although all forms of higher education are flourishing, the largest growth has been achieved by the public institutions. The quantitative aspects of governmentally operated education, therefore, are quite impressive.

In certain respects public higher education seems to be, organizationally speaking, merely another department of government. In many instances the budgetary procedures for the public colleges follow that of the other departments of government: public works, police, fire, sanitation, social welfare, hospitals. Whatever elements are to be found in the others are regulatory for the "department" of higher education. If the other departments submit biennial requests for funds to the state legislature, then the colleges do likewise, even though some other time span may seem more suitable.

In numerous other aspects the public colleges seem to mirror the structure and procedures of government bureaucracy. The composition of the governing board may be governmentally controlled. The retirement arrangements for the teachers may be integrated into a state-wide system, covering retirement age, benefits, etc. There may be the equating of rank and salary for the college staff with other agencies of the government. Policies controlling the printing of brochures or the planting of grass seed may be centrally maintained by the government. In these and other ways the public higher education has been viewed as not merely an adjunct to government itself, but in some respects simply one branch of governmental bureaucracy. In this view the colleges are a subtopic of the general theme of government.

A paralleling argument can be made for the influence of the model of government organization for the organization of private higher education. It is commonplace for students and faculties to consider the college as a miniature political association. The students usually are organized into formal bodies. These sometimes reflect in name the larger political organization: senate; the president of the student body; the assembly; representatives. Faculties also have their own associations which often reflect in name and otherwise the political realities of the larger community. And, in speaking of names, it is possibly significant that colleges often employ titles for their agencies similar or identical to those employed in government: The Bureau of Remedial Reading, The Office of Admissions, the Department of Art. Behind the names, moreover, lie the attitudes and practices of those who administer. They, it would appear, can scarcely be differentiated in their behavior from the bureaucrats who hold responsibility in government agencies.

So it is that higher education may be viewed as reflecting the organization of other bureaucracies in society, if one is willing to begin from the standpoint of a particular bureaucracy other than that of the college. From a business point of view, the colleges may seem like business organizations. From a religious or governmental standpoint, colleges may appear to be little models of the more basic bureaucracy. Probably from a military outlook (see how neatly armed forces units fit into the academic organization), the college is primarily shaped after it.[7] Nevertheless, these interpretations are inadequate for a number of describable reasons.

First, social institutions are interrelated and interactive; one does not automatically or necessarily hold sway over the others. The statement of the influence of other bureaucracies on higher education can be made with some validity. They do influence the colleges. On the other hand, they are each influenced by the others, including the colleges. Since ours is distinctly a business culture it is predictable that business is an influential model for other organizations. For example, business relies upon advertising. In the colleges advertising is called public relations. The public relations of business and the colleges may at points seem much the same. The picture brochures of some colleges have formats strikingly similar to those produced to advertise a Grace Line cruise to Bermuda or the annual report of Standard Oil of New Jersey. Contrariwise, however, the advertisements most common today readily show the influence of scientific experimentation associated with the colleges. Two cleansers are spread on a sink and compared, two beakers of stomach acid respond to the antacid, cigarettes have a definable amount of nicotine and tars.

Similar influence is evident in disputes between corporations and labor unions. A steel strike occurs. Each side presents its case giving careful respect to a mass of statistical details. These reports have been prepared for both sides by persons trained in the colleges and employing methods of investigating, organizing evidence and presenting cases which are characteristic of college teaching on the subject. In fact, each side may be represented by college professors with Ph.D.'s who are employed as consultants.

The battle on the factual front may actually be more between two sets of college professors and their assistants than between the actual participants. In this sense, the business community is strongly influenced by the colleges. But the relationships between organizations and bureaucracies are seldom simple—a one-to-one relationship. Most commonly business, the churches, government, the military, and other bureaucracies are intertwined in their mutual influence in ways that are at times surprising and often difficult to unravel.

Second, each social organization or bureaucracy does not secure its existence by being in the service of another. Each seeks to fulfill a somewhat distinct social function. The social function of business is business. Only incidentally does business seek to educate and even then its efforts may be aimed at the enhancement of itself. So with the other bureaucracies, they have their own particular function to meet. There is overlap among the bureaucracies, but this should not obscure the core reasons for the existence of each. The colleges, at least theoretically, have been established to transmit presently known truth and to maintain the constant search for additional or more nearly perfect truth. They may employ methods, titles, budgets, and other features of other organizations. But the colleges primarily are devoted to their own responsibilities, their own social function.

Third, the colleges in themselves meet the conditions previously suggested for bureaucracies. Aside from what the nature of other organizations may be, the colleges on their own terms are bureaucratic social organizations. As has been suggested, they have their own social function. The nature of this function is "spiritualistic" rather than "materialistic," although a considerable material base is employed. The college, moreover, qualifies as a bureaucracy by reason of its complex specialization of personnel. Surely the mass of rules and procedures within colleges places them in the category of bureaucracy. Also, a hierarchy of authority is prevalent. Finally, a high degree of impersonality reigns within colleges so far as the students (the clients) and staff are concerned. Each of these elements of higher education as a bureaucracy will be described in greater detail in succeeding chapters. Here it may be stated that higher education is a bureaucracy and that by understanding it in such terms it may become more meaningful. It is too much to claim that it will be better liked, but at least it may be better understood. Harold Stoke, in this connection, says:

It is easy to inveigh against the frustrations of bureaucracy and to denounce its incompatibility with the spirit of learning; it is something else to do anything effective about it. The institutional loads exist and grow heavier and they cannot be carried without organization. With organization comes restiveness and a blind, habitual querulousness which can be quite undiscriminating . . . The academic world has much to learn about reconciling the bureaucracy of its new, diverse, and heavier responsibilities with its necessary freedom.[8]

4

The

Anatomy

of

Office

*L*loyd S. Woodburne, an experienced hand in higher education, states: "Universities have been in existence as teaching institutions for more than five hundred years . . . But a careful study of the internal operation of institutions of higher education has almost never been made." [1] Although he may be stretching the fact somewhat to meet his need, essentially he is right. Vast sums of money are spent annually for the maintenance of America's colleges, but few resources are available for extensive studies of the manner in which they operate. Almost any study, however, would need to take into account the bureaucratic character of the modern college.

In this and succeeding chapters the nature of higher education as a bureaucracy will be examined. The main features of the analysis will be taken from Max Weber and those who have modified his theory of bureaucracy. A definitive study will not be attempted, but it is hoped that at least the analysis employed will contribute toward a basic framework from which other and more detailed studies may take off.

This chapter will examine the office which the college worker holds, with its several characteristics of a bureaucratic nature and the educator as a social type.

There was a time, not so long ago, when the personnel in higher education in America was scant and informally organized. Richard Hofstadter, an historian, says:

For over a century and a half American collegiate education relied chiefly on young tutors, having in all its faculties only a handful of professors of some maturity and length of tenure. Harvard had been established for more than eighty-five years, Yale for more than fifty, and Princeton for more than twenty before each had its first professor, and it was to be many years more before regular professors outnumbered transient tutors. The only secure and sustained professional office in American collegiate education was that of the college president himself.[2]

Today by contrast the American college is a major employment enterprise. Its personnel has grown in number and complexity of specialization to a truly amazing degree. Yet, in bureaucratic fashion, practically all, if not all, of the staff of a college holds an "office."

Actually, "office" has at least three distinct meanings all of which are basic to the work of the college employee. The first refers to the status of a person. The status of a person is defined

. . . by a statement of his rights, privileges, immunities, duties, and obligations in the organization and, obversely, by a statement of the restrictions, limitations, and prohibitions governing his behavior, both determining the expectations of others in reference thereto.[3]

Thus, in the first meaning of the term, the office of the librarian is distinct from that of an hourly-paid typist.

The second definition of "office" refers to the place of work. The college employee, mainly the faculty, is characterized by having a physical area provided for at least a desk and a chair. Others (for example, the window washer or the carpenter) in the college may not have an office in this physical sense which generally implies status. The professor, moreover, commonly is faced with continuous decisions regarding his physical place of work. His status as well as his actual work requires that he have a physical area within the college. Yet for much of the academic year, he is not present on the campus. In addition, he generally likes to work in an office at his home (which he calls a "study").

An office in higher education also denotes what Weber called the "organized work process of a group." An office in this sense refers to a kind of organization or bureau. Thus, "the office of the Dean of Students is responsible for counseling," or "the Bursar's office collects all fees." In this third sense the office does not refer so much to a person or even to a status as it does to a function or set of activities.

The fact is, however, that the people who work for a college are generally holders of an office with one or all of the above meanings intended. They are not individual entrepreneurs. They are not associated in a voluntary and informal enterprise. They are officeholders.

The college officeholder does not set his own conditions for employment. These have been established by the college prior to his employment. Qualifications, which are typical of those for bureaucratic officeholders generally, may be listed in part and briefly described. Ten qualifications, not arranged in any particular order, will be reviewed.

First, competence is a basic requirement. The collegiate officeholder is appointed, in Weber's terms, to "a sphere of obligation to perform functions which have been marked off as part of a systematic division of labor." That is, the college worker by reason of education and experience has assumedly demonstrated that he is able to manage a particular set of activities which are deemed important to the total life of the college. He is a specialist or expert at something which the college prizes.

Second, the officeholder is appointed. In most instances he does not secure his office on an hereditary basis. In the medieval period all lay offices tended to become hereditary, but the rise of bureaucracies in modern times with their strong stress on competence has led to the elimination of the hereditary factor as a basis for employment. John W. Gardner describes this feature of the modern bureaucracy:

. . . it should be obvious that the modern large organization could not have emerged without the disappearance of hereditary stratification in its strict form. There have been large organizations throughout history. But in their modern form they require, among other things, flexible movement and interchange of people *on the basis of their usefulness to the organization.* This is impossible in a society which determines status on the basis of relationship. You can't give the Prince of Wales an aptitude test and start him in the stock room.[4]

Appointments are made by one's superiors in tenure, seniority, rank, or status.

Although office-holding in the college is primarily appointive, there are exceptions. In certain instances committees of a department or departments as a whole may elect a new member to the staff. Despite the employment of the voting process and the use of the term "election," the hiring of a new staff member is commonly referred to as an appointment. Again, it appears that the higher status positions within the college are commonly more open to election than to appointment. For example, the president of the college is elected by the board of trustees as is the secretary of the faculty council or senate. On the other hand, recognizing the variety of existing patterns, deans, department chairmen, business managers, and others may all be appointed to their posts by a single man, the president. Still it may be safe to say that the higher one goes in the status system of the college, the more election is employed, while the lower one goes, the less is election practiced for appointment to an office.

Third, the college officeholder, like bureaucratic officials everywhere, normally receives a fixed salary. He may have other sources of income than his college-derived salary, but a precisely formulated salary is one of the characteristics of his appointment to the staff. Not working on a commission basis or some other tenuous arrangement, the college worker is provided with a highly dependable financial income.

The fact that the salary is fixed does not mean that it is unchanging. Colleges, especially those which are governmentally supported, regularly have an official salary schedule which roughly matches the structure of the rank order of the personnel in the college. The employment of manifold differentiations in income within the college is one of its principal bureaucratic features. Such a financial system reinforces the idea of higher and lower positions and holds forth the desirability of upward mobility.

Fourth, the office in the college is characterized by rank. In substantial measure the placement of the person in the salary schedule of the college affords the most obvious index of his status. Gossip sessions in faculty dining rooms and elsewhere illustrate the importance of salary as a criterion of success. Yet the college also depends upon a formally organized system of granting recognition through the assignment of titles despite the unofficial status which may be accorded by a person's colleagues. The system is fairly uniform in American higher education, consisting of such stations as: instructor, assistant professor, associate professor, professor, department chairman, division chairman, dean, vice-president, president, chancellor. In addition, a host of other titles interpenetrate this academic-type arrangement: fellow, tutor, coordinator, director, deputy, physician, superintendent. On many large campuses it may be almost impossible for any but a few top administrators to understand the whole system of tag giving, although most officeholders seem quite willing to spend large chunks of time in trying to keep the system straight in their minds.

Mary Jane Ward tells in her novel about the college teacher who "on the score of absentmindedness . . . rated a full professorship." [5] At times it may seem to some that rank is accorded for no more substantial reason, but in the main, taking a balanced view, the ranking system of the college relates to publicly observable and sensible qualities which are possessed by officeholders. Individual employees in higher education are graded as persons; they also are graded by the status of the offices they hold. In most instances the responsibilities of the office determine its degree in the rank order of the institution.

Fifth, the collegiate officeholder regards his work as a career. It is true that college workers change employment, but it is also true that most regard their function as an end in itself. Usually this end, such as the teaching of physics, is of such a nature as to presume that the individual cannot quickly master it and pass on to more complex or exciting prospects. To be both knowledgeable in a discipline and effective as a teacher is a sufficient objective to constitute a career for a person. Tenure, a benefit granted by the institution and a fundamental feature of college organization, protects the career aspirations of the worker.

Sixth, by and large, work in and for itself is a major commitment of the college officeholder. The professor spends a great part of his life in griping about the size of his work schedule. Every teacher wishes he could teach fewer courses and students, but it seems that his over-all responsibility does not necessarily diminish by granting him a lighter teaching load. Few groups in society complain more about overwork and concomitantly provide voluntarily a more personal basis for the judgment than do college personnel. Work is all in all to them. Absorption, obsession, dedication, enthusiasm, or any similar term may be used to describe the identification of the officeholder with his work. Life for him pivots upon his special function, or upon the activity in which he participates.

A most obvious personal incentive for work in the college is the salary. It is a significant fact, moreover, that by the payment of a salary the organization secures not a specific service from the officeholder but his undifferentiated time and effort. To a significant degree the college worker puts himself, his time and effort, at the disposal of those administering the college. But, in addition, there is placed before the officeholder the attraction and possibility of promotion. He sees himself not merely for what he may be today but in terms of his prospects for tomorrow. On the other hand, neither his salary nor his prospects fully account for his utter devotion to plain hard work. It may be that he is, as the psychologists say, a "compulsive personality" who secures his major satisfactions in diligent and self-punishing work. Perhaps the all-engulfing claim of the objectives of professional development which he has accepted for himself creates a self-induced drive of major proportions. Whatever the reason, the college officeholder commonly finds the major meaning of his life in his work.

In fact, work is so important to the college officeholder that it tends to dominate all of his waking hours, much to the chagrin of his family, and even at times his sleep. Randall Jarrell humorously tells how even a professor's dreams are colored by his waking activities: "The day before, at lunch, I had heard him telling Dr. Willen about the dream he had had that night. He began: 'I dreamed that the Winter number of the *Journal of Sociometric Studies* had come early, and that it was all tables . . .'." [6]

Seventh, the college worker is characterized by a style of life that is developed in various ways. One facet of it derives from the prestige held as a result of his rank in the institution. His prestige elicits appropriate responses from persons on and off the campus. The teacher is recognized as a *professor*. He is considered and considers himself to be an influence over the lives of others.

Such an assumption realistically may be open to question, of course, or even factually denied in some sectors of the academic and general community.

In 1959, six hundred college seniors who had won Woodrow Wilson Foundation Fellowships were asked to write a one-thousand-word statement covering their intellectual interests, activities in college, and career plans. A study of their papers showed that the college seniors had not been noticeably influenced by either their high school or their college teachers in the selection of a career. About 30 per cent said that their incentive had come from actual teaching experience as a laboratory or classroom assistant, tutor, church school teacher, scout or camp leader. Only thirty mentioned the specific influence of a professor.[7] Thus the assumption by the college teacher that his style of life includes influence over the young in their choosing of careers may not be based upon reality. Yet the college teacher goes about his daily chores as if he were an influential person.

Another element in the style of life of the college officeholder is the manner in which he utilizes his leisure. The formal work schedule provides for a notable degree of seeming leisure. The individual is often responsible hour-by-hour for his own activity. A high degree of self-discipline is a characteristic requirement of the academic person. The fact and use of seeming leisure, therefore, is a component in the officeholder's style of life.

By these and other considerations the character of the college worker is formed or strengthened. He becomes, as will be examined in greater detail later, a fairly distinctive social type. Probably both institutional and self-selection factors enter into even the process of appointment so far as style of life is concerned.

Previously it was stated that a fixed salary is a characteristic of the office. Obviously, other appeals and compensations are also provided in higher education. Some of these have already been mentioned. But an eighth qualification is that of security arrangements. In most institutions the officeholder is not only paid materially for his services in money and psychically through the granting of rank, but economically again in terms of "compensation in kind." A report by a committee of the American Association of University Professors for 1959–1960 stresses and illustrates the

. . . wide ramifications of the problem of 'compensation in kind'—such as free housing—we may mention that some institutions provide their faculty free breakfasts or other meals at their cafeterias or dining halls; that some provide free firewood; and that at least one college offers free burial plots for deceased faculty members.[8]

But such security measures do not exhaust the arrangements of most colleges. The granting of tenure, by which the economic security of the individual is maximized, is a principal security feature. Adequate or generous retirement benefits, in addition to the federal social security measures, are also most important. In addition, medical services, research opportunities, sabbatical leaves, secretarial aid, and other elements enhance the office of the college employee.

It is common to assume that "compensation in kind" is a feature only of modern bureaucracy. This it not true; even medieval public servants were entitled to security benefits. Of them Thomas F. Tout says:

Besides ecclesiastical preferment, the worn-out civilian could look for pensions from the Crown, transference to less laborious or nominal service, or, at the worst, to what was called a 'corrody,' that is authority to take up his quarters in some monastery and be fed, clothed, and lodged at the expense of the monks.[9]

The modern college worker may have greater benefits than his ancient counterpart, but he is not historically unique.

Ninth, the separation of personal and organizational property is another feature of the office. Workers in higher education do not themselves own the nonhuman means of production and administration. These are provided and the accounting for them is a responsibility of the officeholder. Thus, the professor does not own any buildings, classrooms, students' seats, laboratories, examination books, and other paraphernalia associated with his office. All of these and others are provided by the institution.

The complex nature of the modern college makes it impossible for the officeholder to do other than to rely upon the institution for the material resources of his functioning. But in this regard he is not socially unique, as Robert K. Merton points out:

More and more people discover that to work, they must be employed. For to work, one must have tools and equipment. And the tools and equipment are increasingly available only in bureaucracies, private or public. Consequently, one must be employed by the bureaucracies in order to have access to tools in order to work in order to live.[10]

No one today can imagine the nuclear physicist owning the equipment necessary to his trade. Even the social scientist also in many instances is dependent upon highly organized and expensive instruments of quantitative analysis. The college Department of Buildings and Grounds, moreover, cannot assume that its workmen will themselves own such equipment as large grass mowers, asphalting machines, die presses, garbage trucks, warehouse lifts.

Yet the separation of personal and organizational property is not always psychologically complete. One of the marks of the bureaucrat is his use of such phrases as "my department," "my research," "my staff." Certain campus groups, such as librarians, perhaps because their physical facilities are more fixed than those of the teachers, regularly take attitudes which assume that they in fact do own their buildings or equipment. Such possessiveness also is shown in the scientist's use of microscopes and other equipment, and the teacher's attitude toward his office (in a sense of physical space).

Finally, the college officeholder is characterized by intense organizational loyalty. Like most bureaucrats he is thoroughly devoted to the system of which he is a part. Such loyalty is not difficult to explain; in part his personal success is dependent upon the success of his unit. For example, a purchasing agent tends readily to believe that his office or his contribution to the office managed by someone else is commendably efficient. If he is not loyal to his bureau (bureau meaning an independent administrative unit), he can scarcely expect others to accept him for what he thinks himself to be. Organizational loyalty also is induced by the officeholder's desire for advancement. Since the incentives of promotion and salary increases are important to him, he tends to give his best to his office.

A constant tendency, moreover, is apparent among college personnel to overemphasize the significance of those activities for which they are individually responsible. To the teacher of anthropology, nothing is more important than anthropology. His loyalty to the discipline tends to flow over into other areas within the institution. Also, by believing that he is part of a first-rate college, he is better able to assume that he himself and his contributions are first-rate. Sometimes the loyalty of the college worker is greater to his discipline or professional association than it is to the college as a whole, but, for the most part, as Robert O. Bowen has shown in some detail, he is warmly appreciative of the obligation which he holds toward the institution which has appointed him.[11]

These ten characteristics, then, comprise the major elements of the office which the worker in higher education holds. In themselves, they are not distinctive from those which characterize workers in other large-scale organizations, but are part and parcel of the bureaucratic nature of modern society and its enterprises. The specific content involved in the ten categories may be distinctive in degree, but not in kind. Taken together and in the manner in which they are organized in higher education, they probably do comprise a distinctive set of employment criteria.

Not only is the college somewhat distinctive by reason of the specific qualifications it establishes for its workers, but the personnel itself is probably somewhat unusual in response to the requirements. It is possible, therefore, to review briefly some of the

presumed characteristics of the educator as a social type in order
that the human dimensions of the office may be more clearly
understood.

Marshall E. Dimock observes that:

When people work together in an organization, they come to have
common understandings, prejudices, appreciations, loyalties, and outlooks similar to those of the members of a family. They have a feeling
of identity and exceptionalness which sets them apart from others.
They think in terms of 'ourselves' and 'others.' They have an awareness that the interests of the program and the symbols which are identified with it are larger and more important than the interests of any
one person connected with the organization. They tend to deperson-
alize their interests and affections and to concentrate them upon symbols
which represent programs of one kind or another—money-making,
construction, education, government, welfare, religion. In this group
spirit which develops, subtleties exist which are not perceptible to the
outsider. The longer the members of the enterprise work together, the
more complete their mutual understanding, and the more pronounced
their common likes and dislikes, the more subtle become the nuances
of meaning conveyed by their words and action.[12]

Although one can believe that every bureaucracy, including the
college, both selects and produces its own social type of personnel,
it is nevertheless difficult in the present state of knowledge to
know precisely what the college worker is like. Clearly this is a
field for investigation.

One person who thinks he knows what a college teacher is like
is Ernest Earnest:

The kind of person who becomes a college teacher is likely to be a
special breed. He has many estimable qualities: intellectual interests,
sometimes high intelligence, integrity and a genuine desire to help his
fellow man. Few college professors have been indicted for rape, swin-
dling, theft or assault and battery. Only one, a professor of chemistry
at Harvard, has been hanged for murder. On the other hand, the college teacher is likely to be introverted, conservative, overconscientious,
and sexually inhibited. Dr. Kinsey has discovered that it is the less
sexually active part of the male population which goes to college; and
it is likely that this applies especially to those men who go on to graduate work and teaching.[13]

Yet, Professor Earnest unfortunately does not provide sufficient evidence for his assertions to make them reliable.

Novelists on occasion have sought to isolate the personality elements which compose the professor as a social type. William Maxwell, for example, thinks that the professor is someone who runs away from making money in life. Thus a professor's wife, Mrs. Severance, speaks to Lymie Peters, a college student, about his future:

'William also tells me that you like poetry,' she said. 'Why don't you become a professor? It's a very pleasant life. So safe. Nothing to worry about as long as you live. You don't make any money, of course, but I can tell just by looking at you that you'll never make much money anyway. You're not the type. If I were you I wouldn't try. Settle down here and teach. William will tell you just how to go about it.' [14]

On the other hand, Kingsley Amis reasons that a person becomes a teacher of a particular specialization out of happenstance. In his novel, Dixon, a college professor, is aksed why he became a medieval specialist. Dixon replies:

. . . the reason why I'm a medievalist, as you call it, is that the medieval papers were a soft option in the Leicester course, so I specialized in them. Then when I applied for the job here, I naturally made a big point of that, because it looked better to seem interested in something specific. It's why I got the job instead of that clever boy from Oxford who mucked himself up at the interview by chewing the fat about modern theories of interpretation. But I never guessed I'd be landed with all that medieval stuff and nothing but medieval stuff. [15]

Both accounts as well as others fail to provide a substantial basis for the character delineation of college teachers or others employed in higher education.

Some college personnel may unconsciously or deliberately model themselves after images which are popular beyond the college. Thus, Theodore Caplow and Reece J. McGee in a study published in 1958 describe an academic type they call the Gentleman Adventurer. He is:

A carefree and somewhat irresponsible sort, the adventurer is a late-comer on the academic scene and wanders from realm to realm singing, telling stories, and doing well-sponsored contract research. When his record of being able to secure foundation support is sufficiently gaudy to emblazon on his shield, he becomes a chairman . . .[16]

Such a Gentleman Adventurer reminds one of the self-made business tycoon or the buccaneer of the high seas of days gone by. He is essentially an empire builder whether his empire is placed primarily within the college or in the larger community. Such a type is justifiably referred to as one of "the affluent professors." [17]

These broad-stroke delineations of the nature of the college teacher are clearly guesses and, therefore, lacking in dependability. Indeed, there are few studies which provide even the slightest idea of what the authentic character of the professor is, only guesses and questions remain.

What, then, are some of the questions? These may comprise a basis for investigation or at least for preliminary thought. Four of a much larger number will be indicated.

Is the college teacher more verbally proficient than others? If so, what others? The common assumption is that the teacher makes his living through the use of words—oral and written. Does the college office of teaching tend to select for appointment and promotion those people who "talk a lot?"

Is the college teacher dependent for his success upon his wife? In 1958, *Third Best Sport*, a popular Broadway play, starring Celeste Holm, recounted the soap-opera like trials and tribulations of the "organization wife." It was a satire on the personal behavior of the corporation man and wife—the ritual of conventions, the hierarchies of corporation life, the professional insincerities, the techniques of salesmanship, company morality, and total dedication to the success of the team. The present question is: To what extent, if at all, does the wife of the college teacher feature in his office-holding? Next to nothing is known about faculty wives, except by the faculty and their wives through the college's rumor system. What a fertile field for social investigation!

Is the college teacher a lopsided personality? That is, does he truly exemplify the cliché of the college catalogue of the "well-rounded person? Aside from his girth, he may not. He may be one-sided, narrow-gauged, specialized beyond reeducation, and defensively antagonistic to disciplines other than his own. Everyone remembers the passage in which Darwin confesses with much frankness that his humane appreciation of art and poetry has been impaired by his partisan devotion to science. How, then, do specialization and general education fit together in the life of the college teacher?

Is the college teacher "idealistic?" Is he a visionary and impractical person? The common view is that he tends to be. But is it accurate, or to what extent is it accurate? These and other questions may be directed to the officeholders within higher education.

It should be assumed that the college officeholder, like other officeholders in religion, the military, industry, and politics, tends to be molded in his personality by the characteristic sentiments, orientations, and expectations of his office. Such influences, to the extent to which their power is felt, create a social type. The "profile" of such a type in the college is not clearly known, although its importance suggests that it is a fundamental field for future research.

Quite possibly the reason why the character of the educator as a social type is difficult to locate and define is the fact that there is no single type available. The modern college is so large and complex, possessing so many attributes of the larger world of which it is a part, and so prone to the appeals and rewards which are available widely in society, that many different types of persons are able to find a spiritual as well as a vocational home within the college. It may be, as certain analytic tests intimate, that different personality types are attracted to different functions within the college. So the teachers in the several divisions, the sciences, the social sciences, and the humanities, require different character orientations. Again, it is possible that administrators represent in degree a different sort of personality organization from that of the holder, for example, of a chair in poetry. Future investigations may provide some evidence.

Another major difficulty in understanding the nature of the educator as a social type may derive from the fact that colleges generally seem unable to make up their minds as to what it is they expect the faculty to be and do. Some present conflicts in the college, which will be described in Chapter 5, give support to this view.

5

Pilgrimage

to the

Charmed

Circle

On the face of it, American higher education appears to be a bedlam. So many interests, activities, problems, aspirations, persons, and organizations exist that whatever integrative forces there are do not always appear at first glance to be effective. The campus' scatteredness is commented upon by Walter D. Wagoner:

The American campus is still an amazing melange of chapel bells, adolescent Willie Lomans, capable young adults, physical culture, convertibles, frat paddles, serious studies and beer-filled alumni, with Professor Jones lecturing sonorously on the width of Roman roads. This confusion is illustrated by the remark of a coed at one of the innumerable intercollegiate Christian conferences. About to go to bed, she remarked to her roommate, 'Oh dear, I don't know whether to do up my hair or to read my Bible.' [1]

Part of the seeming confusion may be authentic, but part of it is derived simply from the fact that the current task of higher education is such that a large and complicated battery of specialists is required for its maintenance. One of the most endlessly quoted remarks in American education contrasts thoroughly with the nature of the present situation. Speaking about Williams College's President Mark Hopkins, United States President James A. Garfield, Williams '56 (who was assassinated on his way to a Williams commencement), supposedly said that "the ideal college is Mark Hopkins on one end of a log and a student on the other." Never the reality anyway, such a notion is today preposterous. Higher education has grown from its simple beginnings to a full-blown bureaucratic venture.

Three factors have chiefly contributed to the current character of American higher education. They enforce specialization among the college's officeholders. First, the college has grown enormously in size and gives every evidence of continuing to expand. Each year an increasing number of students attend college. They require ever-enlarging staffs. Size provides the basis for specialization.

Second, the college has become increasingly more complex in its total organization. Take the curriculum as an example. Charles Homer Haskins sums up the system of education of a prior period:

The basis of education in the early Middle Ages consisted . . . of the so-called seven liberal arts. Three of these, grammar, rhetoric, and logic, were grouped as the trivium; the remaining four, arithmetic, astronomy, geometry, and music made up the quadrivium. The first group was the more rudimentary, but the second was rudimentary enough.[2]

From such simplicity the present day college is a far cry. Instead of four or seven basic disciplines, today's college can boast of several dozen major departmental divisions with, in many instances, detailed sub-divisions within these major categories. A college which does not offer several hundred courses to its students would be considered a freak in the educational world. The curriculum, as well as other aspects of the college, has greatly grown not only in size but in complexity.

Third, the nature of the educational undertaking has changed. The college in the American tradition has increasingly taken more and more responsibility for the direction and control of the student. As other institutions within the community have become more specialized, or have restricted themselves in their functioning, and as the American people have increasingly looked to their schools and colleges as the major formative influence over children and youth, the colleges have increased the scope of their responsibilities. This fact was commented upon by a former dean of Columbia College:

Today we include in our educational scheme, as the responsibility of the school, attention to many aspects of the individual that were not so considered in the early days of American education. This change of attitude means that, while we are giving our attention more effectively than ever to the intellectual development of our students, in addition to this we have become aware that their character, their health, their manners, their vocational plans, their financial problems, and even their family environment are all a part of their educational progress.[3]

The change in the nature of the enterprise of higher education has called for the presence of a larger number of specialized persons.

The personnel of the modern college, then, is distinguished by the differentiation of its work functions. Specialization is the rule rather than the exception. Each staff member has his own particular responsibilities or functions. He claims some degree of uniqueness by reason of the fact that his task is somewhat different from that of everyone else. He finds a source of pride in being needed by the organization to perform activities which presumedly no one else regularly is able to manage. What Emile Durkhein wrote as a theoretical formulation in his *Division of Labor* has become an apparent and controlling factor of higher education.[4]

Size, complexity, and the nature of the enterprise have forced specialization upon the college, but efficiency is the key element in the rationale for its continuing presence. It is assumed that any increase in specialization will increase efficiency—the academic version of the Detroit belt system of production. Although colleges say that they are interested supremely in efficiency, their actions often deny their words. Few have established efficiency studies even so far as the employment of human resources is concerned. In fact, few officeholders in the college would be able to recognize the classic, although limited, contributions on the subject by the Taylor group.[5] Studies which deal with the human and social aspects of college organization, having efficiency as their goal, are even rarer.

Despite its defects, specialization, however, as a feature of collegiate life today, is inevitable. Alfred North Whitehead says:

. . . mankind is naturally specialist. One man sees a whole subject, where another can find only a few detached examples. I know that it seems contradictory to allow for a specialism in a curriculum especially designed for a broad culture. Without contradictions the world would be simpler and perhaps duller. But I am certain that in education wherever you exclude specialism you destroy life.[6]

Knowledge itself has grown too large to be comprehended by a single mind.[7] Even members of a single department in the college have difficulties at certain points in understanding each other. The historian of economic development often faces an uncrossable abyss in his conversations with an expert in the application of statistics to economic phenomena. The professor does fulfill his career by learning "more and more about less and less." Specialization seems inevitable, whether it leads to efficiency or not, and the specialization evident in the curriculum is apparent in all aspects of the college.

Specialization has its defects; two will be mentioned. First, the specialist may become myopic or professionally deformed. He may see only the trees and never the woods. Irving Babbitt wrote of this disability:

The work that leads to a doctor's degree is a constant temptation to sacrifice one's growth as a man to one's growth as a specialist. We must be men before being entomologists. The old humanism was keenly alive to the loss of mental balance that may come from knowing any one subject too well. It was perhaps with some sense of the dangers of specialization that the ancient flute-player replied to King Philip, who wished to argue a point of music with him: 'God forbid that your Majesty should know as much about these things as I do.' [8]

Second, specialization has led in many disciplines to certain rigidities of a bureaucratic nature. The specialist acts as a member of an inner or exclusive group. He believes that he alone has the prerequisites and prerogatives of his office. He is suspicious of outsiders. They may speak about his sphere of knowledge, but always they lack that esoteric stamp which characterizes the specialist. Within the realm of specialization, moreover, there are gradations of acceptability. The profession is viewed in hierarchical terms with fewer and fewer persons being more and more competent. Thus, academic persons like to speak of colleagues who are "first," "among the very best," or "among a handful of the top authorities" within their specializations. Acceptability follows a pattern of social control established by the most specialized. These are commonly found within the precincts of a relatively few graduate schools. Thus, status within a specialization ranks higher even than mere membership within a group of specialists. The resulting exclusiveness is dramatically described by Bruce Stewart:

Specialization, by its development of authorities, has led to a new kind of medievalism. Breaking the grip of the so-called authorities of the Middle Ages was a long and literally painful process. The rebirth of human inquiry was established and the frontier opened to anyone who had sound evidence and logical presentation, regardless of who he might be. On a considerably higher plane, there has grown up a system of schools, authorities, degrees, grades, and sundry paraphernalia which operate in a more modern fashion to divert those not bearing the official stamp.[9]

The college officeholder, while on the campus, is a specialist, but in order to enhance his campus reputation as an expert he also must secure the appropriate recognition of his status from persons and agencies beyond the college. Caplow and McGee say that "success is likely to come to the man who has learned to neglect his assigned duties" in favor of his "private professional interests." [10] Four of the more common ways by which the office-holder in higher education increases his acceptance on the campus by engaging in off-campus activities command attention here.

First, there is the phenomenon known as "reading papers." Reading papers at professional conventions increases one's prestige generally with co-specialists in one's discipline. It is taken as a sign of creativity and leadership. Professional associations organize annual meetings on a regional or national scale for the actual purpose of providing opportunities for mutual status advancement, in addition to the ostensible prospect that some new or old truth may be communicated. The very size of these conventions and the large number of the participants in them would seem to preclude the assumption that advancing the truth is the primary or sole purpose. Professional conventions for the specialist are a form of conspicuous display.

Douglas N. Morgan points out in an article that "pay, promotion, and reputation" for the college teacher depend upon his success in reading papers at professional conventions. He analyzes the pitfalls in the reading of papers (badly read, windy, too complex, pompous, dull, trivial, elementary, underdone, incompetent) and stresses six rules for success. These in the main are the obverse of the pitfalls. Grandly he concludes: "You owe to your discipline the best you have in you. Your research and your analysis do not belong to you, but to the world; you owe them to your colleagues. You owe to yourself the genuine excitement of scholarship." [11]

Second, prestige is secured through off-campus activities by visiting other colleges and universities. The teacher, for example, who is in regular demand to lecture at colleges other than his own is admired on his own campus. His prestige inflates. The reasoning is that his expertness must be valuable to his home campus if other colleges are willing to recognize him and his value. As Dewey W. Grantham, Jr., mildly puts it:

The marvels of modern transportation, in conjunction with the availability of travel funds, have made it possible for a steady stream of college administrators and faculty members to move across the landscape of higher education bent on academic consultation, scholarly investigation, professional association, and student recruitment.[12]

This form of travel is a kind of academic process whereby experts take in each other's washing.

Kenneth I. Brown has perceptively seen that the urge of scholars to visit other campuses has its obverse side. The college, he says, has itself come to believe in "academic salvation by visitation." Although he calls the phenomenon a heresy, it may well have become by now the orthodoxy. Says Brown:

The heresy is attractive by its very simplicity: our faculty has been less than fully successful in achieving the goals of education in a truly significant and exciting fashion; they are good men but neither top scholars nor brilliant teachers and our budget will not allow us to attract such men; therefore, we must turn to the Great-Man-with-the-Big-Name who will come to the campus for several days, or better a week or a fortnight. If the Great Man can be secured for a semester, then do we have a written guarantee of academic salvation for all, by the easy and painless way of visitation.[13]

Third, status is increased by consulting. This phenomenon is known on almost every campus among the physical scientists. Commonly, geologists, chemists, physicists, biologists, and others spend a considerable part of their time in off-campus consultation with industries and other organizations that require their services. To act as a consultant provides kudos to the scientist. But the physical scientist is not alone in his consultative activities. In the more recent years the social scientists have been called off-campus in large numbers. In 1959, for example, the Esso Standard Division of Humble Oil, an affiliate of Standard Oil, New Jersey, employed a total of fifty psychologists, sociologists and anthropologists as consultants. These contributed a grand total of 1,728 man-days of work for the company. All but seven of these came from colleges and universities.[14] Other companies, to a greater or lesser degree, also employ social scientists.

In recent years sociologists have been highly prized in consultative work. Their services mainly fit into two categories: They are consulted regarding consumers. Two Iowa State College sociologists, for example, started the pattern of adoption for new farm products; they studied the kind of people most receptive to innovation and those least receptive, where they got their information, and how long they were likely to wait. Eli Lilly and Company used this information for a campaign for a new beef cattle hormone seed additive. Sociologists also are employed to increase employee efficiency. They hold classes, for example, to teach supervisors about group dynamics.[15]

Fourth, the academic "status seekers" are accorded recognition when they take leaves from the college. Although a leave may be taken to restore health, to engage in private research, or to write a scholarly tome, much of the prestige currently attached to leaves of absence derives from being invited to serve in an important capacity away from the campus. Sometimes it seems as though the prestige increases directly with the distance from the campus to the new responsibility. Thus a call to advise the government of Iran on educational matters may appear to be more prestigious than a leave to work in a chemical industry in the next town. At any rate, college employees, far from living in seclusion from the turbulent events of the world, at times seem to be at their very center.

Time, long before the presidency of John Kennedy, reported briefly on the Harvard faculty under the title "Where Are the Professors?" The magazine reported that David Bell had left abruptly to grapple with the U.S. budget, Edward S. Mason was surveying the economy of Uganda. Arthur A. Maass was off studying the water laws of Spain, John T. Dunlop was mediating for the construction industry, George B. Kistiakowsky, absent for a year, was advising the government on scientific matters in Washington. Boston attorney Francis H. Burr, a member of the Harvard Corporation, admitted that "a lot of people are concerned and so are we," but he was also able to add that "many professors are worth more to the university by spending time away." [16] He did not elucidate on his meaning.

The quips and jokes about the absentee Harvard faculty, which followed the inauguration of the late President Kennedy, tended to obscure the fact that the situation at Harvard is mirrored to a greater or lesser degree by similar conditions in many other American colleges. The specialist is not only one who is recognized as such at home. He is recognized at home because he is recognized away from home.

In addition to these four means whereby the specialist seeks to enhance his position in the bureaucracy of his college there are others. Some of these will be discussed later in this chapter in connection with the unsettled and unclear position of the college teacher's function in the college.

The objective of the enhancement of status in the college is the promotion to a higher position. Promotion comprises a major concern for every college officeholder. To this subject some consideration now will be given.

The basis in motivation for the intense seeking for status on the part of the college worker is certainly complex. Its ramifications are probably as broad as human life itself. One way of giving focus to the phenomenon, however, is to give attention to the status anxiety of the bureaucratic worker. Higher education as a bureaucracy rests ultimately upon the ability of each working member to assume a precise responsibility within it. The status system of the college is a powerful developer of the sense of responsibility. The stability and reliability of the college's functions depend upon the conjoining of status and responsibility.

The individual worker, aside from monetary and security factors, is largely motivated by his status. This motivation takes essentially two forms. First, he is desirous of protecting whatever status he may have. Second, he strongly wishes for an improvement of his status. No matter what his present status may be, he looks to its increase on the morrow.

Robert Michels says that "a mania for promotion" is a characteristic of every bureaucracy.[17] The hierarchical organization of the college as a bureaucracy tends to tease the employee into high aspirations. The worker perhaps too readily assumes that if he is able to climb one rung on the ladder of success that each succeeding rung will be equally within his grasp. The employee who is not upwardly mobile understandably tends to be anxious about his status. Despite the fact that college personnel has regularly been categorized as "idealistic" in comparison with workers in business organizations, the judgment is probably untrue. Collegiate experience teaches that college employees are as fiercely competitive and possess as high personal aspirations as any other group of workers in society. They are intensely concerned about their failures and successes. They, too, have "a mania for promotion." As with chess players, they are looking for a gambit by which the game of promotion ultimately may be won.

The intensity of the current mania may be better understood in contrast to the situation in higher education about a hundred years ago. Richard Hofstadter, looking back to the 1840's, says:

. . . there was no system of rewards for competence; salaries were commonly inflexible, there was no system of raises, no hierarchy of promotion; once installed the professor was treated much the same whether he was an eminent success or a substantial failure as a teacher. Although a professor usually held office indefinitely on good behavior, his tenure depended upon usage and had no legal status; he could be fired at will by the governing board; in many institutions a hearing was not required. Since there was no system of graduate education, no advanced work to look forward to, and no pecuniary reward for distinction in scholarship, the professor tended to settle into the groove of the recitation system and the policing of the students in which he was frequently required to join at much expenditure of time and energy and sometimes at the cost of humiliation.[18]

Advancement from a lower office to a higher office, the desire of every bureaucrat, logically should depend upon a set of objective criteria by which the individual may be satisfied and group consensus may be secured. Such standards, being publicly available, should be general enough to permit flexibility and human judgment. On the other hand, they should be specific and detailed enough to create justice or a sense of justice among the personnel involved. The creation of actual opportunities for advancement depends upon such matters as death, expansion, and resignations. The chief difficulty in the college so far as promotion is concerned is surely not educational expansion. The primary problem is that of establishing sufficiently decisive and acceptable yardsticks for evaluating performance and potential. American higher education has been notably weak in this regard. Higher education has not made up its mind what it values first, second, third, and so forth in its staff. In view of this situation, the anxiety which is to be expected on the part of any holder of a graded office is currently compounded by the vague standards applied by colleges in their promotion practices. As a means of reviewing some of the dimensions of the problem, the following six promotion elements will be commented upon briefly: seniority, teaching, group activities, research, administration, and writing.

Seniority as a basis for promotion seems to be an objective and wise criterion. It clearly and on a chronological basis arranges the college's personnel according to greater and lesser chances for promotions. It has the further virtue of including the valuable ingredient of experience. That person with the most experience on the job is generally first to secure the office above.

Yet seniority is not so much an exclusive principle of promotability as it is simply a fact among other facts. No one would assert that the person with the greatest seniority should by this reason alone be a department chairman. Many other requirements than that of seniority immediately come to mind as being of greater importance. Again, a staff which operates wholly on the principle of seniority assumes that the personal abilities of all its members are equal with the exception of the variable factor length of experience. This, obviously, is a rash assumption. Although seniority is probably used more often than not as a basis for promotion, its uncritical and automatic usage is liable to the charge of injustice and inefficiency.

Teaching, at least for the teaching staff, is regularly and widely conceived in American higher education to be the primary function, and is the one, therefore, which constitutes the first basis for consideration for promotion. Catalogues of colleges loudly assert the claim. Admission officers speaking in high-school convocations are bound to have this element on the list of their institution's strengths. Harried administrators, almost by rote, emphasize the primacy of teaching to their faculties. Yet, despite the propaganda, there appears to be no strong conviction among college teachers generally that excellence of teaching is the *sine qua non* for advancement. Many faculty members agree with a professor in a modern novel: "I'd like to think that classroom performance still determines status, but I've seen too many promotions made in somebody's drawing room." [19]

Colleges, at present, are unclear as to whether they prize more the knowledge of the teacher or his success in making it available to students. If a college stresses the knowledge or expertness of the teacher, it is inclined to look for more than good teaching. It tests the expertness of the teacher by those activities for which he can be basically responsible, such as research and writing, and by those factors which have been discussed previously as constituting the prestige of the teacher off-campus. Excellence in teaching, therefore, well may not be either the lone or the chief basis for promotion.

Participation in group activities within the college (sometimes also in the community) is another basis for promotion. Group activities may be of an informal character, such as those pertaining to the Faculty Club, the departmental picnic, the president's reception for graduating seniors, or, they may be of a formal character, such as faculty and faculty-student committees, legislative bodies within the college, departmental committees. In general, group participation indicates the willingness of the individual to assume responsibilities beyond his private sphere. It also provides others with an opportunity of knowing and evaluating him.

On the other hand, despite the intense attraction they hold for some, group activities are viewed by many of the college's personnel as an unavoidable evil. Some college workers believe that group activities, such as committees, detract from scholarship. Carlos Baker, for example, has a character in his novel say:

'No more committees, please. I'm on enough committees as it is . . . They say it's the price you pay for democratic government in a university. And the places that don't have committee-government are always trying to get it. But who pays the price of scholarship? Who writes the books on Shakespeare, Sophocles, Voltaire? No books were ever written while a man sat at a committee table.' [20]

The late president of Yale University, A. Whitney Griswold, expressed his doubt of the efficiency of committees in these words: "Could *Hamlet* have been written by a committee, or the 'Mona Lisa' painted by a club? Could the New Testament have been composed as a conference report? Creative ideas do not spring from groups. They spring from individuals." [21]

Finally, committees have been criticized for illogical behavior. Jacques Barzun says:

I have sat on a committee so democratic that the chairman, who had received a publisher's circular offering a new syllabus in the social studies, read the letter aloud and asked for a vote to obtain a sample copy. At the other end of the scale, committees meet not to debate over fifty cents' worth of printed matter, but to settle the great imponderables, such as how to insure in wartime the survival of permanent human values. I am told that on one such occasion a blunt logician pointed out that if the human values were really permanent the college might let them shift for themselves.[22]

Such spirited comment recalls the stricture of Dryden's *Achitophel:*

> Yet still he saw his fortune at a stay—
> Whole droves of blockheads chocking up his way.

What is true by report regarding the effects of committee participation may also hold to a degree regarding other group activities. Such an experienced and wise a hand as Beardsley Ruml was able to assert that:

The liberal college faculty *as a body* is not competent to make the judgments and evaluations required to design a curriculum in liberal education. The individual members of the faculty are for the most part chosen as specialists in departmental subjects, and as a result both in knowledge and personal interest each is a special advocate, necessarily and desirably so. A collection of special advocates cannot be expected to be a repository and a voice of judicial wisdom.[23]

Group activities in the college are not held in high esteem by many. The weight that they should be given in an evaluation of performance and potential in connection with promotion is ambiguous.

Productive research is a fourth factor. Research, like teaching, is a basic activity of the college. One can scarcely debate whether it should or should not exist within the college. For some faculty members it is a source of vital interest and prestige, although not every researcher enjoys faculty status. The debate regarding research which usually takes place on college campuses sets up an either–or alternative—either teaching or research. Much of this debate is fruitless and uninspired. The basic questions are what are the interrelationships between teaching and research and how may the quality of both be improved. Alfred North Whitehead answers them in part:

Do you want your teachers to be imaginative? Then encourage them to research. Do you want your researchers to be imaginative? Then bring them into intellectual sympathy with the young at the most eager, imaginative period of life, when intellects are just entering upon their mature discipline. Make your researchers explain themselves to active minds, plastic and with the world before them; make your young students crown their period of intellectual acquisition by some contact with minds gifted with experience of intellectual adventure.[24]

While research is a problem-laden activity for some college teachers, it is at least as vexatious to the college as a whole. The rapid development of research in higher education, especially that supported by the federal government, has created a new category of administrative concern, as Charles V. Kidd has shown. Kidd has catalogued many of the problems, particularly in the natural sciences, in a study of the subject, including: concentration of support in a too limited range of colleges and universities, stimulation of research in the sciences at the expense of other fields, overemphasis on team research, problems related to the indirect costs of subsidized research, classified research and security policies, the development of new institutional activities (including even advertising and the semiprofessional solicitation of research support), the "senseless situation" in which the federal government provides profit-making concerns with money to finance high pay scales that lure scientists from the colleges and universities where the government is attempting to encourage scientific research.[25]

Involvement in administrative functions also constitutes a basis for promotion. The contest between administrative and other functions within the college is not as sharp as most college employees make out. As will be discussed in the next chapter, administration is a characteristic function of every aspect of the college's organization. Thus, many persons are engaged in administration in the college who would not claim the title of administrator. Administrative functioning, however, is a basis for promotion.

In the relationship of publication to promotion, Caplow and McGee assert: "It is neither an overgeneralization nor an oversimplification to state that in the faculties of major universities in the United States today, the evaluation of performance is based almost exclusively on publication . . ." [26] The common cry of the faculty is "publish or perish." Charles A. Fenton describes the situation:

In every American college and university, nevertheless, in the most seedy and in the most honored, the devoted teachers raise the canard of 'publish or perish,' emphasizing the slogan as an unclean discriminatory principle by which, they claim, pedagogical devotion is inhibited and mechanical scholarship is honored. They readily persuade each generation of undergraduates that the odious doctrine of 'publish or perish' is the perverse prescription by which the ancient verities are being corroded and the warm alma mater of former years is being despoiled.[27]

There is sufficient evidence, however, to show that faculties and others are writing as much and probably more today than did their predecessors. This very fact, moreover, may be a basis for the cry rather than an answer to it. But a basic question in connection with all writing is: Is anything important being said? On the basis of this criterion, Eugene P. Chase is able to say:

It seems to me possible that in the fields of which I know something, we have reached a peculiarly low position in research and in the production of books and articles possessing some suspicion of possible originality. There is plenty of writing, but it says little.[28]

Obviously publications cannot be quantitatively weighed; they must be evaluated. Quality is the objective rather than mere bulk.

One of the certain marks of quality for the academic person is the justifiable introduction of novel or creative advances within a discipline. Such a contribution comes about through the challenging of accepted notions and the creation of new postulates and conclusions. Lincoln Steffens reports that he once asked Einstein in Berlin how he had made so many great discoveries. "How did you ever do it," I exclaimed, and he, understanding and smiling, gave the answer, "By challenging an axiom." [29] This, then, is the basis of creative advance in the several disciplines. Such advance is hopefully reflected in publication.

Writing and similar creative responses, then, comprise an important but not necessarily conclusive ingredient in the standards by which performance and potential are judged.

At times all of the promotional elements previously discussed are found in some individuals in combination. A vignette of such a person is found in a novel by Robert Glynn Kelly. He tells the story of Barney Stone who teaches English in a small midwestern university. The plot is tempest in a college teapot. Barney Stone is faced with a decision between following a course that will end with a deanship or one which will bring him the desired affection of his sweetheart, a student who seeks his counsel. The narrative is as airy as a soufflé, but at one point a note of sheer desperation and seriousness enters, when Barney says: "I'm the unadulterated scholar. One of the damned few . . . This is the day when scholars and critics run in schools, like fish, the day of the half-breed —the quadroon—the scholar-teacher-committeeman-administrator." [30] In sum, Kelly pictures the college teacher as a person caught between the several competing functions which the college requires of him for his own success. The teacher's aim may be good, but he is trying to hit a pinpoint with a buckshot gun.

John W. Gustad headed a committee in 1961 which surveyed 584 colleges and universities of every type in order to determine "policies and practices in faculty evaluation." The committee, composed of experienced educators, was surprised by "the extent and depth of the chaos." It found that constant lip service is being paid to the importance of the good teacher. It also found that the colleges have few, if any, really effective criteria by which to evaluate good teaching. Scholarship, according to the report, is evaluated "by bulk rather than by quality." The report warns that the present chaos is compounded by the myth that greater precision and objectivity cannot be sought and found.[31]

If the procedures and standards regulating promotion in higher education are vague and confusing, then it is equally true that the promotion system lacks another dimension—demotion. A system which assumes that persons will progress from lower to higher levels of value in an organization should also develop policy regarding those individuals, even if their number is very small, who according to objective standards are deserving of demotion. The "mania for promotion," however, is not counterbalanced in the college by a system of demotion or even of open restraint in many instances. Arrangements do obtain in many colleges for dismissal under prescribed conditions, but the lesser penalty of demotion is scarcely perceived and rarely applied.

In this chapter the professional activity of the officeholder has been examined in terms of the specialization of its staff. Bureaucratically the college is organized in terms of the expertness of its employees. Specialization tends to fragmentize the college. There are few forces to give it unity. The expert is interested in his own responsibility and in his advancement. He looks not only to various avenues within the college for the satisfaction of his aspirations but, if he is effective, engages in off-campus activities which bring him recognition both on and off the campus. Since the college officeholder, like other bureaucrats, possesses "a mania for promotion" he is driven by status anxiety to succeed, despite the fact that promotion seems to be a sign of aging rather than achievement, with happily a few exceptions. His success, however, is impeded in the present circumstances by the fact that the standards for advancement are not only vague and diffused, but are confusing in their lack of preciseness. The very uncertainty which results, however, is a guerdon to the college, for it stimulates the employee to work all the harder to overcome the ambiguities in his acceptance for promotion.

6

The Great

Chain of

Academic Being:

The System

"*A*sked once how he classified people, Archibald MacLeish replied, 'into two classes: those who divide people into classes and those who dont'." [1] Anyone discussing higher education as a bureaucracy obviously fits into the first class—those who divide people into classes. The college as a bureaucracy, like all large-scale organizations, organizes its offices according to the principle of hierarchy, that is, each lower office is under the control and supervision of a higher one.

The theme of this chapter is the formal organization of the college in hierarchical form. The discussion will center on the nature of the hierarchy, the particular role of the administration and the other graded offices, with some attention given to the satellite formations. The particular subjects will be briefly discussed. The purpose of the discussion is not to provide extensive analyses of the personnel categories particularly, but merely to illustrate the nature of the social system, the bureaucracy, in which they have their place. Other aspects of the college as a social system, deriving from its informal organization, will be delineated in the next chapter.

"Organization implies the tendency to oligarchy," states Robert Michels.[2] In every organization the aristocratic tendency is evident. The personnel is scattered upon a scale of ascending status and responsibility. Those who secure positions near the top are accorded the highest recognition along with the most generalized responsibilities. Those on the lower end of the scale are accorded the least recognition with responsibility for a much more circumscribed field of activity. In such an hierarchical arrangement there may be disjunction at one or more points in the scale, marking off the major steps of ascendancy, but from a theoretical viewpoint a graded system of offices and careers implies a gradual, determined, observable, and responsible social system. No sizeable enterprise exists without a highly rationalized arrangement among the personnel involving super-subordinate personal relationships. The college is no exception.

Higher education has not always been as bureaucratic as it is at present. Charles Homer Haskins says:

Throughout the period of its origins the medieval university had no libraries, laboratories, or museums, no endowment or buildings of its own; it could not possibly have met the requirements of the Carnegie Foundation . . . Such a university had no board of trustees and published no catalogue; it had no student societies—except so far as the university itself was fundamentally a society of students—no college journalism, no dramatics, no athletics, none of those 'outside activities' which are the chief excuse for inside inactivity in the American college.[3]

From its origin the college has been characterized by increasing formality, but for long centuries it could hardly qualify as a large-scale organization. According to Richard Hofstadter, the bureaucratization of the college has occurred in the main within the last century in the American experience. He considers the historical point of origin of the bureaucratic college as having taken place at the time when the university emerged, possibly about the middle of the nineteenth century. He may miss the fact that the rise of the university was a fairly constant and harmonious development from the prior stage of the college, and that the college as a social form has not been extinguished, but rather has in itself become larger and more complex. Also the university as a social form was known much prior to the middle of the nineteenth century. In Hofstadter's view, however, with the emergence of the university:

The academic profession took on, for the first time in a full measure, the character, aspirations, and standards of a learned profession. Within the university, the growth of resources, the proliferation of activities, the assemblage of large faculties gave impetus to bureaucratization—to tenure rules, formal procedures of promotion and dismissal, the delegation of authority.[4]

At any rate, the modern college manifests a bureaucratic form in its distribution of offices.

Max Weber in analyzing the hierarchies of bureaucracies noted three basic forms: the monocratic, the collegial, and the patrimonial.[5] The monocratic system denotes organization in a clearly defined hierarchy of offices with the chief and sole authority being relegated to the top leader. The collegial system refers to the management of an organization by groups rather than individuals, as in the monocratic type. The collegial system rests ultimately upon representative bodies, committees, and boards. The patrimonial system involves unfree individuals, like slaves or dependents.

Obviously the bureaucratic college may be described in terms of either the monocratic or collegial systems of hierarchy, but hardly in the patrimonial. Weber's way of describing hierarchies

The Great Chain of Academic Being: The System

(he always was concerned with the Prussian experience) refers chiefly to the nature of the ultimate authority binding the system. It is not a sociological accounting for the totality of the system. In that regard it is inadequate.

Another and more fruitful way of viewing the hierarchical arrangement of offices in higher education has been provided out of other contexts by Chester I. Barnard. He writes about two kinds of status systems: the scalar and the functional. While not absolutely opposed to Weber's classification, these distinctions are more effective tools for the analysis of the hierarchy of the college.

According to Barnard, status in the scalar system is determined by: "(1) the relationship of superiority or subordination in a chain of command or authority and (2) by jurisdiction." In the scalar system (having only magnitude), the personal relationships are fashioned along vertical lines. The controlling concept is that of super-subordinate offices. Integration of the system tends to fall in pyramid fashion to an even smaller group of responsible persons until ultimately one person is the final authority.[6]

Colleges are organized in part as scalar systems, but only in part. That is, the college is organized in terms of offices which are scaled according to status with increasing authority being granted to persons and bodies on an ascending order until a chief person is reached. This gangliated, direct line of command parallels that which certain military and business organizations manifest, although the precise nature of the relationships within the college differs markedly from at least some aspects of the other bureaucracies.

The exact nature of the relationships within the college hierarchy must be understood from formal sources, such as bylaws, charters, faculty handbooks, or other documents. The formal, and sometimes legal, statements take precedence over oratory. Thus a fair-spoken college president in addressing the faculty may assert that when all is said and done it is the faculty which is the controlling element in the college—the most important. Some faculties even get to believe this propaganda. The fact is, however, that the faculty of the college is clearly several notches down in the scalar system of hierarchical organization. There are a few exceptions to this rule. Similarly, as on commencement day, the students may be told that without them there could be no college, that they are the most important people in the entire organization. Again, some students get to believe such rhetoric. Students, however, rank relatively low in the scalar system of organization. Their level of authority is fairly close to that of those who have no official connection with the college.

Another popular misconception about the college hierarchy is the one which avers that "the administration" is a body apart from all others. Sometimes this assertion takes the form of a war cry against pettifogging tyrants. Faculties, sometimes egged on by such organizations as the AAUP, look with haughty disdain or outward belligerence and resentment upon administrators. Actually, according to the scalar system, administration is what everyone employed by the college does. The form of what each person does may be different, his status and reward may differ, but everyone from the member of the governing board to lowest clerk in the lowest office in the college is a practicing administrator.

The common reference to the administration as those few persons within the college hierarchy with the highest status and the most general responsibility is noted for its lack of clear group definition. Sometimes the governing board of the college may be included. More often reference is made to the president, vicepresidents and deans. Regularly department chairmen are in an ambiguous position; they are both faculty and administration. In addition, there are others, like business managers, registrars, dieticians, who may or may not be considered part of the administration. Accusations against the administration may be more a sign of self-castigation and vague institutional resentment than clear thinking.

The Great Chain of Academic Being: The System

Yet there is no need to hide the fact that college administrators do exercise considerable power. Their task, in the words of an ancient prophet, is to see that "every valley shall be exalted and every mountain and hill shall be made low, and the crooked shall be made straight and the rough places plain." [7] To them falls the responsibility for major decision making. No organization the size of most modern colleges finds it possible to be without such leaders, but quite possible the resentment which administrators lower on the status scale bear toward those on or near the top may be due not so much to the inevitability of the existence of high administration as to the methods top administrators employ and their conspicuous wallowing in material benefits. Jacques Barzun comments:

Nothing so strikes the foreign observer with surprise as the size and power of American collegiate administration. The best offices and the best building, the rows and rows of filing cabinets, the serried ranks of secretaries and stenographers, make the European feel that he has wandered by mistake into some annex of a large business concern. The thick carpets, the hush and polish of the surroundings, cannot form part of an academy. The foreigner is used to a distinctive shabbiness, to hollowed steps and an inky smell, without which no school, college, or university seems genuine, be the place England, Germany, Italy, or France.[8]

Whether administrators are liked or not, they are needed. John Jay Corson points this out as a conclusion of a recent study of American colleges and universities. He points out that just as educational institutions face a population crisis so, too, do they face an administrative crisis. For the increase in student enrollment—and the chain reaction which this phenomenon sets off—requires a reconstruction of the traditional, almost informal, administrative machinery through which the college or university has organized and governed itself.[9]

Not all of the offices in the hierarchy of the college can be discussed within the limits of the present effort, but some benefit might accrue from a few bare comments on several.

Governing boards in the United States and Canada are quite distinctive by reason of the fact that they are composed of laymen. This development came about in the history of American higher education as a response to church and clerical dominance in an earlier period. There also may be a democratic presentiment in favor of boards of laymen. The lay board is in fact the controlling agent of the college. All those who work on the campus may consider the board to have a somewhat tenuous and remote connection with the institution. But the board is the law so far as the college is concerned. It is the body, for example, which legally hires and fires faculty members. If it wishes it may reserve to itself practically all decisions which relate to the operation of the college. Such a development, however, would not only be unwise, it would be impractical. Also, it would be unbureaucratic.

From one perspective the lay board has every responsibility of the college. From another viewpoint, however, and in accepted bureaucratic fashion, it relegates its responsibilities to those lower down in the scalar system. Even the tasks that Donald R. Belcher believes that boards of trustees of colleges possess, such as money-raising and money-giving, watching over the investments of endowment funds, and keeping the physical plant in a state of good repair, etc., are in the main referred to officers of the college for their day by day supervision.[10]

Educators are the only major group of professionals in America who are governed by laymen. Every other group, such as physicians, lawyers, engineers, are led by their own professional representatives. Lay boards of trustees of colleges generally have refused representation from the personnel of the college itself, although it may draw upon professionals associated with other institutions. This fact of lay management may contribute to the lowering of the status of the employees of the college so far as their position in the community is concerned. Obviously it also limits their ability to determine the standards and conduct of their own profession. The board, however, generally works through the college president.

The president currently suffers, next to his faculty, from an unclear definition of his responsibilities. Like the faculty, he has much that he is free to do. But, he is not limited sufficiently as to what is clearly expected of him. There are few standards to evaluate his effectiveness. His dilemma, moreover, derives from the fact that, as Harold W. Stoke says: "The college president as the Man of Learning has given way to the Man of Management." [11] He also is society's Man with the Begging Bowl.

In the scalar view of the organization of the college all responsibility not reserved by the board in theory and in fact rests upon the president. He no longer can use his job in the manner of Increase Mather, a former president of Harvard College. Although Mather served as president of Harvard for sixteen years, he was settled in Cambridge for only a few months. He was always too busy with non-Harvard activities to take his responsibilities seriously. For four years he represented the Massachusetts Colony in England. As a clergyman he thought it was far more important for him to be preaching to a large multitude of Boston's citizens than to be nurturing the intellects of a few hundred students. That day is gone. It went in fact a long time ago.

The former president of Princeton University, Woodrow Wilson, on the other hand, if he is representative of modern times, could reminisce about his days as president as follows: "It was the best period of my life," he said, "and I begin to realize that my contribution to my generation, if I have made any, was in connection not so much with my political work as with my activities as a teacher and college administrator." [12]

"The truth is that a president alone can do much destructively, but little constructively," according to Lloyd S. Woodburne.[13] Beyond such generalizations little is specified as belonging to the functions of the president. Whatever he does, however, is usually done through the agency of his vice-presidents and deans. The dean, as a second-line official, is held in generally low esteem by some members of the college staff. Charles A. Fenton, for example, says of them:

The majority of American minor deans, inept creatures who at an earlier more honorable incarnation could neither manage a classroom nor perform useful research, are themselves compelled to worship the mystic of the luminous teaching which they pretend to have abandoned, with enormous self-sacrifice, in order to assume the labors of administration.[14]

The perceptive and satirical words of W. H. Auden in this connection are too well known to need repeating here.[15]

Among the friends of deans, however, is David Riesman. He recognizes that presidents are overburdened, that they find it difficult even to catalogue all their responsibilities much less act thoroughly on them. Deans, according to Riesman, are the "innovators" of the college. He says:

. . . just as big corporations have left innovations to research and development departments and confined the work of their top executive to that of chief public relations officer, so at the big universities what innovation there is seems to have been shifted out of the president's hands into those of the deans.[16]

Whether deans are unsuccessful teachers or notable "innovator" they do hold important though ambiguous positions in the college hierarchy. Theoretically they cannot take final action without reference to the president. On most occasions, however, such final reference is not required. It may not be even desirable. To the degree to which deans operate in semiautonomous ways, they are able to gather both the power and the effectiveness to facilitate the solving of institutional problems and to enhance the college's growth.

Beardsley Ruml rightly notes that: "the tendency of members of American college and university communities to be classified as either 'faculty' or 'administration' is well known." [17] But, the man who is most in the midle of that dichotomy is the department chairman. The department chairman represents both the problem and possibility of decentralization and integration within the college. He along with his numerous colleagues forms a collection of responsible officeholders far up on the administrative scale of the college. On the other hand, by reason of their numbers and their very real obligations to department members, they form a reflection of the faculty organized in its several disciplines. The department chairman seeks to act as a citizen of the whole college when he is a participant in the affairs of the whole college. At other times, he tends to act as a partisan representative of the fierce and bitter interests of his departmental colleagues. The matter has been expressed this way:

The 'chain of command' in a college is at most a tenuous line of influence. The president and deans must rely primarily upon departmental chairmen to direct and influence the departments. But . . . the chairman's ability to meet this expectation is based upon a delicate and unreliable relationship. He does not have the sanction of dismissing recalcitrant colleagues. In carrying out institutional policies, he requires strong backing from the president and the dean, and he must depend largely upon his skill as a negotiator and upon his ability to persuade colleagues that the decision is at least pragmatically right and that acceptance is in the long-run interests of the department.[18]

Next lower to the department chairman in the hierarchy of higher education stands the faculty member. One tends to think of the individual faculty member as a relatively unorganized person in the sense that he simply has his own existence to be responsible for. He may at times seem to use his vigor to thwart the encroachments of his colleagues at any point in the hierarchy where they may intrude upon him. But, this view of the professor in his isolation is archaic. The modern college teacher is himself a highly organized bureaucrat. In order to secure any kind of success within the college, he must devote a considerable part of his time to understanding the scalar system and the types of pressure he might bring upon it for his own advancement. Quite often in addition to his teaching and research he himself is engaged in the administration of a college bureau.

The contrast between the past and the present, so far as an academic scientist is concerned, is portrayed by Bentley Glass, an eminent scientist himself:

The picture of the academic scientist of 1960 is not complete without some further description of the modest empires over which many of them preside. Consider a fairly typical example. In 1940, as an assistant professor of biology, this scientist had no special fund for his research. An amount not exceeding $100 annually came from the departmental budget and was used for consumable supplies. He actually used one moderately good compound microscope and one good binocular dissecting microscope. He made all his own media, did his own sterilizing in a Sears Roebuck pressure cooker, kept his own stocks without assistance, and was grateful for some help in washing up the glassware. Without even a chest to run at a controlled temperature he worked during the hot summer weeks in a dusty, normally unused but surprisingly cool basement room. Sometimes he lost stocks because of a rise in the temperature—sometimes epidemics of mold made entire experiments a loss—but the research went on in spite of the fact that perhaps 80 per cent of the scientist's time was spent in routine chores. In 1960, the professor has charge of two research laboratories, both supported by funds from the federal government. A senior research associate operates one of these laboratories semi-independently, with a research assistant to aid him. Two research assistants work in the other laboratory. In addition, there are two part-time laboratory assistants to wash bottles, keep animals, and prepare media. The annual research budget of the group is close to $50,000 not including the scientist's university salary; and none of this comes from the regular department budget. There is no lack of equipment; compound microscopes of the best quality; binocular dissecting microscopes for each worker; phase microscopes; photo micrographic equipment; an x-ray machine; a cool room; constant temperature in incubators, refrigerators, and a deep-freeze; air conditioning for the laboratories; special supplies of chemicals; special rooms and equipment for preparing and sterilizing media and washing glassware; animal quarters; in short, everything that is really needed for an experimental program of some size. One might be moved to say, 'But this is exceptional. It reflects seniority as well as the change of the times.' On the contrary, junior members of this scientist's department are about equally well established.[19]

The students also have a place in the hierarchy. They themselves possess both a formal and an informal set of graded statuses in which some of them move as intently and cleverly as do the other officeholders in the college. First, the formal organization of students in student government, sororities and fraternities, subject-matter organizations, etc., creates a "pecking order" of notable proportions. While the adult members of the college may not be too clear on the precise gradations involved in the various student organizations and offices, there usually is a lively appreciation on the part of a large number of students of their meaning.

Second, students are informally ranked. Owen Wister's *Philosophy Four* of 1901 continues to be one of the most remarkable accounts of the informal differentiation among students. In this novel, Bertie and Billy are rich, socially impeccable, and bear old colonial names. They seldom attend class or do any other kind of academic work. They rely upon Oscar Maironi to read them his faultless notes at ten dollars an hour. Oscar is apparently Jewish; his parents came over in the steerage. He is a contemptible fellow by the standards of Bertie and Billy.[20]

There are two major points of stress and conflict within the hierarchy of the college. The first is between the faculty and the so-called administration, the second is between the students and the rest of the institution. The first conflict is intragenerational. It is a conflict of adults. It centers largely upon the formulation of educational policy and the striving for personal promotion.

The second is an intergenerational conflict. The college is a relatively artificial community in that generally it consists of two distinct age groupings: adults and youth. Most of the moods and resentments prevalent in general society between the generations are expressed within the college. The degree of successful management of the first kind of conflict may be greater than for the second. At any rate, students, in a parallel to other bureaucracies, are largely regarded as customers. As customers they do not hold as important, intrinsic, or as permanent a relationship to the hierarchy and its continuance as do the employees of the college. Customers are regularly regarded as out-groups by those who are firmly entrenched in the hierarchy. As Randall Jarrell has a character in his novel say about the relations between the faculty and the students: ". . . there was one allowance they never under any circumstances made—that the students might be right about something, and they wrong." [21] Or as a social science professor says:

The sociologist prefers to regard the college student as a candidate for socialization. Whenever a group must incorporate new members— whether it is a family to which an infant has been born or an army which has just drafted a civilian recruit—the same problem exists: to teach the 'barbarian' to play the roles and to incorporate the values of his new society. [22]

Yet, it does not seem to matter how the students are organized—formally or informally. They represent the second great point of conflict within the college. They frequently are opposed simply for the sake of opposition. Such was the case in the early days of Yale University. Thomas Clapp, a Yale president, sought during his tenure to make the institution truly sectarian, believing in a strictly sectarian test for participation in the college. The students, faced with Clapp's efforts, were adamantly opposed, using almost every stratagem including violence to have their way. Finally in 1766, Clapp resigned. President Daggett who followed him was not embroiled in the controversy. But his successor, Ezra Stiles, reversed Clapp's policy. He favored the admission of all Protestant groups to the college. One might think that the students would have acclaimed him an educational hero in cock-a-hoop fashion. But not so; they disliked his policy, too. The subject of their formal debates was: "Whether toleration of all religions is beneficial to the state."

As part of the organization of every college there are necessarily present certain "satellite formations." Their aims are subsidiary to the major purposes of the institution. These formations are difficult to classify in the hierarchy. In general they tend to be at the bottom of or even an extension from it. On the other hand, at certain times they may become so important that they take precedence over the authorities which are regularly rated high in status. Their management constitutes a major aspect of college administration.

These satellite formations mainly operate either from a base on campus or off campus. The on-campus formations tend in the recent years to be manifold. College sports are an example. They exist in many colleges not only as a part of the college itself, but as a satellite formation. They are as Henry Steele Commager says "organized as a public amusement." He urges colleges to "give the games back to the students." [23] Campus religious groups, like the Newman Club, the Westminster Foundation, the Canterbury Club, the Hillel Foundation, etc., on many campuses tend to operate both as a part of the college and yet within their own autonomies. Various research institutes financed by the federal government comprise another kind of satellite formation as do other institutes, schools, programs, extension courses, adult-education programs.

Another set of on-campus satellite formations is the Department of Buildings and Grounds, the college's "development" program, and the secretaries, mimeographers, and other academic *humildes*. Although all of these tend by certain definition to rank low in the hierarchy of the offices of the college, it is apparent that on occasion and for certain of the personnel of these enterprises there is opportunity for status and recognition which far exceeds their nominal titles. For example, it may be claimed that in certain respects the secretaries of a college, taken as a group, wield effective power far disproportionate to their ranking in the scalar system. Max S. Marshall illustrates this in connection with the role of a dean's secretary:

The most capable secretary I ever knew was elaborately careful never to step out of bounds, yet did a beautiful job, and was not at all appreciated by faculty men who could manage the dean but could not hoodwink her. She was appreciated properly by all honest persons, including deans who fell in that category. She was not unique, but she was an exception. There is the one who bumbles rules and never sees any realities; the cold strategist who runs both the dean and the school with a ruthless hand; the assured one who boasted to perfect strangers that she can and does run the school better than the dean; the inner sanctum type who speaks only the words of the dean but never lets the dean speak except through her; and the hostess type. I have left out some. Any expert on deans knows, however, that these ladies hold key spots in the offices of deans and must be considered with them; in fact, half the time the dean can be ignored.[24]

The importance of the secretary for a department of instruction is illustrated by the procedures employed by the Department of Psychology of the University of Texas in 1961 when it sought to replace its principal secretary one week before fall registration. In addition to using the university's personnel office, the department ran the following advertisement in the local newspaper:

Wanted: Senior Secretary who can make good coffee, laugh, and run the lives of twenty crazy college professors. Low pay, high responsibility, and a good deal of fun for anyone who can stand it.

The ad actually was an exercise in motivational research. The responses sought the following:

Senior was intended to eliminate the young and inexperienced. *Make good coffee* was intended to discourage those hard and masculine women who think it degrading to nurture men a bit. *Laugh, and run the lives of twenty crazy college professors* were ingredients meant to discourage the rigid and frightened. *Low pay* represents a touch of reality. At all levels, universities still seek people who work for non-negotiable rewards; we have no place for anyone whose motivations are mainly economic.
High responsibility was some more reality, and an attempt to ward off the young and scattered-headed.
Fun for those who can stand it was a reiteration of non-negotiable rewards and was intended as a discouragement to those without tolerance for confusion and ambiguity.

Seventy-two applicants responded to the ad. Fourteen of these were interviewed. One finally made the grade. She also could type 99 words a minute.[25] No one knows whether the experiment was a scientific success; probably it was a professional form of enjoyment for a group of somewhat humorous professors. Yet it has its serious aspects. The main import of the experiment, however, is the fact that departments, like other bureaus of the college, are genuinely concerned about the quality of their secretaries, for these factotums constitute in many instances the very backbone of the organization of the bureau.

Satellite formations with their base off-campus also may be considered as a part of the hierarchy. The multiplicity of provisioners, for example, interpenetrate into almost all of the hierarchical offices of the college. Without successful management of them in relation to the efficiency and goals of the college, a demoralizing and even institutionally paralyzing situation may develop. The importance of the provisioners cannot be rated by their lack of mention in the college's catalogue or by the unobtrusive way in which they support the entire collegiate enterprise. A wise administrator knows thoroughly of their importance.

Again, there are a variety of professional associations, with bases off campus, which have a direct relationship to the activities of the college. The several disciplinary-professional groups, representing the departments in the main, have the possibility, through the setting of standards and the providing of a common mentality for their practitioners, to possess a sizeable influence on the campus. A group like the American Association of University Professors has been a principal and energetic agency for the improvement of faculty salaries and other aspects of faculty employment, although there is no indication that the AAUP is cognizant in the same measure of its responsibilities for the elimination of waste in the curriculum or in the genuine advancement of the teaching objectives of the college.

The role of the accrediting association in the United States stands in contrast to the manner in which education is controlled elsewhere and especially in Europe. In Europe, the supervision of education is generally undertaken by a Ministry of Education or some other central agency of government. In the United States, there may be a nominal supervision of education in the locality or the state, but, for higher education, the task is assumed by accrediting associations. These are of two types. There are six regional associations (like the North Central Association of Colleges and Secondary Schools) which are concerned with the total organization of the educational offerings in the colleges within their bailiwicks. Secondly, there are the specialized accrediting associations (such as the American Chemical Society) which in addition to the requirements enforced by the first type of association maintain their own partisan systems of accreditation. If college administrators are not clear-minded on the rationale of accrediting in the United States, they can take comfort. Apparently even the various associations are not able to understand it either—with communicable clarity. Their combined attempts are both a realization and a denial of rationality in higher education (see Chapter 8).

Formerly the Association of American Universities acted as an over-all, national accrediting agency. But its abdication some years ago has left the nation with no national agency for the accrediting of colleges and universities and indeed no effective agency for the governance of graduate education, including studies for the Ph.D.[26]

In the recent decades the many educational foundations also have had a striking impact on local campus outlooks and practices.

Another category of personnel may be considered as contingent to the hierarchy of the college, although its position is probably more remote in the hierarchy even than that of the satellite formations. These are "the outsiders." They consist of citizens in the community, such as potential students, who have an interest in the college. Of course while at times the good will of the outsiders is strenuously sought by the college, no outsider can rank in any way as does an insider. Certain outsiders, however, such as those who contribute financially to the endowment of the college, have their status positions transvaluated; that is, instead of being anonymous citizens of the community they become extremely valuable to the college. Sometimes they end up on the lay board of trustees. No wonder, then, that college administrative charts are as confusing as a subway map!

In the beginning of this chapter, Chester I. Barnard's twofold description of the hierarchy of a bureaucracy was indicated and defined. In this chapter the scalar system has been the guiding concept. By it the college may be described as a social system of graded offices in which responsibility, reward, and status are organized in super-subordinate relationships. The description of Beardsley Ruml is appropriate in connection with this scalar system:

When depicted on an organization chart, a college resembles any other institution following the hierarchical pattern . . . The chain of command runs from the Board to the President to the academic dean, thence to the chairmen of departments, and ultimately to the individual teacher. As in other bureaucracies, there is a division of labor based upon specialization . . . In all of these respects the college resembles the bureaucracy of government, military, religious and business organizations.[27]

Barnard, however, suggests that there is another way in which the hierarchy of a bureaucracy may be viewed—according to its functional system of status. It is to that aspect of the organization of higher education that the next chapter will be directed.

7

The Great Chain

of Academic Being:

The System

(Continued)

A cynic might say that the scalar system of hierarchical organization within higher education, as described in the last chapter, denotes a kind of mechanical meaninglessness, such as is pictured in the form of two factories in Hermann Kashek's *City Beyond the River:* one factory grinds up stone and the other bakes them together again, only to send them back to the first factory to be ground up once more.[1] The difficulty with this view is that higher education is more than the impersonal and the routine that the picture in the previous chapter may suggest. There is another aspect, diametrically opposed to the scalar picture, in which the college may be viewed as a highly informal and unorganized enterprise. Such a point has been made regarding the curriculum, for example, by Richard Livingstone:

But undergraduate education has never been thought out as a whole. It has simply grown, and in its development has been determined by a combination of *vis inertiae*, the present circumstances and a struggle of individual subjects for a place in the sun. We are all familiar with the process by which the curriculum develops. A subject, long neglected, makes its way into the circle, establishes a position, and then pushes out from its bait to seize as much of the country as finance and its rivals in public opinion allow. In fact, university education has grown up in the casual English way. It had never been viewed, much less planned, as a whole. A saint might give a book on the subject the title of 'Drift.' [2]

Curricularly, the college of today is as up-to-date as a galoot with galluses.

Certainly drift was a hallmark of the earlier periods in higher education. Even today, drift seems to dominate much in the college, yet as the college comes to look at itself critically, as its enrollment and staff swell, and as the community makes more demanding claims upon it, the college seems to be veering from its unsteady course of drift to one of planned and centralized management. This tendency is perceived by John J. Corson who asserts that as institutions grow larger, the influence in governance of the faculties grows less, and the creation and extension of central staffs about the president and the deans tend to accumulate authority within a small number of officeholders in the top range of the institutional hierarchy. [3]

In the last chapter primary attention was given to a description of the scalar system of status or organization, as suggested by Chester I. Barnard, although it was noted that this arrangement is only one of two kinds of status systems which are characteristic of bureaucracies. It is time now to mention and describe briefly the second system and to see its implications for higher education.

Barnard calls the second a functional system of status. By this term he means that the location of the individual and his office in the hierarchical arrangements of a large-scale organization depends not only upon authority and jurisdiction, but upon his function as well. Says Barnard: "The ranks are vertically divided into lateral groups of different callings, trades, crafts, metiers, divisions of labor, specializations, and professions." [4] An important and common characteristic of these various divisions of authority is that the command of one over another is generally not permitted. The effect of the functional system is to create a decentralized organization in contrast to the centralized type of the scalar system. The functional system tends to view the college as a series of constellations of authority which in greater or lesser measure are integrated around certain all-college offices, such as those of the board, the president, and his appointed officers.

Both the scalar and the functional systems of organization exist at one and the same time in nearly all organizations. They are partly overlapping and interdependent; yet they also are partly independent and self-contained.

The scalar system of college organization tends to favor administrative centralization, while the functional system is more congenial to decentralization. The first places the primary emphasis upon the neatness of the lines of authority. It aims to grade every individual in relation to every other. The second is oriented toward the recognition of the close tie between activities performed by experts, and their resulting authority. It also tends to see expertness assembled in groups of persons with relatively similar responsibilities. Yet, centralization and decentralization are not precisely synonyms for scalar and functional systems of bureaucratic organizations. Some of the relationships between the terms and the actualities they represent will now be briefly explored.

Centralization and decentralization are matters of psychological import as well as organizational fact. All colleges have some sort of departmental divisions, yet the allocation of decisions in the colleges varies. In one institution practically all decisions are made in the president's office. In other institutions, perhaps characterized by great size, practically all decisions are made within the departments. Thus, the chart of organization of the college, whether scalar or functional, shows little of the realities of authority unless additional details are supplied.[5]

Again, one of the key marks of a highly centralized organization is the presence of highly developed rules. Robert Dubin has observed this for industrial organizations.[6] Like an industrial organization, the college which depends heavily upon a scalar system of organization must create and sustain an elaborate formulation of procedural guides. All workers tend to act *de regle*. Less is left to human discretion and more is granted to "the book." In the functional arrangement, however, the decentralizing tendency places responsibility upon the managers of subunits of the total organization. These, because of their number and their close relationship to the functions of the subunits, more often than not depend upon personal relations rather than written guides for the success of their bureaus.

A scalar chart of the organization of a college, as previously intimated, also may be deceptive in that it may not embody the precise way in which authority is exercised. Varying philosophies of administration bear upon the manner in which authority is carried out in an organization. Lyman Bryson summarizes at least two contradictory viewpoints when he says: "The adage, 'If you want something well done, do it yourself,' is an admonition to an administrator not to trust his executives. The other adage, 'A man who is his own lawyer has a fool for a client,' may incidentally express the other side of the case." [7] Thus in the college an administrator who actually holds power may seemingly not exercise it in deference to his acceptance of a view of administration which makes the distribution of authority to lesser officeholder an important function of his own administrative responsibility. The scalar college, then, may be much more decentralized in its organization of authority than it superficially and formally appears to be.

A case can be made for the prevalence of a situation of equilibrium, between centralization and decentralization, in the college's practical affairs. Absolute centralization is as unreal a limit as is absolute decentralization. No such things actually can exist. They are in fact complimentary to each other. Each needs the other, and each to some degree expresses the other in itself. No college organization can long exist on the basis of orders issued solely by the board or the president, and surely no college can continue if everyone does as he pleases. Some middle course seems not only desirable but inevitable.

Equilibrium is maintained probably because trends toward centralization or decentralization, when they go too far, tend to create counter-trends.[8] Excessive decentralization tends to excessive overlapping which in its turn calls for some degree of coordination and elimination of waste. Excessive central authority leads to the stultification of spontaneous impulses within an organization which in turn leads to a closure on the incentives of the personnel. It also may lead to deeper resentment and even to forms of rebellion.

Authority in the functional system, as is implied in the term itself, is related to the function of the officeholder or bureau. The clearest expression of this formation is in the departmental system of the college. Within departments, teachers may be ranked as instructors, assistant professors, associate professors, full professors, and department chairmen. Each rank will hold an added measure of status over those lower than it. The function of the department, such as the teaching of English, forms the core of adhesion of the departmental membership. The instructor in the department tends to take the wishes of the chairman as an order. All members of a department, with at times striking and irritating exceptions, tend to work for the increasing efficiency of their function within the total department.

Paralleling any one of the departments of the college are other departments organized in the same manner. Each tends to operate with semiautonomy. The lines of authority may pass through the department to other administrative offices in the college, but the lines of authority within a department seldom commingle or interpenetrate with those of the other departments. So, the department of English has a primary responsibility for formulating courses in its subject. It does not expect nor does it tolerate any "interference" from other departments. Similarly, the instructor who takes his chairman's wishes as an order will be less responsive to the wishes of the chairman of a department other than his own.

What is true, moreover, of departments is equally true of all the other bureaus of a college. Thus the instructor in English does not presume to tell the vice-president for development how he should function in fund-raising. Each may be critical of the other and may express his criticism in the rumor system of the institution, but each probably would recognize his own realm of functional autonomy.

The scalar system of college organization also appears to be modified in the face of important legislative and policy-setting bodies—those venerable caves of the winds—within the college. In the scalar system, the lines of authority seem to flow from the board, president, presidential appointees, department chairmen, on downward. But, in fact, this arrangement is seldom as perfect as it appears in the faculty handbook because there are legislative and policy-setting bodies which also play a role in the college. A faculty council or senate may possess an authority to veto or modify the decisions of departments. A college-wide committee on curriculum, for example, may enjoy such security and authority within the college as to frustrate all attempts by the president and his assistants to modify the curriculum of the college. This is to say that in addition to the various departments and bureaus of a college there are other bodies which possess authority. This authority oftentimes is resistive to centralizing tendencies.[9]

The college as a bureaucracy, then, is organized both in a scalar and in a functional fashion. Both systems apply a blending of authority with specialization, yet the distribution of the component factors varies in each system. The scalar system represents the college primarily in terms of authority, while the functional system considers it basically in terms of specialized responsibilities. Both are apparent in the college and both probably are necessary to the organizational well-being of all social institutions.

In addition to the scalar and functional systems of organization within the college there are the latent structures. These consist of the organizational features of the college which seldom if ever get on the organizational charts. They are highly informal in character. Also, they may be viewed as connecting devices for accomplishing in a personal and nonorganizational sphere those authentic purposes of the institution which for one reason or another cannot be carried out in its formal arrangements. These spontaneous lines of communication commonly exist and develop in the face of bureaucratic rigidities. When the artificial differentiation of the rank order within the college exceeds by far the gradation warranted by the technical requirements of the establishment there is a tendency for informal means to develop.[10]

According to Philip Selznick, moreover, latent structures tend to develop because:

All formal organizations are molded by forces tangential to their rationally ordered structures and stated goals. Every formal organization—trade union, political party, army, corporation, etc.—attempts to mobilize human and technical resources as means for the achievement of its ends. However, the individuals within the system tend to resist being treated as means. They interact as wholes, bringing to bear their own special problems and purposes . . .[11]

In sum, the college personnel is motivated not only by the incentives which are provided by the institution but also by their private feelings and goals. The personnel tends to blur the distinctions between the two, believing that their human satisfactions are necessarily bound up with the success of the organization. Where the formal aspects of the organization do not make it possible for them to achieve their private requirements, they often seek by informal ways to satisfy themselves and to achieve the purpose of the college.

The interpretation of private motives, however, should be viewed in the light of Herbert A. Simon's description of them:

The phrase 'personal goals' which is used here should be understood in a broad sense. It is by no means restricted to egoistic goals, much less to economic goals. 'World peace' or 'aid to the starving Chinese' may be just as much a personal goal for a particular individual as another dollar in his pay envelope. The fact that economic incentive frequently predominates in business and governmental organizations should not obscure the importance of other types of inducements.[12]

Informal or spontaneous ties occur at all levels in the hierarchy.[13] The president of the college may have his own coterie of special friends on the board who in a pinch make it possible for him to have his way. Sometimes the informality is second person removed, as when one department chairman may ask his secretary to speak to the secretary of another department chairman in order to make an arrangement which seems easier to achieve by this device than by the face-to-face confrontation of the chairmen. Often, however, the greatest degree of informality or camaraderie exists among those of lowest status. These have less status to lose. Also, the nature of the decisions which they seek is less generalized and more specific; therefore, they are more prone to direct and easy agreement.

In the main, however, informal activities are engaged in, in higher education as elsewhere, by persons of relatively equal rank. If a person of high rank develops an informal relationship with a person of low rank there is a tendency on the part of their colleagues to speak in terms of favoritism, nepotism, or even graft.

The relations between two such persons, in addition, is generally difficult to maintain because of the intrusion of their formal statuses.

On the other hand, the college possesses a high degree of informality generally in its daily life. In contrast to certain business organizations and the military, for example, the college stands out as a prime example of relatively informal organization. This informality may in part derive from values in the general culture. It also may derive from the ancient tradition of the college itself. While informality is found *par excellence* in the college, it appears to be an increasingly prevalent ingredient in all highly and complex-graded organizations. In this connection John W. Gardner says:

One might suppose that the principle most antithetical to the large modern organization would be equalitarianism, since any complex organization is inevitably hierarchical. But the truth is that a rather high degree of equalitarianism is tolerated—even is encouraged within many large organizations. It is not an equalitarianism that extends over the organization as a whole, but governs a given level in the hierarchy, reducing the competition which might have characterized relationships at that level.[14]

Ralph H. Turner, in discussing the Navy disbursing officer as a bureaucrat, outlines three sorts of informal structures which pertain to that office, and which have a relevancy to the latent structures within the college. According to Turner, these are: friendship patterns, simulated friendship, and the exchange system. The friendship pattern occurs when the officeholder belongs to the same basic groups as do his clients. Where this takes place the officeholder personally wishes to help his friends and, in fact, in order to hold friends there is a need for a high degree of on-the-job accommodation.

In the simulated friendship (or, in Navy jargon, "earbanging") the relationships are less lingering and more uncertain. They take a number of forms, such as an officeholder treating one of lesser rank as an equal, particularly in the on-the-job situation. Such simulated friendship often calls for mutual helpfulness.

The exchange system is based upon the granting of mutual advantages. Thus, for the college, the registrar who establishes a final examination system favorable to a particular department may find himself invited to that department's Christmas party. Similarly, the business manager who supplies a new typewriter to the secretary of the department chairman may find that a commending letter by the chairman has been placed in the hands of the business manager or the president. All three of Turner's patterns are found within the college.[15]

Whenever the latent structures of an organization are employed, even to effectuate its formal goals in an efficient manner, there is a reliance upon a defensive ideology on the part of the participants. The status of the participants may be determined mainly by observing which one of two contradictory ideologies is employed. First, those in the lower ranking offices tend to defend their informal actions by attacking those higher up, notably those at or near the top. Such a person claims, for instance, that the top official spends too much time off the campus and does not know what is going on under his nose or that all high ranking officials of the organization are inefficient; otherwise informal means would not be necessary in order to achieve the institution's purposes.

Second, those who are relatively high up in the status system tend to be critical, when they use informal means, of those that are near the bottom. They say that they must take care of the details of the organization because there are so many "blunderheads," inefficient, or malicious people who have unfortunately been employed in the lowest ranks. In either case the expression of a sense of ideology is apparent. In a few situations "inversion" also may be practiced. That is, those in the highest and lowest ranks, as well as those in the middle, may turn upon those close to them in status claiming that informal means are required because of the deficiencies of their immediate colleagues.

Informal organization, as F. J. Roethlisberger and William J. Dickson discovered in their noted study of industrial organization, is not "bad." [16] Informal organization is inevitable in any bureaucracy. Higher education as a bureaucracy encounters it in much the same form as it exists elsewhere.

The top leadership of the college has as one of its principal responsibilities the "synchronization" of the organization.[17] By this term is meant the responsibility to see that the institution, in view of both its formal and informal organization, is administratively tied together in such a way that an over-all organizational harmony exists, that the component parts are related effectively to each other, and that the over-all purposes of the college are succeeding.

One phase of synchronization has been termed, in the study of bureaucracies, "cooptation." According to Philip Selznick, cooptation is "the process of absorbing new elements into the leadership or policy-determining structure of an organization as a means of averting threats to its stability or existence." [18] According to Selznick, this general mechanization of cooptation assumes two basic forms. First, formal cooptation which pertains to the "legitimacy of authority or the administrative accessibility of the relevant public." Second, informal cooptation which occurs when "there is a need of adjustment to the pressure of specific centers of power within the community."

Actually, Selznick's goal for the cooptative process seems unduly limited. It concentrates only on "averting threats to its stability or existence." One of the chief aims of a large-scale organization is not that merely of maintaining stability. It is that of creating harmony and flexibility. Robert Michels refers to this need in connection with an organization other than the college:

The history of the international labour movement furnishes innumerable examples of the manner in which the party becomes increasingly

»*102*

inert as the strength of its organization grows; it loses its revolutionary impetus, becomes sluggish, not in respect of action alone, but also in the sphere of thought. More and more tenaciously does the party cling to what it calls the 'ancient and glorious tactics,' the tactics which have led to a continued increase in membership. More and more invincible becomes its aversion to all aggressive action.[19]

What Michels indicates as a proneness of the international labor movement is undoubtedly true of the college. It requires cooptative processes as a part of the synchronization of its total effort which calls it not only to stability but to coherence and progress.

From an administrative point of view, however, the basic purpose for which the effort of synchronization is rightly aimed is decision-making.[20] "Policy" and "administration" have somewhat different meanings. Policy refers to those standards and agreements which are guiding principles for the operation of the college. Administration refers to the process of graded accountability whereby the college's policies are carried out. Decision-making is a core ingredient of administration. Although decision-making is a specialized function of administration, it is diffused through the various levels of the hierarchy of the college. The bulk of decisions, however, are performed in the lower-status offices—the fag end. This is necessarily so, since the quantitative brunt of the maintenance of the social system rests there. On the other hand, the more important and generalized decisions are made in the upper levels of the hierarchy. While the higher offices may have fewer decisions to make in a given day, the import of their decisions is commonly more far-reaching than of those made by the lower offices.

Decision-making rests structurally upon policy considerations, although every fresh decision is a presumedly new and unique interpretation of the policy. In decision-making the loyalty of the officeholder to the organization as a legal system and as a tradition is counterbalanced by the degree of independence and open-mindedness of the decision-maker.[21] Officeholders, moreover, who feel that required decisions in the interest of the organization violate their own standards commonly tend to pass their responsibilities on to others, notably those above them. As Arthur K. Davis says: "Responsibility tends to be passed upward; work, downward." [22] "Passing the buck" is as old as the hills. Possibly the first instance of it occurred in Genesis 3. When God inquired of Adam how he had come to eat of the tree of the knowledge of good and evil, he quickly declared that it was Eve who tutored him. Eve, in turn, was unwilling to take the blame. She told God that it was the snake who had tempted her. The course of the buck-passing in this case, we assume, was from higher to lower (was the Biblical account written by a man?). In the long course of history, buck-passing has been directed downward, upward, and every other way.

While "buck-passing" is a perfectly normal device whereby officeholders avoid responsibility, it can also be employed as an effective tool in administrative conflicts. The higher officeholder who for one reason or another is disliked may find that he is deluged by referrals from lower officeholders of matters which in peaceful and mutually cooperative times would unquestionably be decided by the lower officeholders. Also, there is a tendency on the part of officeholders to refer decisions to new superiors, for it is not always possible for an officeholder to know precisely what the wishes might be of a new superior.

Obversely, the adherence to "the book" of regulations, to the routine and perfunctory making of decisions by an officeholder, may at times also be an expression of resentment of, or resistance to a higher officeholder. Edmund G. Love, for example, tells the story of a distinguished warrant officer who during wartime had been cruelly forced to give up his perquisites and accept a commission as a major. By way of revenge the fellow did everything in scrupulous obedience to army regulations. This lengthened the war measurably.[23] Such behavior in the college pours a mixture of sand and molasses in the whirling wheels of progress.

The relationships between old members of a bureaucracy and new ones raises special problems for the efficiency of the personnel system. New appointees come about through succession and recruitment. These processes will be briefly discussed.

As Alvin W. Gouldner makes clear, the problem of succession in bureaucracies has seldom been studied, although he has made a contribution to the subject himself.[24] In addition, Arthur W. Macmahon and John D. Millett have studied the selection of bureau heads in government.[25] Studies of this phenomenon in higher education, however, are not yet in evidence.

Max Weber, the classic writer on bureaucracy, is impressed by the importance of charismatic qualities in the transition from old to new leadership. "Charismatic qualities" are indefinite, personal factors that are incapable of complete definition and control. He infers that the primary attribute of a successful successor is his possession of these qualities. Charismatic qualities, moreover, may depend not merely upon their presence in the personality of the successor, but in the system from which the successor is derived. Thus a successor may be readily accepted if the person who appoints him possesses charismatic qualities in a high degree or if the very process (for example, the choice of a new Dalai Lama) is charismatically oriented.[26] The nature of charisma and its relation to the college will be discussed in some detail in Chapter 9.

Alvin W. Gouldner also discusses the prevalence of the "Rebecca Myth" in connection with succession in an industrial organization.[27] W. Lloyd Warner and J. O. Low also provide an account of the operation of myths during a strike.[28] The "Rebecca Myth" refers to the young woman in a story by Daphne du Maurier who married a widower. She was plagued constantly by the memory of the widower's first wife, Rebecca, whose virtues appeared to be held in high esteem. The meaning of the myth for succession is that the officeholder who is absent or retired tends to be idealized. Those who served with and under him tend to magnify his strength and minimize his defects. This is a fairly universal phenomenon. Its presence within the college is evident as are the special problems it creates for the harmonious management of a bureau.

Another widespread consequence of succession is the reinforcement and enlargement of bureaucratic methods. The new officeholder, wishing to be a success, at least in the beginning of his regime, tends to rely upon the traditional procedures. In fact, in order to be sure of himself, he tends to be overdependent upon them. He finds in them a formal and unquestioned basis upon which his relations with his inferiors may be maintained. Only later, when the feeling of security has been satisfied, will the new officer be ready to advocate his own innovations. By that time, however, these tendencies may become submerged or routinized in the plethora of accepted rules and procedures. Thus succession, far from informalizing an organization, may add to its bureaucratic stature.

Recruitment to offices of standing in an organization also comprises a special problem. In a sense, recruitment is the obverse of succession. Succession, in its usage here, refers to the effect of the successor upon his colleagues and those of lesser status. Recruitment looks to the requirements which an officeholder must possess in order to succeed (be promoted) to a higher office. As was mentioned in Chapter 5, the most important qualification is that of seniority. While capability might seem on the face of it to be the most important qualification, seniority far outstrips every other consideration in recruitment. Yet other qualifications may be mentioned.

The age of the person also is a factor. Much depends upon the nature of the office. Often it is assumed that college workers dealing directly with students in informal situations should be young. The assumption is that youthful officeholders will be more readily accepted by the students and will be better able to understand them. But in other offices youthfulness is definitely not an advantage. In the higher ranges of administration in the college, it is assumed conversely that only an older person is an attractive recruit. The recruit to the office of dean, for example, is commonly an older person. The rationale is that by age, denoting experience, the officeholder is able to bring "wisdom" to his daily operations.

A further assumption for the recruit is that he has a broad outlook. This is especially true for higher status offices. Here the conflict between success in specialization and a comprehensive perspective is notably apparent. The lower officeholder who has succeeded, say as a teacher of mathematics, may be largely inadequate for a responsibility of a divisional chairman.

The recruit also should give signs of merit for his selection. The chairman of the college's curriculum committee with long years of experience in such matters, for instance, may aptly become a dean of faculty. His experience as a committee man, it is assumed, has secured for him a recognition within the institution of genuine qualities of intelligence and leadership.

The length of office-holding may be another consideration. It is not desirable in the college that all or practically all the major administrators retire at approximately the same time. Some scattering of age and tenure is a prerequisite to recruitment for such offices. Also, it is desirable that a person serve in his office for such a period of time as will enable him to demonstrate his virtues explicitly while not serving so long as to reach senility or exhaustion.

Finally, the benefits of the office should be attractive to the recruit. The rewards of responsibility may take two forms. First, there are the material elements such as salary, retirement benefits, housing, etc. Second, there are "psychic benefits," such as the office's title, standing amongst professional colleagues, reputation in other colleges, satisfaction to family, and a genuine chance to influence educational policy and procedures.[29]

In these and other ways the qualifications for recruitment play an important role in the successful administration of the college.

8

Driving Forces:

Myth

and

Matter

*I*t is proper and desirable, after look-
ing at the people who make up higher education as a bureaucracy
and its formal and informal organization as a social system, to
consider at least briefly some of the chief ideas and emotions
which provide a driving force to the institution. So that Carl J.
Friedrich is correct when he states:

The discussion of institutional manifolds such as bureaucracy, without
reference to a pattern of objectives toward which their operation is
directed, is like discussing plant growth without taking the sun into
account.[1]

This chapter will be concerned with the myths which guide

the college and the demystification and rationalizing of its basis for existence. The nature of power or authority in the college, the special role of charismatic factors, and the function of ceremonialism will be reviewed in Chapter 9. No effort will be made to provide an exhaustive or even nearly complete analysis of these factors. The prime purpose of their review is to illustrate the fact that abstract and covert forces are at work in the college as they are in other bureaucracies. The mythology of the college is the first subject to be examined.

The greatest myth of all in higher education is that no myths control the college. The common assumption—a gnostic pretension—is that the college of all of the community's institutions is devoted basically and fiercely to the discovery and transmission of the truth. It is further assumed that the college is or should be the most scientific (meaning rational) institution in society, since all of its members are completely devoted to the efficient attainment of the truth.

The same mode of thinking is held by the uninitiated concerning the college teacher. Some believe that the college teacher necessarily must be an almost perfectly reasonable and efficient person since he is so highly a sentient individual. He bears all of the marks, degrees, and recognition that go with the acceptance of such a view.

The college and college teachers, however, are both rational and nonrational. Both elements are intermingled in their lives. In this respect, despite some of its unique features, the college as a bureaucracy is similar to any other. All bureaucracies and their personnel are dually grounded—on rational and nonrational factors. The analysis of the blending of these factors in this chapter and the next lays the basis for understanding the driving forces of the college.

The college does not stand autonomously clear of the rest of society. In certain respects it widely influences community affairs. On the other hand, the college to a large degree secures its guiding ideas from the community. Richard Hofstadter illustrates this point in his comments on the origins of the modern idea of academic freedom:

The modern idea of academic freedom has been developed by men who have absorbed analogous ideas from the larger life of society. From modern science they have taken the notion of a continuing search for new truths, fostered by freedom of inquiry, verified by objective processes, and judged by those who are competent. From commerce they have taken the concept of a free competition among ideas—hence, the suggestive metaphor of a free market in thought. From the politics of the liberal state they have taken the ideas of free speech and a free press and an appreciation of the multitude of perspectives in a pluralistic society. From religious liberalism and from the long historical development which led to taming of sectarian animus have come the ideas of toleration and religious liberty under which they have benefited.[2]

The college, therefore, while it is an influential institution in society, on the whole, is shaped in its basic premises by the society of which it is a part. Such a society also is based both on rational and nonrational assumptions.

Herbert A. Simon speaks about "the proverbs of administration."[3] The college indeed has its own proverbs of administration, that is, certain beliefs which it brings to bear upon situations within the institution in the effort to affect an explanation and motive for the way things are done. But, in addition, and on a larger scale, the college relies upon myths for the satisfaction of its members and the community. Now a myth is usually a traditional or legendary story which is concerned with some superhuman being or some alleged person or event, whether these are with or without a determinable basis of fact or a natural explanation. But myth, in sociological terms, also connotes a collective belief that is built up primarily in response to the wishes of the group. By the sociological definition, it is possible to view the myths of the college, as well as those elsewhere, as essentially nonrational.[4]

Of course, it does not need to be said that "non-rational" in no way signifies "irrational." Myths are extensions of logical ways of thinking to a point where common, universal, emotionalized beliefs become a satisfying explanation for those procedures and events which are close at hand and which, from other vantage points, might respond in explanation to other methods, especially scientific methods. Myths signify that which all thinking must presuppose.

What, then, are some of the myths of the college? Several concrete suggestions may be made.

The late President William C. Fels of Bennington College edited *The College Handbook* in 1951, a digest of self-formulated descriptions by member institutions of the College Entrance Examination Board. These descriptions give insight into the myths or images which are controlling for them. Fels in 1959 wrote a "spoofing exegesis" of his *Handbook*.[5]

The product, aside from being plainly humorous, underlines the contrast between rational pretense and the mythic reliances of the college like a great big hairy spider crawling slowly across a gaily-colored travel poster of Capri.

Fels says, for instance, that almost every college, by one turn of phrase or another, seeks to be both urban and rural. Hood College, Maryland, claims: "To the advantages of the country campus and small town setting are added those of the metropolitan areas of Washington and Baltimore." Brown University in Providence, Rhode Island, however, makes the same claim although its location is clearly urban: "From the historic Market House, one may look straight up College Hill to an elm-shaded campus . . . The almost perpendicular hill has made it possible for Brown to retain the atmosphere of a country college."

Another aspect of the almost compulsive imagery of the college is its concern with topography. Cornell University, Ithaca, New York, speaks of its location on a hilltop: "In a remarkable number of instances, the founders of American universities have chosen a hilltop as the appropriate site for an institution of higher learning. Ezra Cornell chose the top of an especially impressive hill . . ." President Fels, with tongue in cheek, adds: "The higher the hill, the higher the learning." He also indicates that colleges are "obsessed by the need to reveal their exact relationship to nearby water. Beloit is 'on the east bank of the Rock River.' Carleton is 'on the east side of the Cannon River, which flows north'."

Fels also has examined the collegiate lexicon in greater detail. He says:

A women's college is one that has none of the disadvantages of coeducation but has several select men's colleges within a few short miles. Wells' 298 girls have 'many joint activities with Colgate, Cornell, Hamilton, Hobart, Rochester and Syracuse . . .' All colleges are small colleges . . . The advantage of a small college is that it combines unity with diversity. For example, Washington and Lee (900 undergraduates and 160 law students in 1951) 'is small enough to maintain a sense of unity, yet large enough to provide diversity.' On the other hand, Wellesley (1,650 students) 'is large enough to provide diversity and small enough to provide a sense of unity.[6]

Looking further into the notions which form the image of the desirable college, according to the colleges themselves, Fels examines such terms as the "well-rounded" man (women's colleges do not like to use this term), "develop the individual," and "high quality education." In connection with the last idea, "high quality education," Fels admits that he had to go beyond *The College Handbook* to find a definition of this puzzling phrase. He says: "Now, at last, the phrase has been defined by the presidents of Amherst, Smith, Mount Holyoke and the University of Massachusetts . . . 'by high quality education,' say the four presidents, 'is meant a type of education which is equivalent to that which each of our institutions offer'."

On the basis of his research Fels sat down to write a description of Bennington College, employing humorously many of the terms which other institutions use concerning themselves:

Bennington College is a small, rural, private, experimental, women's college of high quality which emphasizes the development of the individual. It shares the cultural advantages of New York, Boston, and Montreal. Its hill is moderately high. From it, on a clear day, you can just see, beyond the toilet paper factory, the historic Walloomsac River flowing northward away from Williamstown, where there is a small, rural, private, experimental college of high quality for well-rounded men.[7]

Thus, each college seeks to fit into a generalized pattern of what it conceives a college as best to be like. Few institutions actively seek to be too much different from the guiding ideal even though the guiding ideal is nowhere to be found. In fact, the myth is still potent enough to control the energies and talents of a considerable body of institutions of higher education.

To the extent to which the guiding ideal does exist, it probably centers in the "Ivy League" colleges. These colleges, despite any efforts they may make to the contrary, tend to be the controlling images for other institutions. When Harvard College, for example, under President Eliot introduced the cafeteria-like elective system, other colleges more or less hurried along to keep in step. Later when Harvard College sought to overcome the excesses of the elective system through the development of a curriculum in general education, many other colleges also reversed themselves and modeled their curricula accordingly. What is true in the case of Harvard College, moreover, is true to a greater or lesser extent for some of the other so-called Ivy League colleges. Fortunately, of course, there have been significant differences in motivation and development among a number of non-Ivy League colleges.

In 1959, John K. Norton, retired head of the Department of Educational Administration at Teachers College, Columbia, made a series of charges at a luncheon meeting of the Eighteenth Annual Work Conference of School Superintendents in connection with the "Ivy League bunch." He stated that these colleges were publishing articles on American public education that were "untrue, low-down, name-calling, and mean." He claimed that the eastern United States is dominated by "an Ivy League psychology" and favored what he called "an aristocratic type of education." Norton claimed that "the Ivy League crowd controlled many of the country's magazines" and that "the attitude among these Ivy Leaguers is much different from people elsewhere." He said: "A good many of them think that if you don't go to the private school, you are of a relatively low cut." [8]

Colleges, whether Ivy or not, tend to think of themselves, despite acknowledged limitations, as in some mysterious manner the best. There is hardly a person, student, faculty member, administrator, etc., in America's colleges who would not make this claim for his own institution. He might add "for me" or "in the circumstances" or some other qualifying phrase, but it is difficult to be disloyal.[9] John Donne's description of a person could well apply to every college, as the one who

> thinks he hath got
> To be a Phenix, and that there can be
> None of that kind, of which he is, but he.

The effectual display of institutional loyalty is particularly keen when new members are appointed to the staff. Few other bureaucracies, if any, by their very nature have the problem of inbreeding which the colleges do. The evident tendency is for colleges to value most highly their own graduates when it comes to the making of appointments. Richard H. Shryock, for example, points out that about 70 per cent of the Ph.D.'s of the Wharton School received them at Pennsylvania, and have done nearly all of their teaching there. In the Arts College about 55 per cent of the faculty over the age of fifty hold Pennsylvania Ph.D.'s, but of the full-time staff, ignoring age, only 47 per cent hold them—a fact which shows that a deliberate attempt to reduce inbreeding has recently been made.[10] This degree of inbreeding of Ph.D.'s may also hold true for other schools, colleges, and universities, but it is a true fact that undergraduate colleges to a significant degree tend to hire those, aside from their advanced degrees, who have their own baccalaureate degree. There's no place like home!

If the college accepts irrelevant and even rationally unfounded beliefs for itself, how about its intellectual pride, the teaching staff? Is it also guided by covert ontological assertions? In this connection Seymour M. Lipset, writing in *Daedalus*, suggests that professors currently suffer from two misconceptions about themselves. Apparently they are able to accept these notions despite the inadequacy of the supporting evidence. First, low status. According to Lipset, the people of the United States respect the professors far more than they imagine. In 1947, the National Opinion Research Center at the University of Chicago polled Americans on how they rated ninety-six occupations. College professors emerged on a par with bankers and corporation directors, were outranked only by physicians and top political leaders. The 1947 study was replicated by the Center in 1963, and the correlation between the 1947 scores and the 1963 scores was 0.99. A similar national poll in 1950 placed professors fourth in twenty-four categories: 38 per cent of those polled called them "upper class." Low status? A myth.

Second, low income. Says Lipset: "There are really two income structures in modern Western countries, the private and the public one." A United States Supreme Court justice earns far less than he could in corporate practice. A cabinet officer in the federal government usually takes a sizeable cut in salary to enter government service. By comparison, a full professor earns a minimum of $12,000 at some top American universities (*versus* a United States District Attorney's $12,500), plus more through books, articles, lectures, and consulting fees. Lipset concludes: "The truth is that professors, like the lawyers who become judges, really believe that the noneconomic rewards of the job are better than monetary gains." [11] Financially undervalued? A myth.

Professors hold other myths. One concerns the nature of the student generation. On this score, as with others, there need not be a single myth controlling all of the college's personnel. Thus Edgar Friedenberg can claim that youth have so few channels for effective expression and growth that they are "vanishing." [12]

Fred Hechinger, a *New York Times* writer on educational matters, can claim essentially the opposite, namely, that today's youth are getting out of hand because their energies are not being controlled by adults.[13]

Teachers also believe themselves to be important centers of influence over their students. That this is a belief without dependable proof has been shown in a limited sphere by Philip Jacob.[14] Lawrence W. Hyman spoofs this conclusion in a satirical article which begins as follows:

A few months ago, a committee was formed to investigate the relationship between higher education and human values. Aided by a $500,000,-000 grant from three leading foundations, this committee has undertaken to find out why the liberal-arts colleges have so little effect on the beliefs, the judgments, and the values of American students. As chairman of this committee, I have been asked to make a preliminary report to the trustees of the foundations, which have so generously contributed to our work.[15]

In the bitter style of the satirist, Hyman proceeds to try to devastate some of "the sacred cows" or myths of the college.

Without going into detail it is possible to name other myths held by college teachers: the college as a "community" or "community of scholars," the teaching effectiveness of instructors, the "liberal arts" nature of the curriculum (*versus* vocationalism), the self-sufficiency of the physical sciences, the ease or difficulty of promotion. Theodore Caplow and Reece J. McGee from their own study add the following myths to the current list:

. . . research over teaching, disciplinary loyalty over institutional, the importance of the prestige factor, resentment toward a colleague who goes to another job, diminishing classroom loads, the 'indelible mark' of the graduate school, the crucial importance of the age thirty to forty in a professional career, the fateful significance of the first professional connection, stresses in the institution, academic feuds, and the influence of departmental budgets.[16]

Substituting "the college" for "modern thought,' the comment of Helmut Thielicke makes striking sense: ". . . the history of modern thought with its succession of 'isms' is like a gigantic parade of idols. And how comical the idols that have just marched past look from behind!" [17]

Ordway Tead says:

> On too many campuses many responsible members of the faculty may know the objectives that they individually are striving to advance, but if asked about the *institutional objective*, they would be hard put to it to give a commonly shared and cogent answer—an answer clearly consistent with the realities of sound campus life and purpose.[18]

Tead is partly right. He is right in asserting that it is almost impossible for a faculty to define its institutional objectives. Aside from some vapid generalities that pass uncritically, it is harder for the college faculty precisely to define its aims than to hit a ping-pong ball in the midst of a hurricane.

But Tead misses the essential point. Higher education also commonly is unaware of its unstated and unstable premises, the bases for its operations which are the silent suppositions of its organized life. These undergirding assumptions comprise its mythology and as such are a prevenient factor of great significance for the understanding of the college.

The myths of higher education may be classified as unconscious and strategic. Unconscious myths are those which happen to spring up in any collection of people. They are not contrived. They exist to serve relatively unstated needs—for protection, grandeur, or some other satisfaction. Colleges are full of them. The athletic prowess of the sports heroes of yesterday is a fertile soil. The misty origins of the college with its almost sacred luminaries comprise another source. The faculty, moreover, when lubricated by a cocktail or two are prone to recount the famous battles of the faculty council or "that odd, young man in the Mathematics Department." There seems to be no overt neceessity for the maintenance of this myth system. It relates to unconscious needs, both individual and collective.

Strategic myths are those characterized by conscious intent.

They are matters of deliberation. They do not possess a folk semblance. Thus a college, by utilizing selective data, may seek to show that it ranks very high in the production of some recognized virtue. The virtue may be physicists, foreign missionaries, college presidents, or just plain school teachers. But the effort to strengthen a collective representation of the college through the deft employment of supporting evidence is characteristic of the strategic myth. The strategic myth which is built upon an unconscious myth—an example of Socrates' maieutic method—is a sure winner.

It is not a sign of cynicism to say that the college may develop its mythic potential in an effort to conceal real goals. Such double-dealing is thought by some to be a sign of defensible cleverness. Thus a college may claim that it is raising its academic standards and, thereby, is limiting its entering class. The fact may be that the college is not financially able to continue with the number of students previously enrolled. Retrenchment of program may be promulgated as the raising of standards.

Regularly the college possesses enough myths, both in number and variety, for the justification of almost any type of action. So a myth in the college may begin in one form and with a particular content; it may change into another form and even secure a different content and the product may not be unplanned or even unpleasant.

But the college has more than myths as its driving forces. Like other bureaucracies it gives lip service and a great share of its energies to the continual processes of demystification and rationalism. Myths constitute the shadow side of demystification and rationalism. Both of these elements, however, are counterbalanced, as will later be explained in the next chapter, by charismatic factors and ceremonialism. At this point demystification and rationalism will be examined for their meaning for the college.

Max Weber considered the bureaucratization of society's institutions to be a paralleling and complementary development in the Western world to the demystification or secularization of the world (*Entzauberung der Welt*). Only as the work activities of modern man were released from their religious moorings in an earlier period did the prospect of a highly flexible and efficient system of human organization become possible. Bureaucracies, in this view, are a human product, accountable to human ingenuity and change. The primary criteria of the success of the bureaucracy are organizational justice and efficiency. These goals are not necessarily a direct product of religious values, although, as Weber believed of the Protestant Ethic, they are a worldly fulfillment of them. Today the organization in itself tends to become a sufficient personal and social goal for its personnel.

Higher education as a bureaucracy seeks to fulfill the requirements of demystification and rationalism. Despite its adherence to myth, it openly and publicly leads a self-justifying existence. It looks to no transcendent goal as a judge of its needs or successes. Although such tenets may be held by the staff of the college for their private lives and may receive respectful enunciation on special occasions, such as commencements, in the main, the college as a bureaucracy gets along very well in its explanation and defense of itself by merely referring to its own nature. The college may claim to be guided by "education" or "the truth" or some other grand idea, but in actuality it assumes that it is the existential embodiment of most if not all such ideas.

The demystification or secularization of the college has been one of the most significant forces in the historical growth of American higher education. As Hofstadter says:

The most significant trend in collegiate education during the eighteenth century was the secularization of the colleges. By opening up new fields for college study, both scientific and practical, by rarefying the devotional atmosphere of the colleges, by introducing a note of skepticism and inquiry, the trend toward secular learning inevitably did much to liberate college work. Secularization was evident in several ways: in more commercial and less religious tone of newly founded colleges; in the rapidly rising number of college graduates who went into occupations other than the ministry; and in vital changes in the curriculum, notably the rise of scientific studies and the modification of theology to include freer philosophical speculation.[19]

Although as an historian Hofstadter is providing comment particularly on the eighteenth century, the fact is that the process of demystification has been gradually increasing. It covers not only those elements of the college's life mentioned by Hofstadter, but the entire ideological, organizational, and procedural existence of the college as a bureaucracy.

Higher education is characterized by rationalism. Rationalism connotes the principle or habit of accepting reason as the supreme authority in matters of opinion, beliefs, or conduct. That which is agreeable to reason is preferred. The reasonable or sensible is the excellent. The originally Greek assumption that man is rational predominates in the college. Rational men, so the argument runs, should bring the test of rationality to all of their beliefs and actions. The college is no exception. College workers regularly appeal to reason as their ultimate guide in preserving or changing the organization.

The guiding doctrine of rationalism in American higher education has many sources. One of them is the inheritance derived from Hegelianism. By this view reason is inextricably tied to essence. Essence rather than existence is the true reality. Education should be concerned, by this line of reasoning, with reality.

Hegelian rationalism was a deterioration of the scholastic position. Scholasticism taught that in God essence and existence are identical. By this it meant that God could not be conditioned by a difference in the orders of reality. In God there is no possibility which is not also an actuality. In finite beings, however, such as man, the distinction is possible. The separation of essence from existence is a mark of finitude.

Hegel, however, introduced the ontological principle into this discussion. He sought to show that reason and essence are closely related if not identical. Schelling termed this identity*Unvordenkliche* or that principle prior to which thought cannot take place.

If reason is so closely related to essence, in the Hegelian view, then existence becomes something less than both reason and essence. This layercake perspective on the relations between reason and existence, then, led to the exaltation of the role of reason in human affairs. It became the *Prius* of all beings.

The college, being rooted to a large degree in German idealistic thought, even today possesses a basically Hegelian assumption regarding the reign of reason. It tends to think of "interests" and "passions" as being inferior to reason. Reason is the instrument by which essence is tapped. It is the means whereby all of the lesser factors in human existence and nature are to be evaluated and finally prized. It is the sole basis for the organization of life. It is the guiding mode for the organization of the college and the conduct of its activities.

There is more anguish shown in the college for a violation of so-called rational principles than for the breaking of the Ten Commandments. The disciplinary officer says: "I am concerned that you acted unethically, but I am equally concerned at least with your failure to see the reasons which justify the moral behavior for which the college stands." Or the teacher announces proudly in class: "I don't care which conclusion you arrive at as a result of your investigations, so long as your reasoning is defensible." Reason, thus, tends to become more than an instrumental virtue. It becomes an end. From an Hegelian viewpoint, such is proper, for reason, after all, is the same as essence.

The result is a form of private autonomy for all persons in which reason is both an end in itself but, also and paradoxically, an instrument for the self-justification of myopic parochialism. One wonders about the strange pride of the college graduate for whom the color of the furniture in his living room sometimes has more interest than Rembrandt's canvasses, and the construction of a backyard swimming pool more fascination than the architecture of the Vatican. Reason is artfully employed by him to support the adoration of his cast-iron, glass-topped dining room furniture, his subscription to the Book-of-the-Month as a standard literary diet, his attendance at the opera once and Broadway plays six times a year, his membership on the membership committee of the local Kiwanis, his Cadillac, his two oil paintings bought on a Greenwich Village street, and his mortgage to a bank for an old Colonial house in Manhasset.

Karl Mannheim has distinguished two forms of rationality: the functional and the substantive. Higher education is characterized by both. The former is the ability to formulate and employ operational techniques to arrive at any goal. The latter is the ability to think and act sensibly, above the plane of intermediate ends, and with reference to perceiving and acting upon the difference between more immediate means and more ultimate aims.[20] For example, functionally, the teacher of a course on juvenile delinquency surveys the available materials on the subject and organizes them in reference to the goal of the teaching of the course. Substantively, the teacher of a course on juvenile delinquency desires to develop attitudes of good citizenship on the part of his students. To that end he organizes the details of the course in such a way that his goal is achieved. The use of reason in both instances is clear.

Similar patterns of action are employed throughout the college. The monocratic or scalar system of hierarchical organization of the staff is a fine illustration of substantive rationality. The use of staplers instead of paper clips is an apt example of functional rationality. The college keys its efficiency by relying upon combinations of both forms. Such is the conclusion of Robert K. Merton: "A formal, rationally-organized social structure involves clearly defined patterns of activity in which, ideally, every series of actions is functionally related to the purposes of the organization." [21]

In the college the personnel is responsible for the maintenance and development of rationally-devised means for the attainment of rationally-defensible goals. These goals largely are found within the context of the organization and are assumed, by the historic process of demystification, to rest upon rational grounds. These goals are the formal and allegedly rational bases upon which higher education as a bureaucracy exists.

"Plagiarism" also marks the college's acceptance of rationality. The college, at least theoretically, is constantly seeking the most efficient principles and procedures for the achievement of its goals. To the extent to which the college is able to devise these from within its own staff and experience, it may be said to be highly distinctive. But in view of the fact that no one college has a monopoly of creative innovation, there is a clear effort made within many institutions to copy the policies and their implementation which are found elsewhere.

Efficiency is the rule, no matter what the source. As intimated previously in this chapter, the Ivy League colleges may be the colleges most plagiarized. The prime stress of rationality is efficiency. It abhors inefficiency as the righteous man hates the flamboyant foxtrot in the middle of a mission compound.

One might wish that the college were absolutely rational in its every aspect. Unfortunately it is not. Previously the role of myths as a driving force in its organization was described. Other factors, now bearing attention, also lead to the conclusion that the college is a mixed field for rational and nonrational forces.

Rationality in itself seems to call for a higher principle to resolve those conflicts which in all conscientiousness are viewed as rationally supported. In the college, one department, for example, may think that it possesses ample rational support for teaching a course on social psychology, but another department with equal rationality as its support will claim the opposite. A faculty senate may be faced with two courses of curricular development as alternatives. The body may be divided regarding the rationality of them. Commonly, such a body decides between alternatives not on the basis of rationality alone, but on the basis of a democratic vote. Voting is a form of resolving power conflicts rather than the achievement of rational consensus. So power or authority also comprises an important mode of organizational action in the college.

Power comprises an important element in the practical affairs of the college. Power is exercised in the name of rationality. It also tends to supersede reason in both the foremost councils and the backwash areas of college activities. Since it constitutes so significant a factor in the college, it is proper that it receive some analysis in connection with the forces which make the college a dynamic organization.

9

Driving Forces:

Power,

Charisma,

and Ceremonialism

The nature of power is a regular theme of novelists who take higher education as their setting. Theodore Morrison's novels, as an example, are concerned with the use of power in the college. In *The Stones of the House*, an ex-professor, acting as president, discovers a taste for, and a humane skill in, using power.[1] In *To Make a World*, a university-foundation sequel, a hinted-at passion deflects a great administrator from the use of his power for great organizational service.[2]

Again, Carlos H. Baker has examined the manner in which power is wielded in the university. In the story, he concentrates on the search for the right holder of supreme power at Enfield University. Edward Tyler, a Voltaire specialist and head of its

French Department, is selected by his colleagues as one of a committee of six to help the trustees select a new president. He speaks eloquently of the professor demoted to a presidency: "When he sits down at the president's desk a light goes out somewhere on the frontiers of knowledge." Tyler's candidate for the presidency is his friend, Cos Cobb, a biologist. Cos, unaware of Tyler's support, emphatically eliminates himself. It turns out that Tyler is the sacrifice agreed upon by both faculty and trustee committees for the presidency.[3] The presidents of many colleges are chosen not on the basis of a rational process of selection, but on the accommodation of power interests.

Although the college may give the appearance of rationality in many of its actions, it is in actuality a hotbed of divisive power blocs. There is nothing new about this. Henri d'Andeli wrote his *Battle of the Seven Arts* about 1250 A.D. At that time the classics were already the older subjects in the universities. They were fighting a losing battle against the newer subjects. As the French poet lamented:

> Logic has the students,
> Whereas Grammar is reduced in numbers.[4]

For the more recent times, David Riesman notes:

Implicit in all I have said is the notion that what my collaborators and I speak of in *The Lonely Crowd* as the 'veto groups,' the political and social blocs and groupings that frustrate political action in the United States, operate also in the intellectual realm, in terms of departments and fields. Each prevents the others from growing too big, from encompassing too much.[5]

The several academic divisions of the college regularly and simultaneously assume defensive and aggressive attitudes towards each other. Robert D. Heilman reports on the humanities:

In the humanities, for instance, it is almost habitual for practitioners to raise their voices in a style that is at once defensive and promotional. Ever since the war, humanists have been protesting, often in a rather accusing way, the value of their services to the human community. I hope I am not disloyal to the humanities if I confess some embarrassment in hearing humanists with loud speakers proclaiming the salvationary powers of their enterprises. What purports to be a disinterested pursuit of grace of mind begins to look like a strengthening of organizational prerogatives, a membership drive for a quasi-ecclesiastical body claiming influence at the gates of a cultural heaven.[6]

Similarly Carl Murchison decries the allegedly weak position of the social sciences:

The social sciences at the present moment stand naked and feeble in the midst of the political uncertainty of the world. The physical sciences seem so brilliant, so clothed with power by contrast. Either something has gone all wrong in the evolution of the social sciences, or their great day in court has not yet arrived. It is with something akin to despair that one contemplates the piffling, trivial, superficial, damnably unimportant topics that some social scientists investigate with agony and sweat. And at the end of all these centuries no one knows what is wrong with the world or what is likely to happen to the world.[7]

In addition to these few illustrations of the divisions in the college according to power blocs, there are others—far too many to be catalogued—such as pro- and anti-administration groups, "old" and "new" departments and subdivisions of departments, "insiders" and "outsiders," alumni and college, students and administration, faculty and community.

The plethoric power divisions within the college dim somewhat the advocacy of rationalism by some college workers. From the perspective of the power relations, the claim for the supremacy of rationalism seems utopian and sentimental. In fact, without the support of psychoanalysis, it is easy to see that rationalism often in the college signifies rationalization, that is, college officeholders first make decisions regarding their individual and bureau interests; then they proceed to think of the reasons that provide intellectual support. This phenomenon is not distinctive of the college; it is apparent everywhere in human life. As Philip Selznick points out for bureaucracies, there is a variety of bases for "organizational commitments," not all of which may be categorized as rational.[8]

From the standpoint of a Christian understanding of man and society, it is possible to aver that the academic community is no more to be identified with the Kingdom of God than is any other sector of the community. The college, no matter what its formal auspices, is indeed an unredeemed community insofar as its members are unable to transcend their private interest in the interest of the larger group or organization.

The presence of power cleavages in higher education, however, must not be taken as an unmitigated evil. Actually, power or the possession of coercive influence over resistant individuals and groups may very well be a good thing. Reinhard Bendix is aware of this fact in his discussion of governmental bureaucracy. He says in reference to it:

. . . there is also much evidence to show that it has furthered the cause of human freedom; and the great critics of 'governmental interference' have often overlooked the latter point. Thus, the classical critics of mercantilism tended to forget that the emergence of absolute monarchy had been a powerful factor in the development of business enterprise, which certainly at the time was regarded as assuring the merchants greater freedom than they had hitherto enjoyed. Likewise, the modern critics of the 'service state' tend to forget that governmental 'interference' has increased individual freedom by promoting social security, just as the earlier governmental aid in the development of corporate enterprise and western expansion increased the freedom of the business man.[9]

So, too, the expression of power in the college cannot always be assumed to be on the side of evil. The president who exercises absolute power over the budget and makes an unusually generous allocation to the library for the purchase of books cannot upon the basis of this action alone be deemed an evil user of power. The faculty senate which passes an enforceable resolution favoring the abolition of athletic scholarships cannot automatically be criticized for the negative employment of power. Power appears to have neutral quality at times, although it obviously is an extension of private interests. Its rootage is not necessarily in universally acknowledged rationality.

Driving Forces: Power, Charisma, and Ceremonialism

It is difficult, moreover, to locate events in the college which may be understood solely in terms of the interplay of power considerations. Negative attitudes toward power are often held by those who fail in its exercise. Those who succeed generally clothe their actions with the defense of rationalism. An administrator who "has his own way" in a particular matter, according to those who are resistive, will to himself be able to provide reasons which he assumes transcend self-interest. And he will use propaganda-like imputations to explain the behavior of the defeated.

The evaluation of the existence and use of power, moreover, cannot be understood without taking into account the preferences of the evaluator. Reinhard Bendix illustrates this truth by referring to contrary evaluations of the power relations between business and government, according to two authoritative evaluators.[10] He points out that Ludwig von Mises holds that business is democratic and government, dictatorial.[11] On the other hand, Beardsley Ruml finds that business is dictatorial and government, democratic.[12] Competent observers with differing prejudices may well come to different conclusions regarding the distribution and use of power within the college.

"Power" suffers from a multiplicity of varying and vague definitions. Its meaning can be whatever the definer wishes it to be. For the present purposes, power is the exercise, either potentially or actually, of coercion in those events where a conflict of interests exists. For example, the humanities departments may hold a different conception of their role in the required curriculum of the college from that of the physical sciences. The resulting curriculum, brought about by discussion and voting, illustrates the exercise of power. Power also may be the effective factor in the settlement of disputes between individuals within the college. Commonly, however, power in this form is a factor where the individuals concerned are of relatively unequal status.

In the monocratic or scalar system of interpreting the college's organization, the term "authority" is more meaningful than "power." The exercise of authority does not in itself signify resistance. It points to a higher plane upon which responsibility is assumed. The exercise of authority does not necessarily imply the exercise of personal interests. Thus, Robert K. Merton says: "Authority, the power of control which derives from an acknowledged status, inheres in the office and not in the particular person who performs the official role." [13] Chester I. Barnard confirms this definition of authority when he says:

If a directive communication is accepted by one to whom it is addressed, its authority for him is confirmed or established. It is admitted as the basis of action. Disobedience of such a communication is a denial of its authority for him. Therefore, under this definition the decision as to whether an order has authority or not lies with the persons to whom it is addressed, and does not reside in 'persons of authority' or those who issue these orders.[14]

Authority, in this definition, exists not only from the top offices downward in a bureaucracy. It exists downward, upward, and sideways. When an officeholder refers a matter to his superior for decision he is implicitly acknowledging the downward aspects of authority. When a department chairman asks his secretary to devise an efficient system of filing, and she does so, and he accepts it, he is accepting the upward flow of authority. In the college there may be many instances in which authority flows upward as downward, since in so many ways, as is true of other bureaucracies, it is the specialized worker on the lower levels who has the most detailed and competent grasp of the situations under review. The higher officeholder may confirm or reinforce the authoritative views or decisions of the lower officeholder; generally he is in no position to dispute the wisdom of the recommendations he receives.

Authority also is exercised laterally. A professor in mathematics may ask a colleague in physics for mathematical illustrations involving physics for his classes. To the degree that he accepts his colleague's recommendations, he is accepting the authority of his office.

Driving Forces: Power, Charisma, and Ceremonialism

Authority, however, is not automatically operative. There are situations in which it is merely tolerated rather than accepted. There also are situations in which it may be rejected as violating either the personal code of the officeholder or the requirements of the organization as he understands them. Of course, both alternatives may be combined. In this connection, Chester I. Barnard speaks of the "zone of indifference." [15] This same phenomenon is termed the "zone of acquiesence" by Herbert A. Simon.[16] Barnard explains his views:

The phrase 'zone of indifference' may be explained as follows: If all the orders for actions reasonably practicable be arranged in the order of their acceptability to the person affected, it may be conceived that there may be a number which are clearly unacceptable, that is, which certainly will not be obeyed; there is another group somewhere more or less on the neutral line, that is, either barely acceptable or barely unacceptable; and a third group unquestionably acceptable. This last group lies within the 'zone of indifference,' obviously the subordinate officeholder is inclined to act freely upon all those expressions of authority which lie in the 'zone of indifference.' He may have qualms about those orders which lie in the neutral zone. Assuming the normality of inter-office relations, however, the subordinate is likely to accept the authority of his superior when it falls in this zone. Rarely, but importantly, when the exercise of authority impinges upon policies or procedures unacceptable to the subordinate, disobedience is likely to be the result.

A variety of personal pathologies must be noted in any discussion of the use of authority. Lyman Bryson notes that: "A more or less conscious desire to dominate and get ahead in administrative hierarchy pervades the behavior of all members of the staff." [17]

Such an observation of human behavior is realistic rather than cynical. Bureaucratic aggressiveness may generally be classified as normal behavior, but there are instances when this behavior becomes extreme. Two forms will illustrate. First, the narcissistic. Some officeholders are greatly enamored with themselves. They cannot trust most decisions to their subordinates. They hold to what they have and seek to get more. Second, the sadistic. Some administrators seem bent on "punishing" those beneath them. They go out of their way to derogate their subordinates. Often an administrator punishes his subordinates with an inhuman amount of work.

Finally, the total staff of a bureaucracy believes in its inherent right to manage its own affairs. Viewed internally, the college may be a house divided against itself. But, in the face of outward interference or attack, as has been immemorially true, the collectivity tends to assert its pseudo-unity. Resistance to outward intrusions are met with claims of rightful (including legal) responsibility for the conduct of the college.

In certain respects other bureaucracies, such as business and government, have explored the relevance of "moral philosophy" more deeply than has the college. The moral philosophy of the college is assumed rather than elucidated. In business, studies have been made of the ethical implications of office-holding. Benjamin M. Selekman has analyzed the businessman's problem of reconciling a successful business with the ethical concepts of the Judaeo-Christian tradition and American democracy.[18]

He states that the business bureaucrat undergoes three dangers: self-righteousness, cynicism, and perfectionism. Each of these he describes in chapters which are related to the total organization of business and to the requirements of the community. Similar studies are not available for higher education.

In Chapter 8 it was asserted that the modern bureaucracy rests upon demystification and rationalism. Both of these forces are evident in practically all aspects of the life of the college. Those who rely heavily upon the claims of rationalism are inclined to assert that all elements of *mystique* have been eliminated from the college, that it is a thoroughly rational enterprise without reference to nonrational compulsions. This view has been seen to be false. Power is operative in the college and it cannot be subsumed under the category of rationality. But, there are other elements in the organizational makeup of the college which also lessen the absolute claim of those who are extreme advocates of rationalism.

An additional factor, not previously mentioned, is the process of sanctification. By this process, elements of rational design within the college, such as a form for recording grades, take on a moral legitimacy which is virtually unchallengeable. These elements are assumed to be kingpin factors in the college's operations. They cannot be changed or denied, it is assumed, unless one maliciously seeks to ruin the organization. They represent in the minds of their believers a Pandora's box the opening of which would automatically lead to disaster.

Charisma and ceremonialism are two further components in the college which deserve consideration. They too reveal the driving forces at work in higher education as a bureaucracy. These now will be discussed briefly.

Charisma refers to an extraordinary personality characteristic, possessed by persons who are thought to have either divinely obtained or otherwise possess "exemplary leadership" powers. Charisma pertains to those qualities of leadership which are viewed by most persons as non-acquirable. In Jacob Bohme's terminology, charisma is *Innerlichkeit*. It does not greatly matter whether the person or office possessing the charismatic mantle actually possesses such characteristics or not. What is important is that there are subordinates who accept such an estimate. In this sense, charisma is counter-rationality. Its presence, moreover, in the college is blended, as are all of the several elements mentioned in this and the preceding chapter, in varying degrees in varying persons and bureaus.

Some may assume that charismatic elements are the very opposite of bureaucracy, that bureaucracy means social order while charisma means exceptionalness. But, such is not the case, as Hans H. Gerth has shown with the Nazi Party.[19] Charisma is very much at home in bureaucracy. Its presence is spread throughout all of the personnel. No one possesses an exclusive monopoly of it. Every officeholder maintains and extends himself through qualities of leadership which come under this heading. The presence of charismatic leadership occurs when, for example, in the face of conflicting alternatives, a person makes a decision which through the force of his personal characteristics is taken to be efficacious by those who accept.

The charismatic element also is in display in the originative processes in higher education. Whenever modifications are made in policy or procedures, leadership is at work. All leadership implies charisma in degree. Creative efforts within the college, therefore, are always characterized by some degree of charisma. Charisma is not irrational; it is nonrational. It is not so much a quantity to be weighed as it is a quality to be observed in persons and events.

Charismatic elements, as Max Weber has pointed out, tend to be unstable. He says: "It cannot remain stable, but becomes either traditionalized or rationalized, or a combination of both." [20]

The existence of the college with its present ramifications of activities, organization and personnel, all may be taken as expressions of former displays of charismatic leadership. In this view nothing comes into existence without persons of innovative force who achieve *this* rather than *that*. Each aspect of the college has its own history of innovation even as the college does as a whole. Thus, a department of biology is an unaccountable entity without reference to the persons and events historically which brought it into being and shaped it to its present existence. The shaping, influencing, elements observable in such a department have at their core some persons of charismatic leadership.

Yet, once an innovation has been secured, it tends to be supported not through the constant implementation by charismatic qualities on the part of the leadership, but on the more routine grounds of rationality. There is a conserving force to tradition. That which was brought about in the college in the past as a result of tremendous personal effort may be viewed today as justifiable without reference to any personalities of the past. It tends to stand on its own feet. It assumes an existence of its own. Fresh charismatic leadership, therefore, if it is to be successful, always must challenge the *status quo*. It must press factors of rationality as far as they will go and add to them those personal appeals which "carry the day" and gain the acceptance of followers. The old yields to the new. But, again, the new becomes rationalized and institutionalized.

One of the difficulties with charismatic leadership is that it is not entirely responsive to the ordinary tests of virtue. The Nazi Party had charismatic leadership in the person of Adolph Hitler. Such pathological expressions, rarely so distorted in the college, may not be challenged immediately and effectively. Restraints to evil leadership of a charismatic sort usually require time for their formation, growth, and effective expression. In many instances it is difficult to discern even in the final shattering of such leadership where the ultimate virtue may lie. Surely rational tests are not entirely convincing.

Charismatic elements are also apparent in the selection and promotion of officeholders. The fraternity, for example, commonly employs this criterion—hopefully, after it has exhausted all others. A hundred students may be technically and formally eligible for membership. The fraternity may be able to elect only a small number of the total. The process of selection, aside from the precise character of its details, ultimately will rest upon the presence of appreciated characteristics on the part of the applicants. These are of a charismatic nature.

The choice of a faculty appointment in a department also may depend finally upon the charismatic qualities of the winning applicant in a field of candidates.

Quite often bodies in the college which are concerned with promotion find that many more persons are technically and formally eligible for promotion than can be promoted. Such bodies may with care apply every rational test that they know to select the most qualified. In the final analysis, however, there are always elusive and nonrational factors present in the candidacy of certain faculty members which cause promoting bodies to put them to the fore. So much so is this condition present in the promotion procedures of the college that some, both deciders and candidates, take the attitude that the stated procedure is merely a formal necessity, that the decisions largely have been made prior to any detailed and rational consideration. Charismatic factors, however, are not to be "blamed"; they are simply present in every decisive situation. As Max Weber says: "Charisma can only be 'awakened' and 'tested'; it cannot be 'learned' or 'taught'." [21]

The charismatic elements of higher education are abetted by ceremonialism. Ceremonies pertain to the formalities observed on certain important occasions. They range from meaningful observances to small gestures or acts of politeness or civility. Even the strict adherence to conventional forms comprises an aspect of ceremonialism. Ceremonies aim to increase the dignity of functions.

Higher education, despite the sharp disclaimers made on occasion, is thoroughly devoted to ceremonialism. Two principal reasons may be given for its prevalence. First, ceremonialism is a way by which the myth system of the college is maintained and reinforced. It is characteristic of ceremonial occasions—academic jamborees—that they are redundant in the phraseologies of the unprovable. They extol extreme virtues. They depend upon the cliches of educational professionalism. The commencement is a most evident example. On this occasion the college is paraded before a sometimes unsuspecting public (certainly before the in-group, which should know better) as the paragon of all that is best. Nobody speaks of the students who have failed, unless it is to refer rhetorically to the success of those who have succeeded. No one refers to the "loafers" among the faculty, for this might ruin the idea of the faculty as a hard-working group of devoted educational servants. No one relates the stresses and conflicts of the institution, for this would not be seemly, unless it can be turned to advantage for the appeal of more staff or buildings. The commencement is bathed in ceremonialism; the major myths of the college are reasserted and reinforced there in public. Ceremonialism as a means of preserving myths is apparent also on other occasions.

Second, ceremonialism is an effective means for the celebration of the status system of the college. In ceremonies the personnel is arranged according to rank. This arrangement is noted in a physical sense in printed programs and observationally in the conduct of the ritual. Thus, to use the commencement again as an illustration, the status of all participants is made clear in the "line-up." The students, the lowest in status, appear on the scene first. Last to appear is the presidential group, including the members of the lay board and invited dignitaries. In-between, in a carefully graded fashion, are all of the other ranks of personnel. Any officeholder knows his "place" when he participates in a ceremony.

The enforcement of status by ceremonialism is particularly difficult as the size and complexity of a ceremony increase. A ceremonial occasion which encompasses the entire college may run into difficulties because the functional system of hierarchy may come into conflict with the scalar system. It may be clear as to how the so-called academic staff will be assembled. But, what the position of the business manager, the public relations officer, the dormitory personnel, and others will be may be in doubt. Regularly, however, colleges facing such a situation have worked out a complete system on paper which may be brought forth on such occasions—as an anniversary dinner. Despite the difficulties, the ceremonial occasion is a collective instrument whereby the college restates its hierarchical order.

The methods or patterns by which formal organizations engage in status-reaffirming ceremonialism have been previously studied.[22] Four of a larger number will be briefly described. First, there are ceremonies of induction. Secularization has led to a de-emphasis upon extensive ceremonialism in connection with the induction of members to the college staff. There is no "laying on of hands" from the top to the bottom of the hierarchy. Some attention is given, however, to the induction of some of the top officers. The inductee to the lay board may undergo a ceremony conducted by the college president, for private colleges, or by an elected official of the government, such as a governor, for public colleges. Induction ceremonies also prevail for the top administrative officer of the college, whether he is termed president, chancellor, provost, or some other title. Vice-presidents, deans, department chairmen, and others of their approximate rank, are today not granted induction ceremonies. On the other hand, those for whom college or community-wide ceremonies are not arranged may find themselves the subject of a more informal process, such as a departmental tea, a special luncheon in the faculty dining room, or a brief speech at the bureau's June picnic.

The main features of induction which pertain to the workers of the college are faithfully imitated by students in their organizational life.

Second, insignia of various kinds comprise another part of the methods of college ceremonialism. Since higher education as a bureaucracy has been greatly influenced by demystification and rationalism, the number and use of insignia have decreased over the years. Currently they are most evident in the office of the chief executive, the president. His office, for example, may be adorned with the flag of the nation. In addition, he may have the flag of the state or an emblematic representation of the community or of the college. On formal occasions he may also carry a mace or some other physical symbol of his status. Top administrators, for obviously secular reasons, sometimes are noted by their daily refreshed flower in the buttonhole.

The faculty of the college also cherishes its insignia. The widespread use of charms (honor society keys) is an indication of status display. The employment of caps, hoods, and gowns at the cookbook-like induction ceremonies of Phi Beta Kappa and other honor societies is also a means by which the faculty cloaks itself in the aura of status.

The college's affection for insignia is found also in the student ranks. Students, some with reason to boast, are classified into a variety of categories: freshman, sophomore, junior, senior, Dean's Honor List, *cum laude, magna cum laude, summa cum laude*, scholarship or fellowship holder, award winner, class president, student government president. For many of these designations there is a formal document, scroll, diploma, etc., which memorializes the status. Students use these, as do their professors, to adorn their rooms at home.

Quite often the academic departments of the college which allegedly have the least claim to academic acceptability are those which employ insignia most generously. The use of loving cups and letters by departments of physical education is an accepted practice in practically the whole of higher education. The organization of the insignia and reward system of a department of history, for example, on the basis of that currently employed in departments of physical education, would prove a challenge to the equanimity of almost any campus. Yet some kind of insignia, awarded for performance to students, is a feature of practically every department of the college.

Third, the ceremonial apparatus includes deference to titles of office and calling. The separation of the title of an office from the person of the officeholder, a bureaucratic characteristic, is observable in the college, particularly on formal occasions. The chief executive officer of the college will be addressed at functions, such as a dinner or the meeting of the faculty council, as "the president." The reference is to the office rather than to the officeholder. The reference, moreover, connotes respect and civility toward one's superior. Similarly in a department meeting, particularly under strain, the chairman may be addressed as "Mister Chairman." The use of a person's first name is frowned upon in any situation in which the status of the members is a significant factor in the relationship.

Much of this symbolic engagement is aimed at the maintenance of the college's status system and the differentiation of the officer from his office. Yet, the office and the officer at times become confused. Such confusion requires prompt reiteration of the distinction. As Chester I. Barnard says:

Much of this symbolic practice related to office in the abstract is transferred to the person of the individual filling the office, and in this way the individual himself by reason of his status becomes a symbol of the organization and of its purposes. This is so true that although it is usually not difficult to distinguish between personal and official acts *per se*, it is not acceptable in general to distinguish personal and official behavior of individuals or for them to tolerate contumelious behavior of others toward them when wearing insignia of office or otherwise publicly known to hold office.[23]

Fourth, the emoluments and perquisites of office also are bound up in the ceremonialism of the college. The nature of the officeholder's physical office is quite often a reliable index of his placement in the status system. It is unthinkable, for example, that the president of a college in his Lucullan splendor should not have the very best office of any of the college's staff. Similarly as one proceeds downward in the hierarchical arrangements, one discovers that the nature of the physical offices by and large are symbolic representations of the degree of status held by the officeholder. In some colleges, symbolic elements, such as private telephone, carpet on the floor, more than one filing cabinet, sheer size of the office, location on campus, etc., are all persistent ways of ceremonially marking off the ranks of the staff. So, too, it is common that the higher status personnel have more material benefits as a function of their offices. Members of the college staff may live in homes which they rent or purchase. The president's house, however, may be provided by the college and indeed may be a physical symbol on the campus of the centrality of the role of the president.

The members of the faculty or other staff members—the college's Janizaries—rarely are the recipients of honorary degrees granted by other colleges and universities. But, generally, so far as the personnel of higher education is concerned, honorary degrees are overwhelmingly granted to college presidents. Such blazonry, it is tacitly assumed, is one of the expectancies of the holding of the office. The granting of such degrees may be considered as a form of recognition to the office mainly, and not entirely to the officeholder. It is the institution in large part which is honored through the granting of the honorary degree to its leading officeholder.

The development of ceremonialism in the college has taken many forms, aside from those mentioned. Often they cannot be distinguished from certain fads or crazes which spring up and sweep across collective life from time to time. Some by reason of their ritualistic patterning of beliefs and actions strike deeply with the intensity of a desperate lover's promise into the character of the college. They may be illustrated by reference to the "progressive education movement" which characterized a section of educational theory in the past and presently still is a vital force. Ernest Earnest in a clearly exaggerated description describes this viewpoint as characteristic of certain colleges:

Teachers' Colleges, cut off from the genuine values of a cultural education, chased after every fad and fancy dreamed up by the so-called progressive educators. They studied English by carving Macbeth's castle out of soap; they did theses on dishwashing and janitorial work; they adopted meaningless slogans such as 'teaching pupils, not subjects' —which implies that a progressive educator can teach a pupil without teaching him anything. They developed a trade language 'pedagese'; their research turned up such truths as the discovery that pupils of different size need seats of varying height; they dealt in large generalizations about government and society like George Sylvester Counts' assertion that 'Capitalism no longer works,' or William Heard Kilpatrick's analogy of the yearly change of automobile models to demon-

>*141*

strate that the Constitution was obsolete. Even their patron saint, John Dewey, denied some of the heresies promulgated in his name.[24]

Fad-like behavior is also a characteristic of the students. Milton Eterow, for instance, reports that the "big college prom is on the decline." In his view: "It is prom time in colleges and universities across the nation, but the big class prom is vanishing." What was once a major ceremonial feature of collegiate life has now passed into a decline. Says Esterow: "The trend is to small informal dances sponsored by fraternities, sororities or other college groups, with local bands supplying the music." [25]

Experienced college administrators are regularly aware of the manner in which student behavior becomes ritualized, often under the impulse of seemingly nonrational incentives. A fresh example of such conduct was provided in 1961 when on Canadian campuses from coast-to-coast a bed-pushing mania became "the thing." Tania Long reports:

The rules of the game are simple, though still in a fluid state. As many as thirty or forty students may take part. The game is conducted somewhat like a relay race. Six or eight students push or carry a hospital bed for varying intervals of time and distance while their teammates follow in cars or chartered buses to relieve them.[26]

The swallowing of goldfish in the Scott Fitzgerald era and the more recent research into how many bodies can be stuffed into a telephone booth are other signs of ritualistic behavior. The description of college students' vacation behavior by Glendon Swarthout, and the later movie version, also comprise a humorous but cruel thrust against the presumed rationality of the college.[27] At other times the ritual takes an individually sentimental form as: "A Wellesley girl returning by train to Virginia for the Christmas holidays happened to look at her watch. 'It's silent time at Wellesley now,' she said. Instantly a hush fell over the Wellesley girls traveling with her." [28]

The student protest movements that sprung up during the academic year 1964–1965 and which continue in various forms today also illustrate the manner in which students are prone to participate in socially deviant behavior in forms that catch on originally in particular campuses and spread throughout higher education. The Berkeley student revolt provides an apt example, now with ample documentation.[29] The slogan of "free speech" became a rallying cry of nonrational dimensions at Berkeley and, later, on many other campuses. Sometimes the objective was tied to civil rights, but at other times it was related to the loosening of parietal rules maintained by the college, the advocacy of international political positions, and the demand for educational reform.

But no matter what the form may be, fad behavior is a significant feature of college life and for all of the inhabitants of the college. Although its content may change from time to time, it is potent in its characteristically ceremonial performance. Ritualistically it depends upon repeat performances and must be carefully and devotedly carried out. The deviant is as popular as a hail-Harry inebriate at the annual convention of the WCTU.

By its nature, fad conduct is nonrational. No one is able to show why one pattern at a given time is found on many campuses. No one knows why a rampant pattern is suddenly *passé* and replaced by another. Little is known scientifically about this sort of behavior on the campus or elsewhere. Yet it provides a satisfying and absorbing experience for many. Its efficacy rests not on reason, ultimately, but upon collective needs which are difficult to apprehend rationally. The task of defining these needs and their relations to their satisfactions falls beyond the scope of this book.

In the last two chapters the effort has been made to describe in general terms the driving forces of higher education as a bureacracy. The ideas and emotions which constitute the dynamics of the college were seen as enormously complex in their nature and in their gangliated relations. They tend to polarize around the nonrational and the rational. Myths, power, charisma and ceremonialism illustrate the nonrational expressions of the collective life of the college. Demystification and rationalism, however, are powerful counteractants, aimed as they are to efficiency.

Nonreason and reason, however, are not disparate elements in the college's makeup. They are closely interrelated. At times it is difficult to distinguish one from the other or to ascertain which is the more influential and dependable.

10

Impersonality

and

Rules

Soren Kierkegaard once remarked: "Take away paradox from a thinker and you have a professor."

It is the abstract and objective anthropologist whose character is delineated by Ian Brook in fictional terms. Caught in all of the tormenting ambiguities of darkest Alabasa Province in an unnamed British Colony in West Africa, the anthropologist in his plodding and impersonal way goes about studying illiteracy among Alabasa's albinos.[1]

Such estimates of the orientation toward prosaic objectivity on the part of college officeholders, whether by Kierkegaard or Brook, indicate the reliance placed by higher education and its personnel upon the value of objectivity. Objectivity is one side of the coin; impersonality is the other.

Impersonality is a characteristic of the interpersonal relationships within a bureaucracy as well as the goal and consequence of

profound scholarship. Max Weber originally stated the bureaucratic requirements of impersonality in these words:

The dominance of a spirit of formalistic impersonality, '*sine ira et
studio*,' without hatred or passion, and hence without affection or enthusiasm. The dominant norms are concepts of straightforward duty
without regard to personal considerations. Every one is subject to
formal equality of treatment; that is, every one in the same empirical
situation. This is the spirit in which the ideal official conducts his
office.[2]

This characteristic of bureaucracies is the basis for "officiousness,"
according to Marshall E. Dimock. He says that officiousness is
"one of the public's strongest objections to bureaucracy," and in
his view "is the evil which must be guarded against." [3]

In this chapter and the next the several attributes of "formalistic impersonality" will be examined. In the present chapter the
nature of impersonality will be delineated and applied to several
aspects of the college's educational functioning. The nature and
the role of rules also will be briefly discussed. In the following
chapter, three other aspects of impersonality will be analyzed:
paper work, red tape, and communication.

At the outset it is well to realize that higher education is not
unique in the present time in laying primary stress upon impersonal and objective factors. Everywhere in society it is the facts,
and only the facts, which are prized. Everett Knight's characterization of "the objective society," is not far off-focus.[4]

Higher education like society generally, is oriented to a marked
degree toward things rather than people. Or, as Martin Buber has
shown, there is one world, but in its manifestation it is twofold.
On one hand, there is the "it" aspect, the objective world of
things with which the person maintains an I–It relation. On the
other hand, there is the personal or human aspect of the unitary
world with which individuals stand in an I–Thou relation. The college in the main has glorified those relationships which can be objectified—the I–It relations—the world of objective fact. It has

tended to neglect those aspects of reality which are expressed in the I–Thou dimension. The objectivism of the college derives partly from this profound cultural distortion.[5]

At many points the college seems to hold an uncritical allegiance to objectivism, but in doing so the college in part is exercising its best intelligence, for a college can never tolerate the mere display of personal bias. It cannot forgive conclusions based on only a segment of the evidence. Loyalty to the complete and impersonal truth—not *my* or *your* truth—is a prime feature of higher education.

Yet Pilate's old question remains: "What is truth?" Can it ever be possible for any person or group to attain to anything more than its own version of the truth. Does the attainment of objective truth, if it is possible, automatically rule out personal commitment? Are all matters reducible in the final analysis to objective terms, making false those areas of human experience in which scientific standards are not obtainable or relevant? Such questions are authentic and at times are debated on the campus in a lively manner. Despite the theoretical "answers" which might be given to them, however, the fact remains that the college, in part because of its basic function and in part because of its nature as a bureaucracy, depends upon "formalistic impersonality" in its organization, procedures, and personal relations.

The pose of objectivity may be interpreted in certain instances as neutrality. Whenever human groups are strongly divided in their sentiments it is well for the honest searcher at least to begin with an attempt to be value-free, that is, to be neutral. Carl J. Friedrich says that a governmental bureaucracy needs to be neutral, not only out of loyalty to the impersonal operations of the bureaucracy itself, but in deference to the divisions that exist within the community. Thus:

It is the essence of *governmental* bureaucracy to be *neutral* with regard to the interest and opinions which divide the community. This does not say that every or even any bureaucrat is in fact neutral, but

>*147*

it is their tendency to be that. Naturally, public services are composed of human beings with opinons and prejudices of their own (although some writers have at times forgot that), yet the neutrality of the whole remains of central significance.[6]

Emerson Shuck, however, has declared that the teacher's pose of neutrality may represent "a fatalistic value judgment, concealed by protective coloration."[7] He claims that teachers by assuming this stance are "abdicating from responsibility." He believes that expertness should be expressed not only in connection with the facts, but in relation to their meaning. No wonder, then, that the student feels at times like the frontierswoman who saw her husband grappling with a wild bear. Not knowing precisely what to do and how to begin, she simply shouted: "Go to it husband, go to it ba'ar!" The result of such neutralism in higher education is apparent in the personalities of many college graduates. They are thin men in a flat world.

Several reasons are apparent for the stress within the college on objectivity. Three of these may be mentioned with profit. First, the rapid rise historically of the importance of the physical sciences in the curriculum, with their accompanying stress upon objectivity, has tended to shape the entire college. Although some humanists and social scientists have objected to this dominance and have sought to express other values, they have generally not been able to turn the tide. In fact, many of them have succumbed to the extent to which they consciously direct their energies toward the imitation of the methodology of the physical sciences. For example, even though the major trends of his work belie some of the minor conclusions which he draws, Albert Camus, a competent and appealing humanist, attempts in *The Plague* to make war, violence, and other ways of committing human injustice value-free and natural by throwing them into the strictest kind of analogy with the biological effect of the plague bacillus.[8]

The growing dominance of science in the college and the

resulting situation has been summarized by dyspeptic Thorstein Veblen as follows:

Whereas it may fairly be said that the personal equation once—in the days of scholastic learning—was the central and decisive factor in the systematization of knowledge, it is equally fair to say that in later time no effort is spared to eliminate all bias of personality from the technique or results of science or scholarship. It is the 'dry light of science' that is always in request, and great pains are taken to exclude all color of sentimentality.[9]

Second, the complexity of the modern college and its reliance upon a bureaucratically extensive material apparatus calls for a spirit of objectivity. In former times, when the curriculum was less diffuse and specialized, there was less opportunity for conflicting truths to be presented to the students. The faculty, possessing a common educational background and value perspective, was more united in its basic presuppositions with the result that a high degree of intellectual harmony confronted the students. Today knowledge itself has grown to such proportions both in size and complexity that only a highly ramified and specialized staff can keep track of it. As the staff member follows out his specialized interests, the possibility of institutional coherence and common agreement upon truth becomes less evident and feasible. Currently the college is characterized not by "the truth," but by "the truths." It is this development which Irving Babbitt saw taking place even at the turn of the last century:

One can scarcely consider the tremendous stir we have been making for the past thirty years or more about education, the time and energy and enthusiasm we are ready to lavish on educational undertakings, the libraries and laboratories and endowments, without being reminded of the words of Sir Joshua Reynolds: 'A provision of endless apparatus, a bustle of infinite inquiry and research, may be employed to evade and shuffle off real labor—the real labor of thinking.[10]

More recently the experience of scatteredness and routinization was met by a foreign visitor:

When I first went to study in the United States, after having studied in European and Canadian Universities, the principal contrast which struck me was how much harder I had to work than ever before. Reading lists were garguantuan, assignments plethoric. I found the work for four courses per semester overwhelming, and considered that two courses would be a more reasonable load for a student who devoted all his time to his studies. My immediate reaction was to feel that the criticisms of American educational standards were sadly misplaced. But then I began to realize that in all my busy round of reading, lectures and paper-preparing I was failing to find time for the only really important activity I had gone there to do: thinking. Shockingly little of what I was reading was I making *my own* in any lasting or significant way. There was never time for reflection upon my reading afterwards: there was always another assignment waiting to be hurried through.[11]

The pluralistic or scattered nature of the college is—to put the matter in another way—simply a reflection of the character of the larger community. In the United States particularly, the society is culturally heterogeneous. Social scientists are prone to be skeptical about any conclusions drawn both within and without their fraternity which would seem to assume the simplicity, unity, or coherence of American culture. More accurately, they speak about the subcultures of America. These taken together do form some vague and even self-contradictory construct. The result, however, is incapable of providing precise guidance for value decisions.

So, too, the diversity of the general culture is found in the college. The college is composed commonly of persons with widely differing traditions, presentments, and convictions. The sheer fact of diversity has led to a tacit agreement that so-called tolerance is a prime rule of successful human management. Everyone is quite willing to grant that everyone is unique so far as values are concerned. Furthermore, it is assumed that no one should deliberately shatter the social harmony by talking seriously about private values. Thus, out of respect for the situation, characteristic both of society and the college, the pose of neutrality is not so much insisted upon as it is loyally assumed as the first rule of good manners and good education.

Third, the manner in which the college conducts its activities currently leads to a high degree of impersonality. The fact that college officers and publications loudly prate their firm belief in individualization and close personal relationships on the campus may be an indication of an awareness of the very opposite. Several illustrations of the college's impersonality will be given.

Even in connection with such highly important matters as admission to college is the trend toward routine and objectivized procedures evident. College admissions officers are deeply aware generally that they depend to a very high degree upon certain objective "scores" which are made available to them through their own efforts and those of others. Jean T. Mather, then president of the American College Testing program, in 1961 announced the achievement of "an electronic robot" which now helps admissions officers with their responsibility. This robot, an electronic computing system, measures a student's academic potential. It should eliminate most of the guesswork in gauging chances of college success. It is expected that the machine will be able to predict the student's over-all freshman grade average and his freshman marks in English, mathematics, social sciences, and natural sciences. About five hundred colleges started utilizing this means for determining admission to college in the fall of 1962.[12]

Sometimes a single machine-provided score is not deemed to be absolutely objective. Thus, in the case of the Scholar Incentive Awards in New York State the primary dependence upon the same examination the Regents now give to decide who will receive regular Regents' Scholarships. But, to prevent a worthwhile student from losing incentive payments because of a single, bad test score, those who fail to get a sufficiently high Regents' mark will be able to qualify on the basis of a good mark in College Board examinations or another recognized entrance test. From one perspective the New York State action seems to be skeptical of the validity of objective tests. From another standpoint, however, it is evidence of an even greater dependence upon them.[13]

The student seeking admission to a college is commonly tested by such objective means. In addition, he must present impersonally the required number of high school credits, usually called "Carnegie Units."

When he is admitted to the college, the student immediately faces a highly organized system of education. The system is described in the college's "Bible," the catalogue. This compendium tells the entering freshman how many academic credits are required of him for graduation as well as for his progression through the college from freshman, sophomore, junior, to senior status. It records the number of credits or courses he is able to take in a given semester. It provides detailed standards for the evaluation of his performance, the "A" through "F" scale. These also may take the form of a secondary grading system, commonly called "quality points." The catalogue further may differentiate his tenuous hold upon the college system by outlining the bases within a term or within his college career as a whole when he may find himself on "academic probation." In these and a multiplicity of other ways the college confronts the students, both upon admission and at every point thereafter, with a highly detailed and objectified system of rules and regulations. Every student is expected to run the same obstacle course; and although some modifications may be possible through an "elective system," even here, departments have rather specific advice for their majors. It is evident that the college is not a highly individualized, personalized experience. For the student it is a highly formalized, impersonal, and rule-managed enterprise.

The classroom provides another area within the college where impersonality prevails. Five aspects of classroom instruction will now be examined to illustrate the point. These fall under the headings of technique, cant, lectures, class size, and examinations.

First, even in the classrooms, where one might expect education to flourish in its most personal form, there is a high degree of rule- or technique-oriented impersonality. Richard Livingstone speaks autobiographically:

Education continually tends to degenerate into technique, and the life tends to go out of all subjects when they become technical. It is possible to read Plato's *Republic*, as I did when an undergraduate, without realizing that it deals with the deepest of all problems—what good life is, why man should wish to live it, how a state can be created in which it can be lived.[14]

Second, so much of the classroom experience is centered in an overriding stress upon cant. Jacques Barzun notes this characteristic:

It so happens that there is one professional disease, or rather vice, which generates precisely this feeling and whose consequences are therefore fatal. I refer to Hokum and I hasten to explain what I mean. Hokum is the counterfeit of true intellectual currency. It is words without meaning, verbal filler, artificial apples of knowledge. From the necessities of the caste, nine-tenths of all teaching is done with words, hence the ever-present temptation of hokum.[15]

Of course, the nature of the subject matter and the quality of the teacher and class affect the employment of hokum.

Third, the routinization and impersonality of college teaching consists of lecture notes and assignments that are maintained from year to year and generation to generation. Very few teachers indeed throw out all of their outlines and prepare fresh notes and examinations each semester, but, on the other extreme, many simply rehash from decade to decade what they discovered while students at their master's seat in their graduate schools days:

In 1877 Bliss Perry discovered that his first Latin assignment at Williams was identical with that given to his father in 1848. And in 1916 his son started with the same assignment. As Perry says: 'For sixty years at least, and probably longer, it was the same squirrel in the same cage.' Perry was talking about students, but the really caged squirrel was the instructor who went through the same routine with the same texts year after year.[16]

Fourth, impersonality of the classroom is related to the size of classes. In most institutions of higher learning a paradoxical situation exists. Teachers in general believe that the aims of higher education can be best achieved through small classes. On the other hand, the board and administration of the college realize that such an arrangement is grossly uneconomical. They reason that it is wasteful for a teacher to say much the same thing to small groups of students. Two different philosophies of the nature of education are here in conflict.

The view that education is primarily concerned with the accumulation of objective knowledge to be tested in periodic examinations as a process of credit accumulation has led in part to the present classroom organization and procedures. Bruce R. Morris comments on the problem from a teacher's standpoint:

Most people do not realize that often more education goes on in the faculty offices than in the classrooms. But one cannot spend much time with a student if he has several hundred others to see. So the professor, out of self-defense, becomes an impersonal voice. Moreover, classroom discussion disappears. Time does not exist for instructions with large numbers of students expressing their views—the subject matter must be covered. Thus, the individual student has no opportunity to try out his ideas, subject to challenge by the instructor and fellow students. Nor does the instructor have an opportunity to probe the student's mind by a series of questions in order to force him to think more deeply than is his custom.[17]

Fifth, the examination system of the American college is also rooted in impersonality and objectivity. Gone are the days of William James who recalls that Oliver Wendell Holmes, his teacher, asked James one question. When James answered correctly, the Autocrat responded: "If you know *that*, you know everything; now tell me about your family and the news at home." [18] Today the reliance upon tests has reached such a point that Mary McCarthy satirically describes the founder of a mythical college as so believing in "the use of aptitude tests, psychological questionnaires, even blood-sampling and cranial measurements," that he hoped "to discover a method of gauging student-potential and directing it into the proper channels for maximum self realization." This educator, in the words of the novelist, "saw himself as an engineer and the college as a reclamation project along the lines of the Grand Coulee or the TVA." [19] No wonder then that Howard Mumford Jones is able to state: "The canny student is not unaware of the relation between academic regularity and job-getting, and he is therefore sometimes accused of giving back to the professor on his examination paper what the professor, or the professor's assistant, wants him to give back." [20]

The great stress placed upon objective examinations in the college has led Jacques Barzun to declare:

Every man of education ought to take a solemn vow that he will never 'check' anything on a printed list. Students should not be asked to pass so-called objective examinations, which are the kind composed of mimeographed questions to be marked Yes or No, or to be solved by matching the right name with a definition.[21]

Or as a fictional professor says: "One can't help but respect an integrity that buckles at putting a check beside 'prejudiced but genial' or 'truly liberal.' " [22]

Recently, however, there have been some signs that the trustful and even worshipful reliance of some educators on the results of objective tests has been weakening. Banesh Hoffman, a perceptive professor of mathematics, for example, has been employed by the Westinghouse Science Talent Search and the Educational Testing Service as a critic of their testing procedures. Both privately and publicly he has shown that such tests are far from adequate. With prophetic stringency he states:

The nation, in short, is placing enormous reliance on machine-graded multiple-choice tests as a measure of ability. But, unhappily, it can be shown that they have grave defects. Our confidence in them can have dangerous consequences, not only for education but for the strength and vitality of the nation.[23]

Such a critical note, however, is far from completely deflecting the widespread reliance upon objective tests. If one means of dependence upon objectivism is found to be faulty, the result will probably not be the elimination of objectivism, but rather the development of newer and better instruments.

These five aspects of classroom activity illustrate the reliance of the college upon impersonality. Undergirding these five and others, however, is the ever-present and increasing reliance in higher education upon automation. Machine-dependent learning is today a widespread fact in higher as well as lower education. The use of various audio devices, films, language laboratories, closed circuit television, and other such means has tended to divorce the individual student from the traditional relations of a personal character with his teacher. The employment of computers beyond the classroom provides the college with an understanding of its activities which scarcely was possible even a few short years ago.

Another illustration of the impersonality and objectivity of the college is provided in the matter of degrees. The college degree today has become what the high school diploma was a generation ago. The B.A. degree or its equivalent currently comprises a kind of union card for admission into the world of work. Those who possess it have open to them a wide range of vocational opportunities and increased lifetime earnings. Those who do not possess the degree may well succeed, but their success will be made in the face of handicap.

There is, of course, little or no individuation in the matter of holding a degree, although a degree "with honors" may be more meaningful than one without. Some hiring agents look beyond the degree to the personality of the applicant. But an almost inevitable starting point for consideration for almost any responsible position in society today is the possession of the college degree. Charles Homer Haskins establishes this contrast: "A great teacher like Socrates gave no diplomas; if a modern student sat at his feet for three months, he would demand a certificate, something tangible and external to show for it—an excellent theme, by the way, for a Socratic dialogue." [24] We do not know whether Socrates' disciples actually did receive some manner of certification, but it is known that the American college student (and his parents) for a long time has looked upon the acquiring of a degree to be the most important product of higher education. The president of the University of Georgia, for instance, discovered in 1865 that "the American people were generally satisfied with the *name* of a college, and sought for their sons not so much an education as a degree." [25]

What is true for the B.A. is also evident for the M.A. and the Ph.D. Sixty years ago William James warned against the corruption of the doctor's degree in his essay "Ph.D. Octopus." He believed that the "decorated diplomas" of Harvard stifled personal and spiritual growth and resulted in professors who were neither good teachers nor great scholars. Dr. George Boas, in 1961, discussed the routinization of the Ph.D. in an article entitled "The Three Magic Letters." Said Boas:

My criticism of the Ph.D. is that he usually is not a great scholar. He is usually a young man who has taken a required number of courses in a given field, written something called a thesis—which defends nothing—and passed an examination in the reading of French and German a few days before taking his orals . . . He is simply a person who has passed certain tests which test endurance, assiduity, and a faculty's charity.[26]

Thus on all levels the degree is a principal sign of achievement and status. Impersonally it comprises the social card of introduction to the grand ball of life.

Impersonality also is created through the use of obscure language. Sometimes the obscure language is a foreign language, as in the case of college diplomas, while at other times it is a strange form of English.

In April, 1961, many educators and others noted the hullabaloo which occurred when the Board of Overseers of Harvard University approved the abandonment of Latin as the language for diplomas. As a result of this switch to diplomas which can be read by nonclassicists, some Harvard students became as angry as a fat bull switching his tail to keep biting flies off. They protested and rioted on the campus. Their demonstrations spilled out on to the streets of Cambridge. The Cambridge police fired tear gas bombs to break up a throng of several thousand students in Harvard Square. Four students were arrested on charges of disturbing the peace and the matter received wide publicity. So serious did the situation become that Dr. John U. Monro, Dean of Harvard College, said that Harvard had been brought "to the edge of serious trouble" and reminded the undergraduates of the standing rule of the college about public disturbances:

A student who is guilty of an offense against the law and order at the time of a public disturbance or unauthorized demonstration or who disregards the instructions of a proctor or other university officer at such time may have his connection with the university severed. The mere presence of a student in a disturbance or unauthorized demonstration makes him liable to disciplinary action.[27]

The demonstrating subsided and a tradition dating to 1636 disappeared.

At Columbia College, on the other hand, the valedictorian, John Vaio, gave his address in June, 1961, in Latin. This was the first time since the turn of the century that the address had been given in Latin. At Columbia a group of students objected to the valedictorian's use of the language. It was Harvard College in reverse. But the Senior Week Committee resolved the issue with a compromise plan under which Mr. Vaio spoke in Latin and a printed English translation of this address was distributed with the program.[28]

The experience with Latin and English in formal occasions at Harvard and Columbia Colleges aptly illustrates the manner in which words in the college's life are utilized to create obscurities

—another form of impersonality. The desire to utilize an ancient and unfamiliar language on diplomas and on ceremonial occasions illustrates, even if in uneven form, the apparent need on the part of college personnel to cloak their ideas in forms that are relatively distant from their hearers.

Although bureaucracies greatly believe in words, both oral and written, they are not above obscuring meanings. This fact was noted by Granville Hicks in some comments on the evasion of clarity:

This is peculiarly a trait of the bureaucrats, whether they are in government, business, or the professions. Evasion of clarity is tantamount to the evasion of responsibility, and responsibility is what the average bureaucrat wants as little as possible of. Evasion becomes a habit, and the imprecise word, the qualifying phrase that obscures the issue, the amplification that is in effect a contradiction, these seem to issue automatically from the lips of most bureaucrats, even when clarity could do no harm.[29]

The indescriptiveness of college catalogues has been described by David Boroff. In speaking to the College Entrance Examination Board in 1961 he declared that American colleges fail to project an accurate image of their individual qualities in the catalogues and brochures they publish about themselves. Boroff claims that many students drop out of colleges because the institutions fail to describe themselves adequately and do not meet the students' expectations. Most catalogues, he asserts, omit any mention of the social atmosphere of the college, which is vitally important to the seventeen- or eighteen-year-old boy or girl who is just beginning to reach out socially. In his words: "The student has the right to know the kind of experience the college has to offer.[30]

At times the college obscures its meaning by the use of terms which it fails to define precisely. Thus, in the words of a novelist: "To whom did it matter, certainly not to the students, whether the college were to drop the term 'progressive' and substitute 'experimental' on page three of the catalogue?"[31]

Similarly, Stephen Minot is unhappy over the use which colleges make of "seminar":

The college professor in his role as defender of the language is quick to point out that the politicians have mauled the word 'liberal' until it is verbally useless, and that the ad-men are now killing the word 'as' by promoting 'like.' But before we cast the stones at well paid professions, we might take a look at what we are doing with our own term 'seminar.' The fact is that we have attributed to this word almost as many definitions as there are college catalogues. This is, perhaps, a privilege as intellectuals; but it is hardly our privilege as teachers to be vague about a rather specialized teaching technique . . .[32]

Higher education also obscures the meanings it wishes to convey through the use of special language. For example, the ordinary luminosity of the common firefly is termed "luciferase" by the biochemist. Such language is the province of the specializations, although there is a degree of commonality existing throughout the college in contrast to the usages in the community.[33]

Teachers within their particular disciplines commonly employ a special or technical language. Dixon, for instance, a character in a modern novel about college life, reflects upon the title of an article he had written: "It was a perfect title, in that it crystalized the article's niggling mindlessness, its funereal parade of yawn-enforcing facts, the pseudo-light it threw upon non-problems."[34] Some disciplines, however, receive more criticism regarding their technical language than do others. Brooks Atkinson, for example, using technical language, believes that the synergy of science and technology leads to a language syndrome of deliberate obscurantism.[35] In the main, however, those most highly criticized tend to be the "newer" and less universally respected disciplines, such as psychology and sociology. An apt illustration of the conflict in the use of technical language was provided in a 1961 discussion in *The New York Times*. Russell Kirk contended in one issue that: "A foolish aping of the outward forms of natural science has led many social scientists into an infatuation with jargon and meaningless statistics." [36] Robert K. Merton responded with a point-by-point answer. So far as the language of the sociologist is concerned, he said:

Perhaps it is time to distinguish between jargon and that essential of all disciplined thought, technical language. Technical language is a more precise and condensed form of thought and communication than colloquial language. It is designed to fix definite meanings in which each word has ideally only one denotation and is deliberately deprived of connotations. Jargon, in contrast, is a muddled and wordy imitation of technical language. The mere unfamiliarity or unesthetic quality of language is no criterion. Jargon and technical language sound alike to someone untrained in the discipline where the language is employed.[37]

Professor Merton, of course, is right in his comments on the nature of technical language. Every discipline worth its salt has its own specialized terms. The specialized efforts of humanists, social scientists, and physical scientists alike cannot proceed without the establishment and extension of such language. One cannot rightly complain about technical language as such. He can only lament the fact that as it has developed and continues to grow it becomes in itself a barrier to effective communication. C. P. Snow has overgenerously concluded that at the present time there are essentially two serious interpreters of man, nature, and society. These are the literary humanists and the physical scientists. He claims, however, that their technical languages are such that they live in two cultural worlds, cut off from each other and unable to transverse the abyss.[38]

Snow is largely correct in his views. He fails, however, to stress sufficiently the fact that there are many more than two technical languages operative in the modern intellectual scene. Their number is legion. Their influence in the college is to obscure intended meanings. The problem of communication, which will be viewed in the next chapter, has reached serious proportions for the college. The logical analysts in the department of philosophy have ample room on the campus for their flourishing activities.

Previously in this chapter consideration was given to the manner in which rules as such tend to support the "formalistic impersonality" of the college as a bureaucracy. It was said at that time that the subject would be renewed as a final phase of this chapter.

At times it appears that the college has so many rules and regulations that it is difficult for anyone, whether high or low in the hierarchy, to be aware of them all. Each officeholder tends to remember a great many which pertain to his particular function in the bureaucracy. He, in turn, tends to depend upon other officeholders for an intimate understanding of their own regulations. Only if one proceeds into the higher offices in the college does he find responsibility for the rules of several offices. In the upper offices in the hierarchy, one tends to find knowledge of general or institutional rules coupled with a disinterestedness in the rules which pertain to the detailed functioning of specific bureaus and offices.

The rules of the college sometimes tend to be so numerous, complex and confusing that one is reminded of the comment of Ernst Ekman who with tongue in cheek provides excerpts of the correspondence of a "university president" of three hundred years ago to his "chairman of the board" concerning faculty rules of order: "Would it be possible for Your Excellency to come to Upsala to look over the rules of order to see if everything in them must be followed? There are some things which cannot be done in practice." [39]

The extent to which the complexity of rules and procedures has developed in higher education is illustrated by Lloyd S. Woodburne, who approvingly describes the manner in which tenure and promotion are handled at the University of Washington and the University of Michigan:

In the first stage the number of divisions has to be settled. At Michigan there are three, Humanities, Social Sciences, and Sciences. At Washington there is also a fourth, Arts and Professions, comprising art, music, architecture, journalism, home economics, drama, and physical education. This is a heterogeneous grouping, but the mem-

bers all have professional responsibilities and are in reality semi-pro-
fessional units contained within the College of Arts and Sciences. The
initial nominations are made by each division on the basis of a preferential ballot. At Michigan the nominations are made by a nominating
committee. The preferential ballots are counted and the eight persons
receiving the highest votes in each division form the nominees. The
entire faculty of the college then votes on which four nominees in each
division have its greatest confidence. On the basis of the faculty ballot
there are sixteen names, four from each division. This voting procedure results in a panel of sixteen names, all of which have received
support from a majority of the faculty voting. From this panel of sixteen names, the president is asked by the dean to name eight as the
actual members of the College Council. This last step is important
since the membership should not include two members of the same
department and there should be a good spread even within a division
of knowledge. In addition this step assures a college dean that he has a
council in which the president has confidence as well as one in which
the faculty has confidence.[40]

The rules at these universities, which make the described
procedures possible, if not necessary, are a first-class illustration
of the degree to which rules can become basic to a college's operation, even though they may be difficult to understand and difficult to defend from the standpoint of the investment of valuable
time.

Robert Dubin speaks of the characteristic "reign of rules" in
a bureaucracy. He asserts that such a reign "is the administrative
answer to the problems of governing in large-scale organizations." [41] Rules as an aid to efficient administration have at least
two important purposes. First, a proliferation of rules reduces
conflicts among the officeholders, since officeholders tend to act
impersonally, that is, without reference to their private values.[42]
Their reliance on the multiplicity of rules is deemed desirable.
Thus, an officeholder does not refer to himself when he turns
down a "customer's" request. He simply points to the regulation
governing the request. He does not act; it acts. Similarly, at any
given point in the general process of the bureaucracy, the officeholder may rely in his relations with other officeholders upon the

rules which govern his activities. Every officeholder has a system of justification for his actions. These are the rules.

Second, rules lead to categorization. According to Robert K. Merton, categorization is a process "whereby individual problems and cases are classified on the basis of designated criteria and are treated accordingly." [43] Example: The college teacher wishes to take a leave for a year. He places his proposal before the dean. The dean outlines certain rules which regulate leave taking. The boundaries in which the decision must be taken, therefore, are already established. Similarly, the student in the third week of the term wishes to drop a course. He makes his proposal to a counselor or to the registrar. The college official in charge relates the college regulations on the subject, thus delimiting the field of action. In this way all requests which are entertained by a bureaucracy are seen as questions which fit into certain ascribed categories. Answers are formulated not on the basis of the fresh asking of the question, but on the basis of the rules which govern the categories.

Categorization is like the pressmark in library science. The pressmark is a sign placed upon a volume to indicate its location in the library. By this mark the library user is assured of the position of the book in relation to others. In categorization the problem is placed in its particular location within the bureaucracy. If a student wishes to pay for a lost gym towel, he is directed to the specific bureau of the college which by administrative arrangement has been given the responsibility for this particular problem or activity.

The rules which obviously limit the element of freedom in bureaucratic transactions are no respecters of persons. They restrict the kinds of questions which can be asked. With the same even hand they also restrict the nature of the answers which an officeholder may provide. Both requester and granter are limited by the rules system. On the other hand, "relaxation of certain rules (e.g., sick leave, lateness, holidays, etc.) increases as one goes up the hierarchy."[44]

Karl Mannheim has pointed out that the bureaucrat generally tends docilely to accept the rules provided to him by the organization. He says that the bureaucrat: "fails to see that behind every law that has been made there lie the socially fashioned interests and the *Weltanschauungen* of a specific social group." [45] The bureaucrat tends to be highly skilled in his knowledge of the organization's rules and their application to the various categories of appeal. His pedantic interests seldom encourage him to challenge basically the rules which he is managing. He is not so much a political being as he is an administrative being. He tends to convert all problems of organizational politics into problems of organizational administration based on the regulations. Yet, as Ralph H. Turner has shown for the Navy disbursing officer, several types of response to the rules are possible on the basis of the officeholder's personality.[46]

11

Paper Work,

Red Tape,

and

Communication

Max Weber, that dogged delineator of bureaucracy, in describing the components of complex organizations notes:

Administrative acts, decisions, and rules are formulated and recorded in writing, even in cases where oral discussion is the rule or is even mandatory. This applies at least to preliminary discussions and proposals, to final decisions, and to all sorts of orders and rules.[1]

The modern bureaucracy, including higher education, gives ample evidence that Weber's words were not misplaced. For as C. Northcote Parkinson so aptly observed: "The flood of paper which now threatens to submerge the world is something peculiar to this century."[2]

Paper Work, Red Tape, and Communication

Reliance on paper work is characteristic of many types of organizations. Businesses, for example, depend upon it. C. Northcote Parkinson relates a program undertaken by the firm of Marks and Spencer, Ltd., a British retail-store organization, operating through 237 branches. This company made a decision in favor of decentralized responsibility. The head office would respect the branch managers and the branch managers would trust the girls behind the counters. By so doing, Marks and Spencer found that it could eliminate the time cards, catalogue cards, complaint records, and stock-room forms. This decision abolished twenty-two million pieces of paper weighing 105 tons. The company took a loss, of course, but only in unnecessary statistics and manpower.[3]

Large church organizations also suffer from paper work. Geoffrey Murray says:

Some of the worst avalanches in Switzerland take place not on mountain sides but in the offices of international organizations, such as the World Council of Churches, where staff members fight desperately day by day to save themselves from being buried alive at their desks by a paper blizzard largely of their own creation.[4]

No wonder, then, that the French in speaking of red tape are inclined to call it *la paperasserie!*

One can scarcely entertain the idea of the college devoid of paper, paper clips, the mimeograph machine, staplers, and files. Enough has been said in the cloister of the Faculty Club about the extension of these devices into the daily work of the college. The mimeograph machine appears to be the principal target of attack. There is probably not a faculty member anywhere who has lived through an academic year (or even a week) without declaiming to his patient wife, intimate colleagues, or even to students, what the collegiate world might be like if mimeograph machines were completely abolished. Yet it must be recognized that such attitudes have been formed largely as a result of the paper-producing activities of others. Scarcely do they pertain to the individual making the criticism. *My* mimeograph materials are generally necessary. They contain information of importance. *Your* mimeograph materials are "made work," unnecessary and deeply resented. There is an egocentrism about paper work.

Paper work also is viewed in terms of super-subordinate relations within the college's hierarchy. Commonly, those mimeograph documents which are issued from superior offices tend to be viewed as unnecessary by those below. Those which are issued by the lower offices for similar ranking bureaus tend to be viewed as justifiable. Thus, paper work is an element in the organizational struggle for status.

As Max Weber has indicated, records are kept even "in cases where oral discussion is the rule or is even mandatory." Although several reasons may be operative, this practice usually connotes the formalistic aspect of the bureaucracy. The oral word tends to be an informal word. Only as it is inscribed on paper, by hand, by typewriter or by some other means, does it take on its proper stature for the organization. There is no implication in the recording process that the human participants do not trust each other or that they doubt each other's "word." The matter of trust is scarcely, if at all, significant for these occasions. All sides wish a written record for there is an assumption at every level in the bureaucratic organization that the written word only is correct. This premise says that it is almost impossible for anyone to recall accurately what was said and done in a given instance. The import of paper work, then, is not as an answer to distrust, but as a practical means of overcoming forgetfulness.

Paper work plays such an important part in the college because as a bureaucracy the college depends heavily upon rules. The college is not an informal and personalized type of organization; it is characterized by "formalistic impersonality." This characteristic leads to the acknowledgment of rules as a primary guide of office action. Rules lead to regularity and dependability in action, as well as to "categorization." The major dependency by the college on rules leads also necessarily to a large and complex development of paper work. The rules themselves must be recorded. Decisions made in connection with the application of the rules and appeals must be preserved. Modifications in the rules and procedures must be kept in writing in order that the orderly growth of the organization may be furthered.

Donald Kingsley has noted that paper work comprises the memory system of the bureaucracy.[5] He notes that an undersecretary of state in the British War Office once described his position as mainly that of "Remembrancer." But, the plight of the undersecretary is that of all bureaucrats. It would be inefficient for any officeholder simply to be called at a moment's notice accurately to report on what had occurred at some point in the past. Human failing is all too obvious in such matters. An unscrupulous person making an appeal would be granted certain clear advantages if the nature of his problem and the decisions made by the organization were not available in objective form to the person making the review. Paper work, then, is the memory system of the college.

Paper work as such tends to be ethically neutral, although it can be utilized to memorialize both the good and the bad. The personnel folder of the college graduate may indicate that he has graduated *cum laude*, that he won an important prize in geology, and that one of his teachers considered him to be most outstanding in laboratory techniques. Such a record simply stands for the future. Its utilization may take many forms, despite the fact that the person under consideration may have greatly changed. In the final analysis such a record is a positive testimony for the student.

On the other hand, record keeping also tends to reenforce and make permanent unfavorable information. Ralph H. Turner points out that the "fitness reports" submitted periodically to the Bureau of Naval Personnel contained notations at times of a negative sort. The fact that there was this practice was well known among the Navy personnel and the procedure tended to act as a control factor over behavior.[6] So, too, in the college. A student who has been reprimanded for poor behavior by a college officer may be told: "This matter will become a part of your permanent record." The use of recording constitutes one of the most effective forms of punishment. The student may not like to take an immediate punishment which is promptly forgotten. He will wish less to have any negative matter, no matter how large or small, included in his permanent record.

Also, just as students have individual records of their successes and failures, so in many institutions do the faculty and other college workers. While the records as a process may be viewed neutrally, their consequences often take a different form.

Records to be effective must be readily available. They also must depend upon some system of review and interpretation by the officeholders. Illogical or unused information merely creates bulk rather than efficiency. The experience of Hans-Jochem Kehrl, a traveling salesman, fully illustrates the point. Kehrl checked into a different hotel in Germany night after night in his travels. Every time he encountered the registration form that infuriates thousands of visitors to Germany. It always asks the same information: name, address, date and place of birth, occupation, passport number, where issued, when issued, by whom issued, wife's maiden name, number of children in party. "Useless, bureaucratic nonsense," thought Herr Kehrl eleven years ago. So, he began a campaign to see if it mattered what one put down on the form. "Regularly, I listed myself as rat-catcher, bear-trainer—whatever my fancy told me." "I listed birthdates that never have appeared in any calendar. I was born mostly in the Himalayas or in Sodom or in Gomorrah. My identification number I listed as 1234567 or my automobile license."

Kehrl noted that nobody ever seemed to notice what he was doing. This exhausted his patience. Says Kehrl: "I consulted the criminal code and I began to list myself as burglar, forger, and embezzler. Finally I listed myself as a swindler and gave my correct name and address." That did it. The excited hotel porter called the police, the police called Herr Kehrl's hometown of Kassel and found that he was a respectable salesman for a publishing house. The police, however, arrested him. The police record said: "Hans-Jochem Kehrl, a hotel guest from Kassel, was charged with violation of Article 25, Paragraph 2, of the ordinance concerning registration. He listed himself as a swindler, although he did not carry on this trade." [7]

The people or officeholders who are primarily responsible for the maintenance of the paper work of the college are called clerks. Today that term indicates a person of skill who is devoted to the mechanical task of writing, bookkeeping, accounting, and copying. Historically, however, a clerk meant simply a clergyman, one who was a member of the general class of actual or potential ministers of the church. All men of education in the early Middle Ages were regarded as clerks. Writing and accounting were not commonly found in the population, especially since all letters were written and all accounts maintained in Latin. As Thomas F. Tout suggests, the medieval clerks were not necessarily "clerks in holy orders" or even "clerks in minor orders." He says: "You could enter the clerical profession as soon as you had induced some prelate to give you the 'first tonsure.' "[8] The modern clerk also plays a highly skilled role in the college; he or she is depended upon for the oiling of the smaller cogs without which the larger cogs would never be able to move.

Any officeholder in the college who bears the responsibility of a clerk should keep Thomas F. Tout's contrast between the medieval public servant and the modern on hand for ready reference in those moments when a fellow clerk may have fallen into the slough of despondency:

The mediaeval public servant had plenty of disadvantages as compared wth his modern successor. All the devices by which book-keeping, letter-writing, account-keeping and the like are made easy were unknown to him. His works of reference were unpractical rolls that had to be unrolled in all their length before he could verify a single entry. His material for writing on was parchment so expensive that abbreviation of his matter was necessary and to waste by a slip something of an offense. The exchequer clerk had to keep books and do sums of extraordinary complexity. The very addition of Roman numerals was painful enough in itself. It was made more laborious by reckonings by scores and by hundreds, by sums, calculated indifferently in marks and in pounds, shillings and pence being all mixed up together in the same columns of figures. Yet you will very rarely find mistakes in arithmetic even in the most complicated of accounts; and if you take the trouble, which some of our modern historians have not done, to understand the accountant's system before you make use of his figures, you will not often catch him committing many serious errors. No one can turn over mediaeval office records without admiration for the calligraphy, the immense pains taken to facilitate reference and eliminate blunders, the careful correction of erroneous entries, and the other innumerable evidences of good honest workmanship on the part of the ordinary rank and file of official cards. It is the same with the innumerable writs and letters, all neatly drafted in common form, and duly authenticated by the appropriate seals and by the signatures of the responsible clerks. The system of enrolment of the accounts past and the letters written, in every office, leaves nothing to be desired in completeness and precision. Anyhow, the mediaeval official took plenty of pains to discharge his daily task, and his labour was all the more praiseworthy since mediaeval casualness and mediaeval indifference to labour-saving contrivances exacted the maximum of effort and trouble in every case. Similarly, if returned to the collections of examples, precedents and forms, which were from time to time written for the guidance of the various offices, we strengthen our impression of sound business traditions, laboriously developed and meticulously maintained.[9]

One popular line of comment on the nature of higher education as a bureaucracy would conclude that all paper work is essentially red tape. Such, however, is not so, as will be seen. Red tape may involve one form or another of paper, but it is not a synonym for paper work. Red tape is essentially an organizational problem or a series of problems. Although it may refer to complications in the record-keeping system of the institution, it refers also to every other aspect of the life of the college.

The term "red tape" was introduced into the English language more than a century ago.[10] Lord Lytton in 1838 stated that: "The men of dazzling genius began to sneer at the red-tape minister as a mere official manager of details." Carlyle spoke of an acquaintance as "little other than a red-tape talking machine." Although Herbert Spencer gives red tape a clearly sociological meaning in the 1870's it was not until a decade or two later that the term was employed in American literature.

As the term is commonly used, one can distinguish a variety of meanings for it. Some of these will be reviewed briefly.

First, red tape may simply mean what a bureaucrat does in his daily behavior. Some use the term in this sense to include everything that an officeholder does whether what he does helps or hinders.

Second, red tape may signify the projection of the means of an organization into ends. In this sense red tape implies a finality and rigidity which in certain instances may even deny the primary and obvious goals through which the bureaucracy was formed.

Third, the term may connote decisions based on clearly ascribed procedures which work against the interest of the person making a request of the organization. A college regulation may require that a student wishing to drop a course must make his request on two forms. The student whose request is approved may think that the college has an excellent system of handling the problem. The student who is denied his request, however, may castigate the procedure as red tape.

Fourth, the use of the term may hinge on the separation of public and private spheres. When a person is asked for information in filling out a form which he considers to be of a public character, such as the color of his eyes, he may be quite willing to oblige. But, if the same person is asked about his age, especially if he is an older person, he may criticize the request as "another illustration of red tape." An invasion on one's personal or private life, especially where the substantial justification for such an invasion is not immediately obvious, may be termed red tape.

Fifth, red tape may constitute a threat to the ego. If a student must secure the review and signature of a faculty advisor before the registrar will grant him official registration, he may view the procedure as red tape in the sense that the college has provided a procedure whereby his "integrity" is being questioned.

Sixth, red tape may signifiy secondary frustrations whereby primary functions are complicated or denied. Edmund G. Love provides an illustration in the story of the awesome executive in a motor car company who installed so many checks and balances on the people working there that they had no time for anything but filling out reports.[11]

Seventh, the term may be used when rights seem to be threatened. A veteran, for example, who is entitled to educational benefits may resent the college inquiring too closely about his receipt of these benefits. He may assert: "But, these are my rights."

Eighth, a sense of powerlessness may lead to the charge of red tape. The student who applies for admission to the college may resent the forms and the procedures established by the institution because he has no means of controlling or overcoming them. He is simply one individual in the face of a carefully prescribed and complicated set of office procedures. He can only influence the final decision slightly; ultimately the decision for or against him is out of his hands. He feels like a backseat ticket holder in the Hollywood Bowl at the onset of a thunderstorm during the first minutes of a performance.

Ninth, complexity may be taken as red tape. The student who wishes to change his major from one department to another may not charge red tape if he is required merely to report this fact in one department. His resentment will increase if he is required to report the fact to the two departments. His critical spirit will enlarge as the number of reporting offices increases. Each person then may have his own bureaucratic "boiling point." Red tape is a subjective matter.

Tenth, red tape may be charged where the probability of deferring gratifications is present. The faculty member who applies for a leave of absence may intellectually know that his request will necessarily be reviewed by his department chairman, the dean involved, the college president, and ultimately the board. Such a review may defer a decision for weeks or even months. Although the faculty member may theoretically understand the necessity for such a system, he may be resentful of it, calling it red tape, because he is not able immediately to secure the decision which he wants.

Finally, red tape may be taken as an expression of resentment against conditions which cannot readily or even finally be modified. In this connection, J. M. Juran speaks of "duplication" as "the common cold of the bureaucratic world." He says:

The most usual form of government duplication is that of duplicate libraries or files—pamphlets, books, circulars, etc. This is also one of the least expensive forms of duplication for the cost is largely in extra copies and involves paper, printing, and file space rather than original preparation. The civil servant who keeps many copies of many things must from time to time come forward with a request for filing cabinets, file clerks, and space. If this is turned down, he is in the clear. On the other hand, if he voluntarily fails to keep the given set of papers, he may be subject to criticism for not having them, or subject to irritation when he endeavors to borrow from someone else. Frequently, it is easier to ask for the equipment, space, and clerks.[12]

From the preceding descriptions of the various meanings which red tape may have for higher education, it may be seen that two sets of factors are commonly involved. First and most important, there are those subjective or personalistic elements by which the individual evaluates the performance of the organizations. A variety of highly subtle and partially dependable motives supports charges from this source. The organization, moreover, regularly is not able to provide satisfactory countermeasures to eliminate all personally-based judgments, as was seen. What is red tape to one person may be green tape to another.

Second, red tape also properly refers to certain features of the bureaucratic organization. When these features are cumbersome, too complex, evasive, impersonal, intrusive, etc., they may bring the charge of red tape against them.

Higher education as a bureaucracy properly needs rules. Rules involve procedures of individuation, but such individuation is possible only in terms of a more comprehensive structure of relationships in which the prerequisites of the system at many points seem to be more significant than the wishes or even the rights of requesting individuals. Paper work is the method of maintaining both the rule structure of the organization and the results of the decision-making process. Red tape, therefore, may be clarified, streamlined, and even reduced in the college. It cannot, however, be diminished past the point of institutional effectiveness. Certainly it cannot be entirely eliminated.

Alvin W. Gouldner discusses bureaucratic organization in terms of the conservative-radical orientation of the persons making charges of red tape. He states that the group which is most sensitive to red tape suffers from a particular alienation in reference to the organization. He characterizes them as "conservatives." It is the conservatives who seem to be most concerned with red tape as a social problem. They are inclined to attack minor rules and minor officials of a bureaucracy. They tend to accept the higher officials and their rules.

By contrast, the "radical" makes his primary attack upon the major rules and officials of a bureaucracy. A radical aims at the core meaning of the organization. He tends to be unwilling to accept its major premises and leadership.[13] If Professor Gouldner is correct in his analysis, the problem of red tape is more complex than is commonly assumed.

Institutional attack upon the problem of red tape rests upon the flexibility of the organization's administrative apparatus. The extreme form of the scalar organization of the college tends in the final analysis to increase the resistance of the organization to the unusual request or person. The organization which is able to provide a high degree of "categorization" is likely to develop fewer charges of red tape. Decentralization and informal organization within the college often lead to the reduction of personal and institutional frustrations.

A second means of reducing the charge of red tape (also related to the first) emphasizes personal decision-making rather than the efficacy of rules. Rules are intended as guides to the actions of officeholders. When they are taken as ends in themselves, they restrict the creative employment of responsibility on the part of the officeholder. If the officeholder, on the other hand, is formally required to be not only a follower of the rules but a person of judgment and discretion, a diminution of red tape may occur. Peter M. Blau, a serious student of bureaucracy, comments:

No system of rules and supervision can be so finely spun that it anticipates all exigencies that may arise. Moreover, some impediments to efficiency, such as the feelings of anxiety and other emotional tensions which often develop in the course of operations, cannot be eradicated by official decree. Maximum rationality in the organization, therefore, depends on the ability of operation officials to assume the initiative in establishing informal relations and instituting unofficial practices that eliminate operational difficulties as they occur. This ability, in turn, presupposes the absence of acute feelings of inequality among the members of the bureaucracy.[14]

A third way of reducing charges of red tape (also related to the previous two) is by effective communication. The problem of communication in the modern college is formidable. Few colleges would wish to claim that they have solved the problem. Yet, by means of effective communication, it may be assumed, the machinery of the whole institutional apparatus runs more smoothly. Comments, findings, and even complaints in one sector of the college ought to have readily devised and easily used channels whereby they may reach the awareness of those who hold responsibility.

Most, if not all, colleges have a public relations office. This office is conceived as a college-wide agency for the communication of needful information to the community at large or to special publics within it. Public relations officers are often skilled persons with fairly adequate resources at their command. In many instances they give their full time and efforts to the task of communication.

The responsibility for internal public relations, however, is usually not so clearly defined, from the institutional view, nor so adequately staffed and supported. Yet, the internal public relations office is a foundation of the efficiency of the entire college enterprise.

The inadequacies of the communicative systems of many colleges are surprising in the face of the fact that, unlike some other bureaucracies, there is generally little need for secrecy. Obviously every bureaucracy including the college rightly practices some degree of secrecy. Perhaps "discretion" is a better term for non-governmental organizations, although Carl J. Friedrich uses the words interchangeably.[15] This is to say that not everything that every officeholder knows must be communicated to everyone. The communicative process is selective in the college as well as elsewhere. The federal government by contrast necessarily has a formal system by which official secrecy is enforced. Of it William Lederer says:

The cult of government secrecy is growing. The practice has become so widespread and routine that, according to testimony given before the House government information sub-committee, more than a million federal employees are empowered to classify information. This means that one out of every one hundred eighty Americans is stamping the word 'secret' on papers. Thus our protective machinery has become so bulky it no longer is effective for really classified material; and, instead, it is turned into a monster which often swallows information which should be public knowledge.[16]

The college, at least nominally, wishes everyone to know what it is necessary for him to know in order that he might be an effective functionary. There is no effort made in most colleges to shield individuals from information. Commonly, the minutes of most or all committees are publicly available either from the secretaries of the committees themselves or through the college library. The official and guiding materials, such as the charter and the bylaws, are also open for inspection. The primary difficulties in the internal public relations of many colleges seem to be their system or lack of it.

The problem of effective communication has increased in the recent years as colleges have grown in size and complexity. Robert H. Shaffer, for example, undertook one-week visits to eight campuses of major universities in order to study the impact of institutional size and complexity upon student personnel services. He was able to draw two general observations from his study. First, he came to believe:

The mature development and organization of student personnel services reflect the personality, traditions and general characteristics of the particular institution rather than its size. A second conclusion was: The basic problem involved in the administration of these services on the large campuses is one primarily of effective communication, not administrative organization in itself.[17]

Shaffer's observations on the role of communication in relation to the student personnel services of the college and its size and complexity probably hold true from most of the other aspects of the college. If communication is more important even than the administrative arrangements, then many colleges are not placing the appropriate emphasis with their staff resources where it should be. As Herbert A. Simon says: "There is nothing to guarantee that advice produced at one point in an organization will have any effect at another point in the organization unless the lines of communication are adequate to its transmission and unless it is transmitted in such form as to be persuasive." [18]

There are principally two lines of communication within the college. First, there are the formal means. Among these are the student newspaper, a faculty newsletter, department meetings, public occasions, legislative bodies, etc. Naturally, the kind of subjects which are discussable through such formal channels is necessarily restricted. They are appropriate to the particular forum. They also undergo a handicap of the format in which they are surrounded. The statement by a college president, for example, to the faculty regarding the policy of the college on the numerical growth of the student body may be put so abstractly that apathy and confusion result instead of clarity and conviction. Some official memoranda have as much effect on a college community as an olive makes noise as it slips into a martini. Yet, the formal modes of communication can be effective channels.

Second, informal means also are available. One college president indicated that if he wanted a subject not to be considered and widely discussed he would comment on it in a general meeting of the faculty. On the other hand, if he wished it to be rightfully and energetically considered by the faculty he would have a rumor planted in the faculty dining room. Such an informal method of communication, despite this erratic example, can be effective. Sometimes "gossip" is able to communicate facts about the college which the formal means could never effectuate. Officeholders regularly, although not always consciously, rely upon certain informal situations in which they are able to glean many of the significant events of the organization.

H. E. Dale, in discussing the civil servant in Great Britain, relates the role of informal communication in daily activities:

After lunch our Assistant Secretary looks for a few minutes at a paper or book in the smoking-room, or even perhaps plays a game at snooker; or he may join himself to a small group of friends where in the strictest confidence the gossip of the Service is passed about—what the permanent Head of a Department really thinks of his Minister, what a horrible nuisance it is to have a Parliamentary Secretary who 'seems to himself to be somewhat,' why C. refused such and such an appointment before it was offered to and accepted by D., which Minister's stock is rising or falling in the political market. Not a great deal happens in Westminster and Whitehall of which the inner truth is not sooner or later exhaled among civil servants in their clubs.[19]

The higher officeholder has a responsibility to communicate to the lower officeholders, but he also has a need to be communicated with, for commonly it is the top officials in the hierarchy who have the weakest means of knowing what is believed and done in the lower levels.

Max Weber has pointed out that the absolute ruler often is completely in the power of his bureaucracy since he, unlike the democratic leader, has no means of discovering whether his policies are being enforced.[20] So the higher officials in colleges need informal occasions regularly to keep abreast of what is happening in the entire organization. Those within a particular bureau tend to learn on the job, during slack or informal moments, what is the gossip of their units. The higher officials, however, who have responsibility for more than one unit, do not have such means available to them. It is not deemed proper for them to inquire about the "rumor system" of their subordinate bureaus. They must learn what information they can, mostly from their equals. This cannot be done best through formal means. Generally it is accomplished by informal devices.

Another form of informal communication is "griping." Superficially, griping may seem to be a pathological form of communication deriving chiefly from the less constructive motives of officeholders. Such gripers are as popular as a Goldwater Republican at an ADA meeting. Undoubtedly, where griping is not well founded, it may be an indication of personality deficiencies. On the other hand, griping can be an important thermometer to judge the health of the social system. Gripes at their best are expressions of institutional resentments, lack of information, or inadequacies in management. On occasion they may be taken as accurate and knowledgeable suggestions for improvement.

The manner in which a gripe or complaint is dealt with in higher education is a clear index as to the hierarchy's openmindedness and flexibility. The very existence of griping may indicate that the organization is not prone to listen to the suggestions of its officeholders, that they are unable to go directly to a superior to have their suggestions heard. In one study of the barriers to understanding between officers and enlisted men in the Army's social system it was discovered that about half of the men studied said that during their Army careers they had felt the desire to bring a complaint to the attention of the Inspector General. But, only one in five actually took their troubles to him. The men who failed to exercise their prerogative were asked to tell their reasons. The men fell into three groups. First, some noted that there was considerable difficulty in getting to see the Inspector General. Here the charge of red tape was regularly employed. Second, others said that it was useless to see the Inspector General. They felt that it would not do them any good, that he would not act upon their complaint, or that they knew of other occasions when no action was taken. Third, others feared reprisal. The assumption was made that the immediate superior would learn of the complaint or deal and would hold it against the man. At other times the soldier was coerced by an officer not to make his complaint.[21]

These three restraints upon the openly declared prerogative for the expression of complaints in the Army may not hold true for college personnel. For one thing the rank order of the personnel in the college is not so rigid and formalistic. Also, the elaboration of specific procedures for the expression of complaints is not commonly provided for in the college. On some campuses, however, it is known that the college chaplain, as is true of the military chaplain, is a ready confidant of those, both students, faculty and others, who wish to register a complaint without employing formal channels. The college chaplain tends to be a "middle man"—someone who is difficult to define in the rank order of the social system. He is, therefore, more accessible for those who wish to complain. The nature of his office also may tend to attract complainers. He in turn must be a highly skilled individual in interpersonal relations if he is to succeed in maintaining both the confidence of those who complain and those to whom the complaints are addressed. On some college campuses, where there is no college chaplain, the dean of students tends to act in the capacity of the chaplain.

For whatever mode of communication may be employed, Chester I. Barnard has indicated three conditions for effectiveness. These pertain to the college as well as to other bureaucracies. First, communication must be authentic. The office issuing a memorandum, for instance, should identify itself with the name, position, title of the communicator. Such provisions are employed not so much for reasons of enforcing status as for the purpose of proper identification.

Second, communication should be authoritative. Authoritativeness means that the content of the communication may be relied upon as a basis for action. Barnard sees two kinds of authoritativeness: functional and scalar. Applied to the subject at hand, however, authoritativeness signifies that the opinion of the business manager on the teaching of Cicero in Latin may be suspect, since this is not a field of functional expertness for him. Again, the issuance of an order by an officeholder who fails to possess the formal responsibility for the matter tends to mitigate the authoritativeness of the order.

Third, communication should be intelligible. In this connection it may be readily pointed out that generality is one of the prime curses of collegiate communication. Statements are issued without sufficient attention for details. Everyone may be required to read and to pay attention to what is essentially meant for a few. Technical terms may be employed which are not understood by the recipients of the communication. Procedures, such as the dates on which forms are to be returned or the precise type of clothing to wear for the commencement, may leave the reader more confused than he would otherwise be. Communication to be effective must be organized in terms of the audience rather than the issuing office.

These three conditions for effective communication, suggested by Barnard, offer practical lines upon which an effective system within the college might be organized.[22]

12

Disabilities

The college is far from perfect. Like other bureaucracies, it has its stresses and strains, it high purpose and low achievement. At times its very strengths become its dismal weaknesses as is illustrated, for example, in Howard Nemerov's novel *The Homecoming Game*. He depicts the chicanery and hypocrisy arising from the question of whether the flunking star will participate in an annual football rite—a case of the institution's rules getting in the way of its interest in a particular satellite formation.[1]

Or, to take another example from fiction, the autonomous existence so preferred and preached by philosophers of higher education crashes on the rocks of practical experience, as Frederic Morton portrays in his account of Iris Leavis's first five days after her graduation from Hunter College. Intensely modern, Iris rejects everything her environment has given her: the Bronx-Jewish atmosphere of her home, the petty-bourgeois values, the entire desperation of her parents, the "subway education" she has received, even her virginity which she resents as an artificial and old-fashioned imposition. The high purposes of a quality education end in personal confusion and personal stress.[2]

Yet another fictional account of trouble in the educational

paradise is provided by William Manchester. He tells the dreary story of President River of a mushrooming state university—all new buildings, sexy cheer leaders, and football team. Too late he discovers that his football star is a bum, his Gridiron Queen a strumpet, his ambitious career a shallow farce, and the degrees offered by his university worthless. At the time River is running for governor, scandal explodes and the walls of *academe* fall in.[3]

Beardsley Ruml in nonfictional terms has expressed concern for the inefficiencies of the modern college. He is concerned with the problems of the traditional, independent, four-year liberal arts college. His comments center upon the curriculum which he regards not as a carefully planned educational whole, but as the patchwork product of a number of special advocates, the least of whose objectives is the efficient use of resources. He is concerned with the better utilization of faculty. He decries the proliferation of courses, the costly effort to redeem the lecture course by attaching discussion sections, and the maintenance of great numbers of courses for which the demand is represented by less than ten students.[4]

The concerns of Ruml, however, are typical of those expressed by many others including perceptive individuals outside of higher education as well as within. In fact, higher education for a number of years has been characterized by breast-beating, a sedulous effort to confess inadequacies and wrongdoings to outsiders even before charges from without are made. A similar spirit increasingly in the recent years has also infected the high school personnel. Criticism of education has become not only possible, it is apparently a necessity for the establishment and maintenance of status.

For many people the term "bureaucracy" comprises an opprobrious reference that signifies everything that is wrong with life. It is employed with resentment and vehemence to criticize out of hand every aspect of large-scale organization. John H. Crider, for example, comes close to this position when he says:

The bureaucrat, then, is a composite of all things known of the species. He is, for our purposes, unless otherwise indicated, an abstraction. The term includes the bulk of all, male and female, who feed from the public trough, thereby obtaining a degree of authority of which they remind us in various ways . . . The bureaucrat most conspicuously, is more concerned with solidifying his position and extending his authority than in performing a public service. Indeed, to the true bureaucrat, public service becomes merely an object of exploitation. And, if you fail to find him any other way, you can surely spot the bureaucrat as the fellow who always knows what is best for you and me.[5]

The bureaucrat, in Max Weber's terms, however, included officeholders in all bureaucratically-organized social organizations, whether governmental or otherwise. Thus, any worker in a large organization is a bureaucrat and likely, by such a definition as Crider's, to come under his castigating comments.

There are others who have an automatically critical reaction to bureaucracy. These appear to be opposed to all sizeable and complex social organization. Their anti-organization stance derives from several bases. First, those with utopianist bent are inclined to be critical of every fallible aspect of existence. They declaim against any form of organization where some measure of injustice is present. They look forward to a perfect future. Surely every organization, including the bureaucracies, is prone to certain inadequacies—those which are inherent in human behavior and man's organizing tendencies.

If the utopianists are forced by their ideological blinders to face into the future, then another group of critics of bureaucracy tend overly much to be oriented to what they think was the past. Rousseau fell into this category when he said: "Man was born free, but everywhere he is in chains." This romantic school tends to believe that at every point in the past human beings possessed greater freedom than they do in the present, and that the increasing size and complexity of social organizations are evidence of deterioration and decline. Commonly they are highly selective in their historical references. It is true that simple and personal relationships dominated in less highly organized societies.

Perhaps the extremes of both schools of criticism adhere, whether consciously or not, to some form of anarchism, the belief that social organization in any form restrains individual liberty; therefore, it is evil. Although anarchism is rarely used in its full potency, it may be found in diluted measure in the arguments of many who *in toto* are opposed to bureaucracy. It would appear, however, that no effort to increase the personalizing tendencies in modern life can be built upon anarchistic notions if they are to be effective. They must begin where people and organizations are in the present.

The observer and describer of any social system cannot divorce himself from his own values. These values, like eyeglass refraction, tend to bring discrepancies and distortions into focus. For example, while the basic aim of this book is to provide a descriptive and analytic account of higher education as a bureaucracy, with a conscious restraint upon the injection of purely personal viewpoints, the achievement of this dedicated task is not absolutely possible. Perspective gained from many sources cannot be denied in the process of examining data. So everyone's approach to bureaucracy must contain bias. No one can be so vacuous as not to like certain features of higher education as a bureaucracy and to disdain others. It is one thing for the observer to claim that the preferences he holds are his own or those of a special group of which he is a part. It is quite another matter for him to aver that his preferences are objectively to be found in the bureaucratic social organization. Thus in any account of the disabilities, as well as the virtues, of higher education as a bureaucracy serious thought must be given to the subjective factors which often are controlling.

The reader who has reached this point in the analysis of higher education as a bureaucracy has probably more than once declared to himself what he thinks to be the disadvantages of bureaucratic organization. The previous chapters may have provided him mainly with justifications for his views. By this point, however, he may say in effect that he does not wish any extended discussion of the disabilities of bureaucracy, that he is well aware of them in the light of previous discussion. It would be well, however, to point out the possibility that another reader might arrive at this point and make quite the opposite conclusion. He might think that the advantages of bureaucratic higher education so far outweigh the disadvantages that no time really needs to be spent in a discussion of disabilities.

Since the advantages of bureaucracies were outlined and described in Chapter 2, it is appropriate that some attention be given in this chapter to their disabilities.[6]

The present state of knowledge does not provide a uniform interpretation of the types of disabilities which characterize bureaucracy. There is the widest discrepancy in the basic categories employed to describe malfunctioning.[7] Four systems of interpretation, presently available, will be reviewed to illustrate both the diversity of interpretation and the kinds of disabilities to which bureaucracies generally are prone.

First, it has been asserted that the disabilities are of two major types. The first is overorganization. This "involves an excessive development of those bureaucratic routines which, kept within limits, are functionally necessary to the operation of a large administrative apparatus." [8] Certain examples in the college come readily to mind. The use of titles is a prerequisite to the maintenance of the hierarchical-status system of the personnel. Used reasonably these titles tend to reinforce the organizational objectives of the college. Used unreasonably, that is, employed excessively and routinely, they tend to stultify the organization's objectives.

The second type, under the first heading, is underorganization. This occurs when the bureaucratic requirements of the college are not highly developed. Disabilities are created through the inadequate development of bureaucratic features. Thus a disability is created when a college lacks a precise and objective set of criteria for appointment. If such criteria have not been developed, there is created the opportunity for nepotism, favoritism, and other forms of mismanagement. Such may not be claimed to be a part of an efficiently operating bureaucracy. Rather they are the consequence of too little bureaucracy—underorganization.

The idea that the disabilities of higher education as a bureaucracy derive from overorganization and underorganization implies a desirable state of organizational equilibrium in which there is a properly sufficient amount of bureaucratic development. This concept suggests that the abuses of the social system are created when disequilibriums are present. The concept in itself throws no light on whether it is ever possible for a bureaucracy to achieve an ideal state of equilibrium. Probably, given the fact of human nature and social organization, a state of equilibrium as pure form is impossible. The fact that an absolute state of equilibrium is not feasible, however, does not lead one to conclude that efforts at improvement are not possible and desirable. These would fall into the realm of mediate objectives, requiring continuous and persistent exploration, experimentation, and reformulation.

Second, another system of categorizing the disabilities of bureaucracies, suggested by Chester I. Barnard, involves six topics.[9] The six are:

1) The status system tends in time to distorted evaluation of individuals.
2) It restricts unduly the "circulation of the elite."
3) It distorts the system of distributive justice.
4) It exaggerates administration to the detriment of leadership and morale.
5) It exalts the symbolic function beyond the level of sustainment.
6) It limits the adaptability of an organization.

Some if not all of these kinds of disabilities have been illustrated in previous chapters. Some will be touched upon in this and the next chapter. Taken together these categories provide a comprehensive system for classifying a bureaucracy's disabilities. Yet the analysis suffers from a high degree of generality which calls for deduction to more specific features.

Third, Marshall E. Dimock, upon a careful review of the nature of bureaucracy, is able to conclude that the disabilities of a bureaucracy may be understood in terms of twelve basic categories. All of these, however, are dependent in his view upon one basic fact, namely, that bureaucracy signifies complexity. Upon the back of complexity he lays the full burden of all of the disabilities: "Complexity is the most general underlying cause of bureaucracy . . ." In further commenting on the relationship he says:

The term 'bureaucracy' not only describes a given institutional situation but may be used to characterize a way or stage of life. It is the state of society in which institutions overshadow individuals and simple family relationships; a stage of development in which division of labor, specialization, organization, hierarchy, planning, and regimentation of large groups of individuals, either by voluntary or by involuntary methods, are the order of the day. There may be a question as to whether individuals prefer such a system or feel that their chances of success and happiness are as good under it as under some simpler system. Let us not deceive ourselves, however, as to the inevitable conjunction between complexity and bureaucracy.[10]

The twelve "more specific institutional and administrative causes" of bureaucracy as listed by Dimock are: (1) size, (2) organization, (3) specialization, (4) rules and regulations, (5) character of executive direction, (6) improper staff activity, (7) central staff controls, (8) group introversion, (9) lack of sales motive, (10) security, (11) seniority, (12) age and tradition.

As with the previous systems of classification, Dimock's categories appear to be based upon certain selective premises which are not always made apparent in the categories themselves. Undoubtedly higher education as a bureaucracy gives evidence of each of the twelve types of disabilities mentioned by Dimock. So, too, do other bureaucracies. Yet the picture is not black and white. Only by assuming negative premises entirely can Dimock reach his conclusions. Thus size may not be a virtue, if one is not predisposed to the virtue which size in itself produces. Here size may provide "the tendency toward red tape," as Dimock asserts. Yet size in bureaucratic organization also provides the basis for the virtue of efficiency. As Ruml says, the college which caters to sections of courses comprising under ten students may be creating a disability thereby. What seems to be a disability from the standpoint of Dimock's premise regarding size may be a virtue according to someone else. So it is with at least a number of the other categories, if not all. Again, the subjective perspective of the observer determines to an appreciable extent the advantages and disadvantages which he imputes to the social system.

The analysis of the disabilities of a bureaucracy does not necessarily involve the classification of "evil" or the cataloguing of certain general conclusions about bureaucracies—prevalent no matter where they may be found and by whatever form they may take. It may depend upon guide lines from which an observer may start in his effiort to analyze the disabilities of a particular bureaucracy. The guide lines are general and in themselves lead to no particular or necessary conclusions. What well may be an advantage in one bureaucracy may be a disadvantage in another. A feature of a bureaucracy may bring success for the low-level bureaus and a lack of success for the higher ones. In this view the universal principle should bend before the concrete facts. After all it is the function of the bureaucratic feature under consideration which is paramount rather than a set of conditions imposed from without. From this perspective bureaucratic disabilities arise from: (1) organizational conditions; (2) the nature and functioning of the personnel; (3) the ideational base, and (4) interrelated factors. The nature of these guide lines will be briefly explored in serial fashion, although it is clear that at many points they are interrelated.

First, certain organizational conditions, when maintained in disequilibrium, may lead to disabilities. Size and complexity of the college, for example, may contribute to delay in decision-making. An illustration is provided by an experienced academic observer of a situation at a state university:

. . . the latest general appropriation bill was introduced in the Legislature on March 2, 1959, to cover the two-year period of July, 1959, to June, 1961. Final Legislative agreement came on November 10, 1959, and the Governor signed the bill on November 21, 1959 (meanwhile, the University has been running from July to November on student fees and similar income and on money advanced by the State in anticipation of the later appropriation). The budget for salaries was held at the previous biennium's figures, though new employees had to be given contracts. In short, there were no raises in rank or salary until February, 1960, and some persons received no increases then.
The results of this delay were destructive to faculty morale. Competitive offers from other employers could not be rationally considered since nobody knew what Penn State would eventually offer. From July 1, 1959, to March 1, 1960, all the faculty except new members didn't know what salaries they were working for, and so could not budget their expenses, vacations, Christmas presents, rents, etc. Many borrowed in the hope of raises that sometimes didn't come.[11]

Again, the manner in which the college is organized departmentally, with its resulting frictions and conflicts among the members and the departments as a whole comprises another illustration of the significance of organizational conditions. C. P. Snow's novels in part are devoted to this theme. Though it has some of the fascination of the detective story, *The Affair*, for example, is a novel of the interplay of character in the intimacy of the small, autonomous community. Pervading the whole is the perennial conflict of the new and the traditional, the consistent struggle between the young and the old, the newcomers and the established, those with rank and tenure and those striving for permanence and place. More important than this conflict, however, is the characterization in *The Affair* of the estrangement between the "two cultures," the traditional-literary and the scientific.[12] Although evident in Snow's *The Masters*, that estrangement is intensified in *The Affair*. In the Cambridge College of which Lewis Eliot, the person through whose eyes the series are seen, is an ex-fellow, a young scientist, Donald Howard, who has published a paper depending on state data and has been quietly dismissed from his fellowship. *The Affair* starts with the discovery of new evidence suggesting that Howard may not have been aware of the fraud. The story goes on to tell of the slow conversion of several of the scientific fellows and of Eliot himself to the clear but reluctant conviction that an injustice has been done and that the case must be reopened. When the case is finally retried Lewis Eliot plays a prominent part as both a participant and manipulator.[13]

In the story of *The Affair* one finds a variety of factors relevant to the organizational conditions of the college as a bureaucracy; the estrangement of "the two cultures," the partisan loyalties of the specialists, the slow-moving organizational apparatus for condemnation and retrial, the ambiguities and fatuousness of the institutional procedures.

Another organizational condition which may lead to disabilities for the college is the ramification of administrative organization. The university, of course, provides an even more apt illustration of the potential than the college. A former university administrator, Edward H. Litchfield, comments:

I am equally troubled by the divisiveness which characterizes our own institutions—the universities. There are few among us who regard the university as a total institution. It would be more accurate to say that we treat it as a miscellaneous collection of faculties, research institutes, museums, hospitals, laboratories, and clinics. Indeed, it has become a commonplace to observe that most of our large university organizations are held together by little more than a name, a lay board of trustees, an academically remote figure called a president, and a common concern for the power plant. On most of our large university campuses, our individual faculties tend to live in an isolated proximity.[14]

What Litchfield observed for the university is undoubtedly true for the large and complex college.

Organizational conditions also at times lead to the devotion of an extraordinarily large share of resources to essentially routine and trivial activities. This also may be called over-organization. Mary McCarthy pokes fun at the importance give to trivia in a mythical college:

. . . for example, students in the dining-hall, when surrendering their plates to the waiters, should pass them to the right or to the left, clockwise or counterclockwise; at an all-college meeting, held in December of this year, compulsory for all students, faculty, and administrative staff, President Maynard Hoar had come within an ace of resigning when his appeal for moderation in the discussion had met with open cat-calls from the counterclockwise faction.[15]

Second, bureaucratic disabilities within higher education may be determined by the examination of the nature and functions of the personnel. By such a device the officeholders are viewed as a primary locus of disability. They are viewed in terms of their personalities and performance.

Previously some attention was given to the nature of the college teacher. Although scant evidence is available regarding the college teacher as a social type it is apparent that some of the disabilities within the college may derive from the character of the officeholders as persons. Not all of the evidence on the subject is commendable. William Van O'Connor, for instance, has written a collection of twelve stories about academic persons. They are mostly about troubled people: rebellious against authority, lacking in power of self-direction, helpless in an emotional entanglement, childishly committed to the performance of a disagreeable role, pursuing a hate-neurosis to the inevitable breakdown, and so on. There are two suicides and one attempt, two instances of bastardy, an assortment of neuroses, insanity, alcoholism, homosexuality, desertion, divorce, incipient juvenile delinquency, and, of course, seduction.[16]

George Williams, another college teacher, speaks in the same critical vein. He claims that between 76 and 80 per cent of college professors are smug, self-satisfied, and uninterested in self-criticism, lazy, timid (here the figure goes up to 90 per cent), and sycophantic. He is not surprised, however, that the typical professor is like this when he considers his background. The teacher, a bookish boy, was neglected by his peers and withdrew into a lonely, private world. When in college he found his scholarly attainments appreciated. He began to develop the characteristic schizophrenia: a personality "underlain with a deep sense of inferiority, fear, and maladjustment yet overlain by an almost frantic sense of superiority . . . further complicated by a latent hostility to that which is non-bookish and non-intellectual." No wonder then that Williams concludes that, all in all, the college teacher is "a quite abnormal personality." [17]

As wide of the mark as these two reporters may be in their attempt, fictionally and descriptively, to delineate the personality of the college teacher, there is a sufficient basis for inquiry and wonderment regarding the role of the officeholders as a source of the disabilities experienced by the college.

The performance of the personnel of the college may be another source of its disabilities. The overriding emphasis currently placed upon specialization provides an unparalleled degree of professional and social isolation for the officeholder. The dependence upon objective criteria of competence to the virtual exclusion of humane virtues may create performances within the college which mitigate or even nullify the stated purposes of the institution. Irving Babbitt, a wise if misguided sage of former times, put the matter succinctly:

There are persons at present who do not believe that a man is fitted to fill a chair of French literature in an American college simply because he has made a critical study of the text of a dozen mediaeval beast fables and written a thesis on the Picard dialect, and who deny that a man is necessarily qualified to interpret the humanities to American undergraduates because he has composed a dissertation on the use of the present participle in Ammianus Marscellinus.[18]

The dependence of the college for its staff upon the requirements and programs of the graduate schools is an ambiguous virtue. There are those, such as Earl J. McGrath, formerly United States Commissioner of Education, who censure the graduate schools for their failings, particularly at the point of their training of college teachers.[19] The claim is widely made that such narrow specialization in graduate school as that suggested by Irving Babbitt is insufficient to sustain the national tradition of "liberal education."

On the other hand, in terms of specialized professional training, Bernard Berelson does not concede the alarmists' estimates of American inferiority in the performance by college teachers, not even in scientific and technological areas. Berelson denies that it is properly a major function of graduate education to coach teachers for the rest of the system, certainly not at the cost of their competence in the field of specialization. Critics have undervalued, he feels, the importance of careful, substantive preparation for effective teaching in whatever level. It is chiefly this component which graduate education must be expected to provide and which it is already providing quite satisfactorily in Berelson's judgment.[20] Aside from, or because of, the conflicting opinions regarding the source of the inadequacies of college teachers, there is justification in searching for the disabilities within the college in this sphere.

Third, the disabilities within the organization of the college may be viewed from an ideational base. In Chapter 7 some attention was given to the unclear and sometimes confused ideational objectives for which the college believes itself to be organized. Some of these elements of belief are not rationally provable, although they are held with the tenacity of the fanatic by some academics. The fact that so much discussion in higher education is concentrated on its aims and purposes may belie the fact that this fear is basically subjective, unscientific, and rationalized.

The college ambiguously holds to both efficiency and moral character. "Vocationalism" and "liberal education" are other terms for the ambiguity. While many colleges prate their affection for character-training, there is little evidence to show that they are successful.[21] Education for work, however, is patently demonstrated by the success stories told by the public relations officers.

Ages ago, Xenophon declared that it was the aim of Socrates in his training of the young not to make them efficient, but to inspire them in reverence and restraint, for to make them efficient, said Socrates, without reverence and restraint, was simply to equip them with ampler means of harm.[22] The failure of the college to educate in reverence and restraint also has been expressed by Herbert E. Hawkes:

Almost anyone who is not intimately concerned with college discipline is surprised to find that many a college youth has never really waked up to the importance of some of the most vital ethical questions. There is no doubt that much of the misconduct on the part of grown men and women is due to the fact that, mature though they may be in years, they are still children as far as some of their behavior is concerned. No one has helped them to analyze their attitudes, and they have never happened to do it for themselves. They have no appreciation of the moral differences between the true and the false, the bad and the good, the ugly and the beautiful. It is easy for a college official to say that the home ought to have inspired such appreciation. Many homes, of course, perform this service completely; but, if the home or the church or the lower school has not been successful in producing such an awakening in a boy or a girl by the time that he or she enters college, then the college must undertake the job and attempt to bring the individual to the point where he will, of his own initiative, choose the higher levels of human behavior, instead of the lower. Here, as always, we must start with the student where he is.[23]

While the college may assert the preeminence of its character-building rule, this assertion is qualified by at least two factors. First, in the hierarchy of stated goals for the college there are at times other virtues which take an equally prominent place along with it. At times the constellation of ultimate goals for the college may be unclear; at other times they are clearly confused. Second, despite the proud belief in character-building, to use this aim merely as an example, there is little dependable evidence to show that colleges are organized in such a way as to achieve this objective. Thus the disparity between the stated aims of the college and the achievement of them is a source for investigation of the college's disabilities.

The ideational base of the college, moreover, in line with the characteristic sentiment in American society, is liable to a generous estimate of its capacities and that of its personnel. The college suffers not so much from a conscious restriction of function as it does from a vaguely diffused dispersion of its energies. This dispersion is based on the assumption that the college is a service institution. The college seeks to meet the widespread needs of its students and the community. No human activity seems to fall beyond its scope. It tends to promise all things to all men.

Such a thrust may be, ideationally speaking, too heroic and sentimental for a community-oriented bureaucracy. Pragmatically its claims cannot be perfectly actualized. Theoretically one might doubt whether they should. As John W. Gardner says:

Although a modern society is wise to foster talent on as wide a scale as possible, no society, modern or traditional, can promise every talented individual the opportunity to earn a living in the exercise of his talent. Some years ago I wrote an article describing the need for talent in modern society and shortly thereafter received an aggrieved letter from a correspondent who described his own talent along a certain line and asserted that he could not market it. He believed that society owed him a living for the exercise of this talent, and he was deeply embittered by the treatment he had received.
But the truth is that no society will ever provide a living for every kind of talent.[24]

What Gardner says about society is undoubtedly true also for the college. The disparity between the college's glibly stated ideals and the limitations of human resources and social utilization provide another sphere in which the disabilities of higher education as a bureaucracy may be explored.

The ideational base of the college may reveal discrepancies between its avowed aims and the procedures it employs to achieve them. In Chapter 9 it was indicated that the bureaucracy which paramountly depends upon the meticulous meeting of rules and regulations tends to dwarf the individualized and personalized aspects of its organizational process. Other illustrations also were provided of the manner in which the objectives of the college fail to be realized because of the existence of certain seemingly necessary procedures. The manner in which the formalized routine of the college can all but smother its deeper purposes is provided autobiographically by a leading educator:

We have not quite given up reading. Here and there, in a few homes, in a few educational institutions, it still hangs on in competition with ethics and methods in processes, such as the extrasensory and the audiovisual. A few teachers still prefer written essays to intellectual bingo games that can be scored by electricity. A few students still like to read, a few statesmen, I suppose still carry books with them when they travel. I am still reading in bed, and you who write and publish the books I read are still earning a modest competence.[25]

Another illustration of the way in which routinized procedures and attitudes diminish the grandly stated objectives of the college is reflected in the beliefs of a college teacher:

To realize at the end of a semester of our inspired teaching how little students have learned wounds professional vanity. It is especially painful because we like to think the students beat paths to our classrooms in search of our brilliant insights. In truth, many students are not eager to come to college; they are responding to the pressures of parents and neighbors. They feel compelled to register for courses and perhaps to attend class meetings; so they make the best of a bad business. They hunt for teachers who are amusing, who have a reputation for giving high grades and short assignments, whose courses are 'interesting' and meet at convenient times.[26]

Fourth, a final guide line is the interrelationship factors within a college as a bureaucracy. The college, despite its formalistic pretenses, is a congeries of disparate bureaus held loosely together by a scalar system of administration. Within the social system various phenomena may be found, not all of which are in harmony with each other. A bureaucracy, moreover, has its own internal stresses which may lead on occasion to disabilities. For example, as has been previously noted, bureaucracies regularly experience conflicts between rules and superiors. The officeholder is obliged to follow the rules of his bureau, but a superior officeholder may request that he disobey the rules. The conflict in this instance between the rule system of the college and the rank system comprises a disability. A study of this conflict in the Navy led to the conclusion that it is most acute in the intermediate levels of the personnel hierarchy.[27] Probably the same is true for the college.

Taken together these four guide lines illustrate possible approaches to the disabilities of the college as a bureaucracy. Again, it should be stressed that what appears to be a disability to one person may not be to another. Also what may be a disability in one situation may be an advantage in another. Only the patient building of factual information regarding the actual operations of colleges in their bureaucratic aspects will provide the answers which are sought.

13

Community

Higher education as a bureaucracy exists in a larger social context. This context may be termed "community." By "community" is meant the local, state, regional, national, and even international spheres of social participation in which the college is to a greater or lesser extent an active force. The college, despite its insularity and at times almost religious disdain of the "world," is, nevertheless, not an autonomous social organization. Rather, the college, especially the large and complex urban institution, is bone and marrow in the anatomy of the large community. It is proper, then, that some consideration be given to the relations which exist between the college and the community.

Previously in this volume the main emphasis has been upon a description of the bureaucratic character of the college as a social system. The primary focus has been upon the internal workings of the college. Only incidentally has any reference been made to the college's community relationships.

In this chapter, therefore, some attention will be given to a variety of themes: college-community relations, bureaucratic tendencies in society, bureaucracy and democracy, the conservative propensities of bureaucracies, the possibility for creating change within the system, and finally the manner in which goals are displaced. None of these themes can be investigated exhaustively, but taken together they may provide a set of suggestions for further consideration.

A high degree of generalism is characteristic of essentially rural living conditions. The family-oriented general practitioner in medicine, the school teacher available to many grades, the lawyer who practised in isolation or within a small firm, all were characteristic of a earlier and more simple society. So, too, was the college worker. Located in a relatively isolated rural community, he tended to favor nonbureaucratic modes of organization. Personal relations were relat'vely more intense, rules were pushed into the background, hierarchical distinctions were less meaningful, and the devotion of the worker to the college was more complete.

Today, as urbanized colleges predominate, the blatant callings of bureaucracy are readily heeded. The teacher tends to look upon his employment more in trade-union terms than ever before even though he may loudly assert his professional status and the lack of recognition of that status by the community. He may not wish to work from nine to five, as do other bureaucrats, but at least he wants a regular work schedule which will provide him with a sector of unattached time; that is, time which he by rights is not obligated to give to the college.

Although influence is a two-way street, it is important to note that the teacher is strongly controlled by images which he derives from his fellow-workers in the larger community. The distinctions between the college worker and others in the community have largely evaporated. So far as work arrangements, residence, community participation, etc., are concerned, the college office-holder has lost much of his distinctiveness. The *mystique* (charisma) of his vocation has lessened. In sum, the distinctions previously held between the college and the community have to a large extent become unimportant in current practice.

Yet interrelationships now increasing between the college and the community have always existed. Galileo provides an apt illustration for former times. On the first page of his *Dialogues Concerning Two New Sciences* he expressed his indebtedness to the skilled artisans at the arsenal at Venice. Said he: "Conference with them had often helped me in the investigation of certain effects including not only those which are striking but also those which are recondite and almost incredible." The history of higher education from Galileo's time and earlier until our own provides a huge catalogue of illustrations of college-community interrelations. Today the interrelations also are apparent, as is illustrated in May Sarton's fictional account about the students and faculty of a New England college for women. She tells how each faculty member is forced to revaluate her profession and motives when the community becomes aware of a scandal which touches the lives of the students.[1]

"Danger spots" surrounding the campus, where incidents of crime and rowdyism occur, also form a basis for new developments. In 1961, for example, the Board of Estimate of New York City approved a construction project for Columbia University on 2.12 acres of the 31.2 3/8-acre Morningside Park of an $8,000,000 athletic center that will serve both teen-age boys of the Morningside Heights neighborhood and students of Columbia University. Regarding this project, *The New York Times* commented: "Columbia University will develop this project in the spirit of neighborhood betterment. Along with other cultural institutions and groups of interested citizens of the area, it has been struggling for a long time against the blight which for years has affected much of Morningside Heights." [2] Ground breaking for the project took place in the spring of 1966.

The college in fact finds itself in the community, yet withdrawn from the community. This ambivalent situation creates tensions and problems for the college as well as for the community. The college would like to think of itself as completely autonomous, not simply because of self-interest, but because it feels the academic enterprise requires it. Much of the college's activities, however, both begin and finish in the community.

The ambivalence may be illustrated by the nature of research in the college. The college as an entity withdrawn from the community asserts the primacy of pure research. The college, it is said, is a place where sheer curiosity reigns. Search for the truth without regard to personal or group interest is the glory of institutionally-sponsored research. The influence of the German university of the second half of the nineteenth century in part shapes this belief.

But the college, as far as research is concerned, also lives in the community. Much of its research begins outside of the college through agricultural, military, and industrial initiatives. The federal government in support of its military requirements apportions large sums of money to the colleges and universities of the land for the accomplishment of specific purposes. Pure research goes by the board. What is required is concrete results for the solution of particular problems. Such research may be called "applied" although the distinctions between "pure" and "applied" are at many points tenuous and interrelated. The point is that the college does not exist only for the pursuit of the truth as it wishes to pursue it. It does this in part. To a large degree, it is the community that influences the nature of college research. Research, moreover, is taken here merely as an example of the complexity of college-community interrelations.

Bernard I. Bell has characterized American society as "crowd culture." [8] From this culture it is not possible to exclude the college. The college, as has been seen, is essentially a bureaucratic social organization like others in the community. In this regard it is not distinctive. In an age of conformism, practically all human pursuits are organized bureaucratically—from the sublime to the visceral. George Derbner provides this striking example:

It takes 17,000 different job classifications to produce an ordinary can of peas. Thousands more are needed to market the millions of cans that must be sold to pay the producers and make a profit. A small army of specialized talent must convince us, therefore, that one brand of ordinary peas is like no other brand of ordinary peas. Finally, we need a detachment of artists, performers, and technicians to create the popular cultural atmosphere in which the vibrant image of the brand and the corporae profile of its provider may be etched in the public mind. All this is a genuine aspect of mass culture.[4]

In this technological age, when efficiency is the predominant value, the most powerful centers in society are the bureaucracies. Increasingly comprehensive organization in all spheres of life is the common rule. The college, like other organizations based on wealth, war-making, love, religiosity, politics, etc., has been bureaucratized. The personal relations between individuals in our time have been dwarfed by the overriding importance of the inter-relationships between the bureaucracies. The individual is enclosed by the "anonymous apparatus of a bureaucracy in which I am only a cog."[5]

Bureaucracy, with its stress upon disenchantment and rationalism, has paradoxically tended to tear man from his traditionally rational moorings. As Hannah Arendt has shown, the tradition which began with Plato and Aristotle and continued into the middle of the nineteenth century was able to comprehend the separation of philosophy and politics, of thought and action.[6] The introduction of new scientific concepts, however, such as those undergirding political revolutions and modern production, upset this long tradition. Such modern heroes as Marx, Kierkegaard, Nietzsche, and others laid the groundwork for a submerged rationality and a deeply personalized individuality. In Marx, for example, man is no longer a rational being who apprehends truth through intellectual processes. Rather, man is a laboring animal who reveals reality through revolution. The autonomous character of man as individual being gave way to movements and organizations of great size and complexity. Bureaucratic organizations filled the cultural bill. They became the most common and accepted form in advanced societies for human living.

Bureaucratization as a process as well as a social structure operates in both public and private spheres. It tends to deny the rationality of the individual while it maximizes the rationality necessary for the maintenance of the modern national state and its complex activities. It is in this vein that Franz Neumann speaks of "total bureaucratization and the powerless individuals." [7]

Some students of the subject speak of the "irreversible trend of bureaucratization." By this they imply that modern society, no matter what the nature of its political system may be, is dominantly bureaucratic and will continue to be so. Small-scale organizations and heightened personal intimacy may be found only in relatively inconsequential spheres of life. The trend toward "privatism" in some sectors of human activity constitutes more a revolt from than a dependable assumption for the organization of society. The several forms of mass communication suffer in the main from an inability to face life as it is. They seek through the escapism of fictional portrayal to enlarge the scope of importance of the individual and to draw off his resentments against a highly organized existence. Romanticised and sentimentalized forms of cultural expression, whether within the college or the community, appear to be inadequate thrusts against the thick breast plate of bureaucracy.

Reinhard Bendix says: "It may be that today a revolutionary change . . . is only possible after a destructive war." [8] But even the destructive First and Second World Wars had little if any impact upon the all-encompassing character of bureaucratic society. Both Franz Neumann and Robert A. Brady share the idea that the ultimate development will be the dominance over all bureaucracies, including the governmental, of the economic concentration of power. They point to the ascendance of the "business system of power." [9] Whether this condition ultimately will happen is not possible to predict with surety. Certainly the social situation currently seems to be more complex than that delineated by Neumann and Brady.

The resistance and growth of bureaucracies, therefore, comprise a fundamental problem in relation to certain nonbureaucratic values which men hold. The threat of bureaucracy to meaningful personal existence has been commented upon previously. The current civilization of man is thought by some practically to eliminate all transcendental beliefs, such as the belief in God.[10]

But bureaucracy also is viewed as a threat to certain proximate values, such as democracy. In this connection Peter M. Blau says:

> Bureaucracies in a democratic society pose a paradox. They seem to be necessary for, and simultaneously incompatible with, modern democracy. In a mass society, democracy depends upon bureaucratic institutions, such as complex machinery for electing representatives and efficient productive units that make a high standard of living for all people possible. Yet, by concentrating power in the hands of a few men in business and government, bureaucracies tend to destroy democratic institutions.[11]

It would be inaccurate to claim that bureaucracy is a characteristic only of communistic forms of life or that it represents a trend toward communism. Crawford H. Greenewalt, the chairman of the board of a very large business corporation, in viewing the role of the individual in the United States and in Russia asserts that the social organization of the two countries is strikingly different at several points. For example, in Russia the leaders of the Communist Party hold almost absolute power over all of the other bureaucracies. In the United States organized power is more highly dispersed. But in both countries there is a prevalence of bureaucracy. In fact, according to Greenewalt, the Russians may be outdoing us in giving more attention to the individual. He says: "What troubles me is to note that at the very time the Soviets are embracing our principle of incentive and show signs of benefiting thereby, we ourselves seem intent upon abandoning it." [12]

One of the strongest criticisms made by ex-communists is not against the bureaucratic nature of communist social organization. They do make such strictures. Yet, their principal target is the concentration of power over all bureaucracies in society by the political bureaucracy. Milovan Djilas held membership in the Yugoslavian Communist Party for twenty-five years. Then in October 1953, he began publishing in *Borba*, the Party's official newspaper, a series of articles in which he suggested among other things, the disbandment of the Communist Party on the ground that political and economical power had long since been seized and there was no further need for a revolutionary party.[13] As in *The New Class*, Djilas did not revolt against work, family, politics, as such. Despite his histrionics, he sought to be critical of the dominance over them of sheer political power.[14]

Bureaucracy, then, is not a prime characteristic of communism. It is not an essential characteristic of other political forms, such as national socialism, as Hans H. Gerth has shown.[15] It is not even a fundamental characteristic of democracy. But it has been found to be necessary in all of these political forms of society. No matter which bureaucracy is in the ascendancy or actually holds dominating power, bureaucracy is a form of organized life. Its content, whether political, military, educational, etc., may vary from time to time and place to place. The goals which transcend it and to which it is directed also may vary, but as a social form bureaucracy not only exists, it promises to be a permanent fixture of life for as far into the future as one may see.

Bureaucracy cannot be placed in juxtaposition to democracy. Bureaucracy is not an enemy of democracy. The claim may be made, moreover, that bureaucracy is a specific form of democracy, that is, it is a social form which discriminatingly differentiates the abilities and limitations of citizens, provides them wth the organizational sources for self-fulfillment, and enables them to play an effective, though limited, role in meeting the human needs of others. Dogmatic assertions about "democracy" or "democratic methods" are not a subject for review here, but cautions against them must be made, lest a too simple identification between a supposed meaning of democracy and the particular social forms which seek to give it expression be maintained in exclusion to all others. Two examples may suffice. First, bureaucracy organizes its members in a hierarchical fashion, but hierarchy in itself is not opposed to democracy. Again, the relegation of authority to specialists is not contrary to democracy.

Second, the bureaucratic organization of life, as in the college, does not nullify political rights and responsibilities. The president of the college and the department chairman as well as the student of age and the maintenance worker each has an equal vote in the community's polls.

Bureaucracy, contrary to some sentiment, may in fact be a strong support of democracy. The very existence of bureaucracy tends to stave off haphazard, quixotic and even irrational efforts on the part of powerful minorities. Bureaucracy is a stabilizing and regularizing influence on the social body. Its reasonable fulfillment may be a condition for the realization of a more perfect democracy. Thus, Carl J. Friedrich argues:

Not only must we reject the idea that democracy is opposed to bureaucracy, but we must recognize that the future of democracy depends upon its ability to maintain a fully organized bureaucracy. For the industrial system which demands it is with us for better or worse since the life of millions of human beings depends upon it. If a popular government is incapable of maintaining a bureaucratic hierarchy, it is bound to give way to a form of government which will accomplish that, whether it be the dictatorship of an individual or of a small group in the name of the nation, the people, or the proletariat.[16]

A. Whitney Griswold describes the problem: "How we can make all this organization serve us instead of our serving it: that is our problem." [17] On this score the obligations and the opportunities of the college officeholder are as open and as great as those of any other person in the community. While every citizen may respond to the challenge laid down by the late President Griswold, the professor possibly has a distinctive contribution to make to it. He, unlike all of his neighbors, has a primary obligation to exercise free inquiry. The college teacher, as a professional person, has taken upon himself the obligation to search for an understanding of those conditions under which human life in harmony with the truth may find its greatest fulfillment. This obligation for the college teacher has existed from time immemorial, but it was cast in modern language in 1958 by a committee of the American Association of University Professors:

A Professor's obligations to the community, like the Professor's rights within the community, cannot be less than those of any responsible citizens. His responsibility both to his profession and to the outside community is mainly the fulfillment of his responsibilities to his subjects, to his students, and to his parent institution. As a citizen and as a member of a profession which depends upon freedom for his health and integrity, furthermore, the individual scholar also has an obligation to maintain and advance the conditions of free inquiry. This obligation reaches beyond the classroom or laboratory.[18]

The college worker, however, cannot assume that he is automatically able to enjoy the fruits of free inquiry. More often than one can be proud of, the college worker is more amenable to the dictates of interest groups than are others in society. Hans H. Gerth and C. Wright Mills say: "Precisely because of their specialization and knowledge the scientist and technician are among the most easily used and coordinated of groups in modern society . . . the very rigor of their training typically makes them the easy dupes of men wise in political ways." [19] It is disheartening to realize, again, that teachers, mostly elementary-school teachers, were the best represented of all the professional groups composing the Nazi Party—97 per cent of all German teachers were members of the Party or its affiliates.[20] Previous experience, therefore, does not lead to the expectancy that the personnel of the college is the wisest of all in the community in their discernment of social demonries and virtues.

Some say that the dominant characteristic of bureaucracy is

organizational expansionism. The claim is made that the bureaucrat is never so happy as when his organization is multiplying personnel and functions. John H. Crider makes this claim when he says: "As long as there are bureaucrats, and the proper atmosphere for their propagation, they will multiply prodigiously." [21] The popular but somewhat misleading stress upon the so-called Parkinson's Law has also tended to further this belief. Undoubtedly organizational expansionism is a persistent problem in all bureaucracies, but an even greater problem is that of the conservatism of bureaucracy. Whatever organizational expansionism may exist in the college, and its marks are quite clear, there is also another tendency, at times counteractive, toward the sheer maintenance of the *status quo*. If it is not the present which comprises the extolled glory of the college it is the distant past. That which is traditional tends to be normative. All organizations possess a conserving tendency; it is fairly apparent in the college. In this spirit Charles Homer Haskins proudly declares: "The essentials of university organization are clear and unmistakable, and they have been handed down in unbroken continuity. They have lasted more than seven hundred years—what form of government has lasted so long?" [22]

The conservative basis of the college is apparent in its functions. Three of these functions may be cited here. First, the college seeks to apprehend reality. General education or the liberal arts is a presupposition of this kind of education. Truth, beauty, and goodness are the generalized objectives. Wherever these may lead, the collegiate mind must follow.

Second, the college also possesses an instrumental or citizenship function. To the degree that the college recognizes and supports vocationalism it veers from the search for ultimate truths. Its function becomes that of relating what is known to the needs of the students as present and future citizens of the community. While vocational education clearly falls into this category, much of general education also is directed toward fitting the student for his role as an intelligent citizen. Under this banner the parade of liberal-arts courses is at times wildly cheered.

Third, the college also possesses an inducting function. It seeks to aid the student in his assimilation of the code and practices of society, but not merely in a vocational or even a citizenship sense. The college as an agency of induction aims to transmit the cultural heritage to the present generation.

Naturally, in almost any college these three purposes are intertwined; actually they tend to serve each other. But for the present purposes the conservative function of the college is made more apparent by reason of the fact that the college holds as one of its basic functions the transmission of the past to the present.

The college, like any bureaucracy, places a fundamental value upon successful participation in it. For the student success is clearly defined in terms of progression from admission to graduation. For the officeholders, success is defined largely in terms of promotion. In both cases success is secured by playing the game, that is, by adhering to the formally prescribed rules. The stud nt who does not adhere to the rules meets with failure rather than success. The faculty member, for personal motives if not out of conviction, is likely to be a conformist. Beardsley Ruml describes the faculty member:

. . . the average faculty member is likely to be quite conservative about educational matters. The status system is a conservative influence. The younger members of the faculty might be expected to provide the impulse for change. But their retention and advancement in the institution rests largely on the favorable judgment of their departmental seniors. Until the young teacher has made a firm place for himself in a department, it is natural for him to be cautious about stirring things up. In any event the 'innovators' in life are relatively few.[23]

Conservatism in the staff is enforced both from within and from without the college. The status system, as Ruml insists, comprises an internal control. But external to the college stands the community with its ever-present influences of restraint. Academic freedom in the college is truly an ideal in that its existence is far from everywhere actualized. The history of academic freedom consists of at least as many denials as expressions. For the community, as well as for the college itself, there remains the massively complex task of education—education as to the nature and requirements of academic freedom.

Paul S. Lazarsfeld and Wagner Thielens, Jr., in 1955 extensively studied the attitudes, feelings, and expectations of an extensive sample of college teachers of the social sciences during the period of McCarthyism. They found among other things that the more productive social-science teachers are also the more liberal ones, that they tend to be more apprehensive, sensitive, and courageous with regard to threats to academic freedom, that they tend to congregate in the superior colleges and to vote Democratic. The study further reveals that during the period of its concern, depressive attacks were directed more against the liberal teachers, who were also the more productive, and against the the superior schools, with the consequence, as the authors conclude: "What was really under attack was the quality of American education." [24]

Lazarsfeld and Thielens also show that the factor that intervened to save as much of that quality as was saved was the superior administrative functioning of the better schools where administrators stood between the hackers and the faculties. Thus the community, not only at the time of Senator Joseph McCarthy, regularly seeks to control threatening developments in the college. Whether tacit or expressive, these restraints tend to strengthen the conservative nature of the college.

Viewed positively, moreover, the conservative character of the college as a bureaucracy derives in part from the genuine attachment of the officeholders to the traditional ways of operation. The officeholder cannot maintain his day-by-day zeal for his job without an accompanying conviction on his part that what he is doing is clearly defensible—it is rational. An officeholder who does not hold this conviction is hardly an efficient worker. From a position beyond the bureau, this conviction looks like an unhealthy emotional defensiveness. But viewed from within the bureau the challenge to change appears like the Nazi threat to Alexandria. Seymour Martin Lipset in discussing a Canadian political movement as an example of a bureaucracy says:

Civil servants, of course, do not operate in a social vacuum. Their opinions about relative 'right' and 'wrong' are determined, like those of all persons, by pressures existing in their social milieu. A department official is interested not only in whether a minister's proposal can be put into practice, but with the effect of such policies on the traditional practices of the department and on its long-term relations with other groups. A reform which may be socially desirable, but which disrupts the continuity of practices and interpersonal relations within the department, will often be resisted by a top-ranking civil servant. He is obligated to protect those beneath him in the administrative hierarchy from the consequences of a change in policy.[25]

Robert Michels also affirms the conservative results of the officeholder's devotion to current policies and operation: "We may even say that the more conspicuously a bureaucracy is distinguished by its zeal, by its sense of duty, and by its devotion, the more also will it show itself to be petty, narrow, rigid, and illiberal." [26]

Related to the conservative nature of the college is the phenomenon, as described by Robert K. Merton, of "displacement of goals" whereby "an instrumental value becomes a terminal value."[27] Merton describes the way in which the displacement of goals in a bureaucracy is related to the career aspirations of the officeholders:

The bureaucrat's official life is planned for him in terms of a graded career, through the organizational devices of promotion by seniority, pensions, incremental salaries, etc., all of which are designed to provide incentives for disciplined action and conformity to the official regulations. The official is tacitly expected to and largely does adapt his thoughts, feelings, and actions to the prospect of this career. But *these very devices* which increase the probability of conformance also lead to an over-concern with strict adherence to regulations which induces timidity, conservatism, and technicism. Displacement of sentiments from goals onto means is fostered by the tremendous symbolic significance of the means (rules).[28]

The manner in which bureaucracy distracts the individual from goal-centeredness is strikingly told by Robert Michels in his description of the bureaucratization of so goal-centered a social movement as socialism:

But in proportion as, in their own country, paths of activity were open for the socialists, at first for agitation and soon afterwards for positive and constructive work, the more did a recognition of the demands of the everyday life of the party divert their attention from immortal principles. Their vision gained in precision but lost in extent. The more cotton-spinners, boot and shoe operatives, or brushmakers the labour leader could gain each month for his union, the better versed he was in the tedious subtleties of insurance against accident and illness, the greater the industry he could display in the specialized questions of factory inspection and of arbitration in trade disputes, the better acquainted he might be with the system of checking the amount of individual purchases in co-operative stores and with the methods for the control of the consumption of municipal gas, the more difficult was it for him to retain a general interest in the labour movement, even in the narrowest sense of this term. As the outcome of inevitable psychophysiological laws he could find little time and was likely to have little inclination for the study of the great problems of the philosophy of history, and all the more falsified consequently would become his judgment of international questions. At the same time he would incline more and more to regard everyone as an 'incompetent,' an 'outsider,' an 'unprofessional,' who might wish to judge questions from some higher outlook than the purely technical . . .[29]

The application of this phenomenon to higher education as a bureaucracy is fairly obvious. The college, too, with certain seasonal exceptions, is inclined to accept its own ultimate purposes as so sacrosanct that they need not be formulated, far less criticized and reformulated. In fact, the ideational basis for the existence of the college is generally taken for granted; its results are assumed to be efficacious. The college in the extreme state of rigidity tends to be a self-justifying social system. As such it displaces its pristine goals with a consuming concern for operational details.

Such a development not only reinforces the conservative character of the college; it leads also to its spiritual decline.

The fact is, however, that the college is not alone among the bureaucracies in the displacement of goals. The illustrations provided previously indicate how political and other organizations suffer from the same occurrence. One of the consequences of a highly bureaucratized society, moreover, is the failure of such a society as a society to examine its goals, to reinterpret perennially its ultimate values, and to live under the tension between the real and the ideal which genuine goal-centeredness creates. While he is far from an ultimate solution to the problem, Walter Lippmann supports this view in his advocacy of "the public philosophy." Lippmann analyzes the causes for the precipitate decline of liberal democracy and the alarming rise of totalitarianism that has occurred in our century. The source of the trouble, Mr. Lippmann argues, lies first of all in the fact that mass public opinion and legislatures have come to exercise a dominant and dangerous influence over the executive functions of government. The result has been that the modern democracies have grown steadily more incapable of ruling wisely in times of war and peace.

The second root of the trouble, Mr. Lippmann thinks, lies in the failure of the Western democracies to defend and maintain the political faith or "public philosophy" which formed the basis of the convictions of the Founding Fathers when they established the Constitution, and which in general underlies the liberal way of life. Without such a generally accepted philosophy, the enjoyment of private property becomes an end in itself, and is destructively used, wealth is ruthlessly accumulated, and freedom of speech degenerates into freedom of abuse. Unless the constraints of this public philosophy are duly recognized and an effort is made to stem the tide of agnosticism and godlessness in Western society, says Mr. Lippmann, democracy will perish.[30]

The case for the conservatism of bureaucracy, however, is

not all black. Some rays of hope shine through the seemingly impenetrable darkness. Bureaucracies are not always fighting in defense of the *status quo*. Not everywhere are the transcending goals forgotten or neglected. Could life stand the intense heat of unmitigated sunlight from so unshaded a source as ultimate reality? Michael Young has written a satire which foresees the application of sheer intelligence as the basis for the conduct of a future society. In a sense he brings Huxley's *Brave New World* up to date. His book tells with roundabout humor of the events which led to a blossoming utopia, the Meritocracy. Here intelligence, guided by education, holds the key role in the creation of the Meritocracy. The result, of course, is one which in its wake destroys so many cherished values as to result in quick rejection.[31]

Bureaucracies, such as in higher education, in order to survive over long periods of time must adapt the totality of their organizations to changing conditions. Even organizational objectives change. As Herbert A. Simon points out:

The organization objective is by no means a static thing. In order to survive, the organization must have an objective that appeals to its customers, so that they will make the contributions necessary to sustain it. Hence, organization objectives are constantly adapted to conform to the changing values of customers, or to secure new groups of customers in place of customers who have dropped away. The organization may also undertake special activities to induce acceptance of its objectives by customers—advertising, missionary work, and propaganda of all sorts.[32]

"Customer" is used by Simon to refer to any individual for whom the organizational objective has personal value. The college, from this standpoint, has not remained static over the centuries, despite the earlier remark by Haskins. It, too, has modified its structure and activities to keep pace with the changing requirements of its customers—potential and actual students. As colleges modified earlier aristocratic appeals to become instruments of mass education for a highly complex industrial society they have perceptively modified their traditions and have introduced new features.

The striking growth of cooperative arrangements among colleges in the recent years provides a good illustration of the manner in which colleges are able to change. In the past, and to some extent still today, colleges, whether public or private, tended to view themselves as competitive entrepreneurs. The rule was: each college for itself and the devil take the hindmost. That day of fears and free enterprise is drawing to a close. Colleges today are appreciative of the values of cooperation.

In this spirit five colleges in upper New York and Pennsylvania agreed in 1961 to a cooperative venture aimed at combining sound economies with high academic standards. The resulting corporation, the College Center of the Finger Lakes, located in Corning, New York, represents colleges with a combined enrollment of almost 4,500 and includes academic categories of great variety: Alfred University, an independent coeducational college, Corning Community College, a two-year institution, Elmira College, an independent women's college, Hobart and William Smith College, an independent coordinate college, and Mansfield State College, a public institution.

The Great Lakes College Association, composed of twelve colleges in Indiana, Michigan and Ohio, forms another illustration of the cooperative venture discernible today in higher education. The association plans to develop educational programs, improve administrative operations, and cooperate in experiments. The colleges involved are: DePauw, Earlham, and Wabash in Indiana; Albion, Hope, and Kalamazoo in Michigan; and Antioch, Denison, Kenyon, Oberlin, Ohio Wesleyan, and Wooster in Ohio.

In recent years the cooperative movement has been gathering momentum in the Middle West and the South, but has not made significant headway in the East. Yet such efforts, aside from their durability and wisdom, represent significant changes in the bureaucratic nature of higher education. Such a modification, moreover, is merely an example of innumerable others which have occurred in the long course of higher education's history. The college from this wider cultural and historical perspective may be termed a "conservative innovator."

In this connection the church-sect analogy developed by Ernst Troeltsch is suggestive. According to Troeltsch the church "is that type of organization which is overwhelmingly conservative, which to a certain extent accepts the secular order, and dominates the masses; in principle, therefore, it is universal, i.e., it desires to cover the whole life of humanity." On the other hand the sects, according to Troeltsch, "are comparatively small groups; they aspire after personal inward perfection, and they aim at a direct personal fellowship between the members of each group." [33] Both terms are used in a descriptive rather than a polemic and apologetic sense. They may be extended, moreover, to describe the ethos of the bureaucracy.

Some bureacracies, it may be claimed, are dominantly church types, possessing many of the characteristics of the universalizing, mass-oriented and secularized organization. Other bureaucracies, including colleges, may feel themselves to be living in tension with the society that surrounds them, but also warmed by the strong convictions and personal relationships in which they flourish. The assumption may be tentatively made that the church-type of college is most prone to maintain itself as a tradition-bearing, conservative, compromised social organization. The sect-type college on the other hand does not readily conform to the demands of the whole community. It perceives its role to be elitist. It strives with a zeal nurtured by rare motives to attain a perfect state of devotion to its primary principles. The church-type college is primarily conservative. The sect-type college is fundamentally open to change. Few colleges fulfill the requirements of either type in pure form. But the typology may throw light upon the possibilities for organizational change in the bureaucracy. In non-Troeltschian terminology, Peter M. Blau describes briefly the possibilities of the bureaucracy being a conservative innovator:

Indeed, the dynamics of bureaucratic development is not confined to the emergence of new instruments for the accomplishment of specified objectives, but in the process the objectives themselves change, too. Particularly in innovating organizations, although not only there, competent officials tend to become interested in assuming new responsibilities and in expanding the jurisdiction of the agency, since this would increase their works satisfaction and benefit their career.[34]

Little is known at the present time of the manner in which creative change may be introduced and maintained in a bureacracy. This is a theme which sorely calls for investigation. But, perhaps, it is the nature and quality of leadership in the final analysis which contributes most heavily to the final character of a bureacracy. As Marshall E. Dimock says:

An institution tends to take on the character of its leadership. If the leadership is bureaucratic, the institution will become progressively bureaucratic also. If the leadership has a fresh viewpoint and one that is attuned to social forces and social change, then there is at least hope of carrying the bureaucracy along with it.[35]

Notes

PREFACE

1. *The New York Times*, August 11, 1961, p. 21.
2. Martin P. Mayer, *The Schools*, New York: Harper & Row, 1961, p. 22.
3. *Reader in Bureaucracy*, edited by Robert K. Merton, Ailsa T. Gray, Barbara Hockey, Hanan C. Selvin, New York: The Free Press, 1952, pp. 451–464.

CHAPTER 1

1. John Q. Academesis, "A.B.—Academic Bureaucracy," *The New York Times Magazine*, October 12, 1958, pp. 10, 63, 64, 66.
2. Robert Lewis Shayon has written an amusing description of the manner in which "private eyes," so far as radio and television are concerned, have become bureaucratized. Instead of the lone man battling against overwhelming odds, including the police, the organization private eyes operate a business complete with research assistants, switchboards, and private secretaries. See "The Corporate Private Eye," *Saturday Review*, August 8, 1959, p. 29.
3. Probably no definitive study of the sociology of business now exists. But Professor Paul F. Lazarsfeld has given a first report in the July, 1959 issue of the *American Journal of Sociology*, surveying some 150 books and articles.
4. The B-58, America's first supersonic bomber, for example, a product of the Convair Division of the General Dynamics Corporation, is a product of more than 4,700 participating suppliers and subcontractors located in every part of the nation. A dependable summary is *Sociology and the Mili-*

tary Establishment by Morris Janowitz, New York: Russell Sage Foundation, 1959.

5. See Fritz Morstein Marx, *The Administrative State: An Introduction to Bureaucracy*, Chicago: University of Chicago Press, 1957.

6. Leo Katcher, *The Big Bankroll: The Life and Times of Arnold Rothstein*, New York: Harper & Row, 1959, p. 9.

7. *The New York Times*, August 10, 1959, pp. 1, 4.

8. Marshall E. Dimock, *Administrative Vitality: The Conflict of Bureaucracy*, New York: Harper & Row, 1959.

9. Beardsley Ruml, *Memo to a College Trustee*, New York: McGraw-Hill, 1959.

CHAPTER 2

1. This characteristic of American society was vividly portrayed by Alexis de Tocqueville in *Democracy in America*, 2 volumes, New York: Vintage Books, 1958.

2. Max Weber, *The Protestant Ethic and the Spirit of Capitalism*, New York: Chas. Scribner's Sons, 1958.

3. William H. Whyte, Jr., *The Organization Man*, Garden City: Anchor Books, 1957.

CHAPTER 3

1. Thorstein Veblen, *The Higher Learning in America: A Memorandum on the Conduct of Universities by Business Men*, New York: Sagamore Press, 1957, p. 62.

2. William H. Whyte, Jr., *The Organization Man*, Garden City: Anchor Books, 1957, p. 69.

3. *Ibid*, p. 116.

4. Beardsley Ruml, *Memo to a College Trustee*, New York: McGraw-Hill, 1959, p. 8.

5. Margaret L. Habein, editor, *Spotlight on the College Student*, Washington, D.C.: American Council on Education, 1959, p. 29.

6. *The New York Times*, November 17, 1958, p. 45.

7. How significant is it that the University of California operates Los Alamos, and the University of Chicago, the Argonne Laboratories, or that more officers are trained in the more than five hundred officer training corps in colleges than are trained in the Army, Navy, and Air Force, including the academies?

8. Harold W. Stoke, *The American College President*, New York: Harper & Row, 1959, p. 152.

CHAPTER 4

1. Lloyd S. Woodburne, *Principles of College and University Administration*, Stanford: Stanford University Press, 1958, p. 1.

2. Richard Hofstadter, *Academic Freedom in the Age of the College,* New York: Columbia University Press, 1961, p. 124.

3. Chester I. Barnard, "Functions and Pathology of Status Systems in Formal Organizations," in *Industry and Society,* edited by William F. Whyte, New York: McGraw-Hill, 1946, pp. 47–48.

4. John W. Gardner, *Excellence: Can We Be Equal and Excellent Too?,* New York: Harper & Row, 1961, p. 25.

5. Mary Jane Ward, *The Professor's Umbrella,* New York: Random House, 1948, p. 268.

6. Randall Jarrell, *Pictures from An Institution: A Comedy,* New York: Meridian Books, 1960, p. 61.

7. *The New York Times,* June 12, 1959, p. E9.

8. "The Economic Status of the Profession, 1959–1960; Annual Report by Z Committee," *AAUP Bulletin,* Volume XLVI, Number 2, June, 1960, p. 161.

9. Thomas F. Tout, "The Emergence of a Bureaucracy," *The English Civil Service in the Fourteenth Century,* Manchester, England: University Press, 1916, Volume III, pp. 192–213.

10. Robert K. Merton, "Bureaucratic Structure and Personality," in *Reader in Bureaucracy,* edited by Robert K. Merton, Ailsa P. Gray, Barbara Hockey, Hanan C. Selvin, New York: The Free Press, 1952, p. 363.

11. Robert O. Bowen, editor, *The New Professors,* New York: Holt, Rinehart & Winston, 1960.

12. Marshall E. Dimock, "Bureaucracy Self-Examined," *Public Administration Review,* Volume IV, Number 3, 1944, p. 202.

13. Ernest Earnest, *Academic Procession: An Informal History of the American College, 1636–1953,* New York: Bobbs-Merrill, 1953, p. 81.

14. William Maxwell, *The Folded Leaf,* New York: Vintage Books, 1959, p. 182.

15. Kingsley Amis, *Lucky Jim,* New York: Viking Press, 1958, p. 35.

16. Theodore Caplow and Reece J. McGee, *The Academic Marketplace,* New York: Basic Books, 1958, p. 197.

17. Spencer Klaw, "The Affluent Professors," *The Reporter,* Volume XXII, Number 13, June 23, 1960, pp. 16–25.

CHAPTER 5

1. Walter D. Wagoner, "Protestantism on the Campus," *The Christian Century,* Volume I, Number 16, April 20, 1955, p. 475.

2. Charles Homer Haskins, *The Rise of Universities,* Ithaca: Cornell University Press, 1957, pp. 27–28.

3. Herbert E. Hawkes and Anna L. R. Hawkes, *Through a Dean's Open Door,* New York: McGraw-Hill, 1945, p. 3.

4. Emile Durkheim, *Division of Labor in Society,* translated by George Simpson, New York: The Free Press, 1947.

5. F. W. Taylor, *On the Art of Cutting Metals,* New York: American Society of Mechanical Engineers, 1907.

6. Alfred North Whitehead, *The Aims of Education: and Other Essays,* New York: Mentor Books, 1955, p. 22.

7. *See* C. P. Snow, *The Two Cultures and the Scientific Revolution*, New York: Cambridge University Press, 1959.

8. Irving Babbitt, *Literature and the American College*, Boston: Houghton Mifflin, 1908, p. 107.

9. Bruce Stewart, "Reflections on an Ant Heap or What Happened to the Ph in the Ph.D.?" *AAUP Bulletin*, Volume XLV, Number 2, June, 1959, p. 256.

10. Theodore Caplow and Reece J. McGee, *The Academic Marketplace*, New York: Basic Books, 1958, p. 221.

11. Douglas N. Morgan, "So You Want to Read a Paper!" *AAUP Bulletin*, Volume XLV, Number 2, June, 1959, p. 249.

12. Dewey W. Grantham, Jr., "A Community of Scholars," *AAUP Bulletin*, Volume XLVI, Number 4, December, 1960, p. 388.

13. Kenneth I. Brown, "Academic Salvation by Visitation," *Foundation Stones*, Volume V, Number 1, March, 1961, pp. 1–2.

14. Spencer Klaw, "The Affluent Professors," *The Reporter*, Volume XXII, Number 13, June 23, 1960, p. 21.

15. "Sociologists Invade the Plant," *Business Week*, Number 1542, March 21, 1959, pp. 95–101.

16. *Time*, December 19, 1960, p. 60.

17. Robert Michels, *Political Parties*, New York: The Free Press, 1949, p. 189.

18. Richard Hofstadter, *Academic Freedom in the Age of the College*, New York: Columbia University Press, 1961, p. 230.

19. Mary Jane Ward, *The Professor's Umbrella*, New York: Random House, 1948, p. 57.

20. Carlos Baker, *A Friend in Power*, New York: Chas. Scribner's Sons, 1958, pp. 23–24.

21. A. Whitney Griswold, *Liberal Education and the Democratic Ideal and Other Essays*, New Haven: Yale University Press, 1959, pp. 131–132.

22. Jacques Barzun, *Teacher in America*, New York: Anchor Books, 1954, p. 159.

23. Beardsley Ruml, *Memo to a College Trustee*, New York: McGraw-Hill, 1959, p. 7.

24. A. Whitehead, *op cit.*, p. 102.

25. Charles V. Kidd, *American University and Federal Research*, Cambridge: Belknap Press of Harvard University Press, 1959.

26. Caplow and McGee, *op cit.*, p. 83.

27. Charles A. Fenton, "The Sweet, Sad Song of the Devoted College Teacher," *AAUP Bulletin*, Volume XLVI, Number 4, December, 1960, p. 364.

28. Eugene P. Chase, "Does Research Need Revival?" *AAUP Bulletin*, Volume XLI, Number 3, Autumn, 1955, pp. 530–531.

29. Lincoln Steffens, *The Autobiography of Lincoln Steffens*, New York: Harcourt, Brace & World, 1931, p. 816.

30. Robert Glynn Kelly, *A Lament for Barney Stone*, New York: Holt, Rinehart & Winston, 1961, pp. 191–192.

31. John W. Gustad, "Policies and Practices in Faculty Evaluation," *The Educational Record*, Volume XLII, Number 3, July, 1961, pp. 194–211.

CHAPTER 6

1. Huston Smith, *The Purposes of Higher Education,* New York: Harper & Row, 1955, p. 4.
2. Robert Michels, *Political Parties,* New York: The Free Press, 1949, p. 32.
3. Charles Homer Haskins, *The Rise of Universities,* Ithaca: Cornell University Press, 1957, p. 2.
4. Richard Hofstadter, *Academic Freedom in the Age of the College,* New York: Columbia University Press, 1961, p. VIII.
5. Max Weber, *The Theory of Social and Economic Organization,* translation by A. M. Henderson and Talcott Parsons, edited by Talcott Parsons, New York: Oxford University Press, 1947, pp. 329–340.
6. Chester I. Barnard, "Functions and Pathology of Status Systems in Formal Organizations," in *Industry and Society,* edited by William F. Whyte, New York: McGraw-Hill, 1946, p. 49.
7. Isaiah 40:4.
8. Jacques Barzun, *Teacher in America,* New York: Anchor Books, 1954, p. 157.
9. John Jay Corson, *Governance of Colleges and Universities,* New York: McGraw-Hill, 1960.
10. Donald R. Belcher, *Board of Trustees of the University of Pennsylvania,* Philadelphia: University of Pennsylvania Press, 1960.
11. Harold W. Stoke, *The American College President,* New York: Harper & Row, 1958, p. 3.
12. Raymond B. Fosdick, "Woodrow Wilson among His Friends," *Harper's Magazine,* Volume CCXIII, Number 1279, December, 1965, p. 62.
13. Lloyd S. Woodburne, *Principles of College and University Administration,* Stanford: Stanford University Press, 1958, p. 11.
14. Charles A. Fenton, "The Sweet, Sad Song of the Devoted College Teacher," *AAUP Bulletin,* Volume XLVI, Number 4, December, 1960, p. 361.
15. W. H. Auden, "Under Which Lyre: A Reactionary Tract for the Times," *Nones,* New York: Random House, 1950, p. 41.
16. David Riesman, *Constraint and Variety in American Education,* Lincoln, Nebraska: University of Nebraska Press, 1956, p. 21.
17. Beardsley Ruml, *Memo to a College Trustee,* New York: McGraw-Hill, 1959, p. 57.
18. *Ibid,* p. 56.
19. Bentley Glass, "The Academic Scientist: 1940–1960," *AAUP Bulletin,* Volume XLVI, Number 2, June, 1960, p. 151.
20. Morris Bishop calls Wister's work: "An innocent picture of the snobbery, meanmindedness, anti-intellectualism, cruelty of class and wealth, and the pitiable spiritual and moral valuations of the Nineties." "The Phoenix Nest," *Saturday Review,* Volume XLIII, Number 34, August 20, 1960, p. 4.
21. Randall Jarrell, *Pictures from an Institution: A Comedy,* New York: Meridian Books, 1960, pp. 81–82.
22. Jackson Toby, "The American College Student: A Candidate for

Socialization," *AAUP Bulletin*, Volume XLIII, Number 2, June, 1957, p. 321.

23. Henry Steele Commager, "Give the Games Back to the Students," *The New York Times Magazine*, April 16, 1961, pp. 27, 120–121.

24. Max S. Marshall, "How to Be a Dean," *AAUP Bulletin*, Volume XLII, Number 4, Winter, 1956, p. 642.

25. Information supplied by Fillmore H. Sanford, University of Texas; later published as: Fillmore H. Sanford, "One Way to Hire a Secretary," *The American Psychologist*, Volume XIV, 1959, pp. 191–192.

26. William K. Selden, *Accreditation: A Struggle over Standards in Higher Education*, New York: Harper & Row, 1960.

27. Ruml, *op. cit.*, pp. 55–56.

CHAPTER 7

1. Helmut Thielicke, *Nihilism: Its Origin and Nature—with a Christian Answer*, New York: Harper & Row, 1961, p. 97.

2. Richard Livingstone, *Some Thoughts on University Education*, New Haven: The Hazen Foundation, 1947, p. 8.

3. John J. Corson, *Governance of Colleges and Universities*, New York: McGraw-Hill, 1960.

4. Chester I. Barnard, "Functions and Pathology of Status Systems in Formal Organizations," in *Industry and Society*, edited by William F. Whyte, New York: McGraw-Hill, 1946, p. 48.

5. See Herbert A. Simon, *Administrative Behavior*, New York: Macmillan Co., 1947, pp. 20–22.

6. Robert Dubin, "Decision-Making by Management in Industrial Relations," *The American Journal of Sociology*, Volume LIV, Number 4, 1949, pp. 292–297.

7. Lyman Bryson, "Notes on a Theory of Advice," *Political Science Quarterly*, Volume LXVI, Number 3, 1951, p. 322.

8. Carl J. Friedrich, "Some Observations on Weber's Analysis of Bureaucracy," in *Reader in Bureaucracy*, edited by Robert K. Merton, Ailsa T. Gray, Barbara Hockey, and Hanan C. Selvin, New York: The Free Press, 1952, p. 30.

9. Beardsley Ruml, *Memo to a College Trustee*, New York: McGraw-Hill, 1959, pp. 58–59.

10. Karl Dreyfuss, *Occupation and Ideology of the Salaried Employee*, translated by Eva Abramovitch, Works Progress Administration and Department of Social Science, New York: Columbia University Press, 1938, Volume I, pp. 1–18.

11. Philip Selznick, "A Theory of Organizational Commitments," *TVA and the Grass Roots*, University of California Publications in Culture and Society, Berkeley: University of California Press, 1949, Volume III, pp. 250–259.

12. Simon, *op cit.*, p. 111.

13. Chester I. Barnard, *The Functions of the Executive*, Cambridge: Harvard University Press, 1938, pp. 223–224.

14. John W. Gardner, *Excellence: Can We Be Equal and Excellent, Too?*, New York: Harper & Row, 1961, pp. 25–26.

15. Ralph H. Turner, "The Navy Disbursing Officer as a Bureaucrat," *The American Sociological Review*, Volume XII, Number 3, 1947, pp. 342–348.

16. F. J. Roethlisberger and William J. Dickson, *Management and the Worker*, Cambridge: Harvard University Press, 1947, pp. 558–562.

17. Frederic S. Burin, "Bureaucracy and National Socialism: a Reconsideration of a Weberian Theory," in *Reader in Bureaucracy*, edited by Robert K. Merton, Ailsa T. Gray, Barbara Hockey, Hanan C. Selvin, New York: The Free Press, 1952, p. 39.

18. Philip Selznick, *TVA and the Grass Roots*, University of California Publications in Culture and Society, University of California Press, 1949, Volume III, pp. 259–264.

19. Robert Michels, *Political Parties*, New York: The Free Press, 1949, pp. 371–372.

20. Paul Wasserman with Fred S. Silander, *Decision-Making: an Annotated Bibliography*, Graduate School of Business and Public Administration, Ithaca: Cornell University Press, 1958.

21. Chester I. Barnard characterizes this phenomenon: "The practical difficulties in the operation of organization seldom lie in the excessive desire of individuals to assume responsibility for the organization action of themselves or others, but rather lie in the reluctance to take responsibility for their own actions in organization." *op cit.*, pp. 170–171.

22. Arthur K. Davis, "Bureaucratic Patterns in the Navy Officer Corps," *Social Forces*, Volume XXVII, Number 1, 1948, pp. 143–153.

23. Edmund G. Love, *Arsenic and Red Tape*, New York: Harcourt, Brace & World, 1960.

24. Alvin W. Gouldner, "The Problem of Succession in Bureaucracy," *Studies in Leadership: Leadership and Democratic Action*, edited by Alvin W. Gouldner, New York: Harper & Row, 1950, pp. 644–659.

25. Arthur W. Macmahon and John D. Millett, *Federal Administrators*, New York: Columbia University Press, 1939.

26. Max Weber, *The Theory of Social and Economic Organization*, translated by A. M. Henderson and Talcott Parsons, edited by Talcott Parsons, Oxford University Press, 1947, pp. 364–373.

27. Alvin W. Gouldner, *Studies in Leadership: Leadership and Democratic Action*, edited by Alvin W. Gouldner, New York: Harper & Row, 1950, pp. 644–659.

28. W. Lloyd Warner and J. O. Low, *The Social System of the Modern Factory*, New Haven: Yale University Press, 1947.

29. Marshall E. Dimock and Howard K. Hyde, *Bureaucracy and Trusteeship in Large Corporations*, TNEC Monogram, Number 11, Washington, D.C.: Government Printing Office, 1940, pp. 45–54.

CHAPTER 8

1. Carl J. Friedrich, "Some Observations on Weber's Analysis of Bureaucracy," in *Reader in Bureaucracy*, edited by Robert K. Merton, Ailsa P. Gray, Barbara Hockey, and Hanan C. Selvin, New York: The Free Press, 1952, p. 33.

2. Richard Hofstadter, *Academic Freedom in the Age of the College,* New York: Columbia University Press, 1961, p. 61.

3. Herbert A. Simon, *Administrative Behavior,* New York: Macmillan Co., 1947, pp. 69–70.

4. Clarence Randall recently has shown that management in American industry possesses foibles and self-deceptions. In today's hyperorganized business community one finds the following: the new breed of specialists, top-heavy executive pay, magic expense accounts, what balance sheets do not show, and the myths about retirement. Clarence Randall, *The Folklore of Management,* Boston: Little, Brown and Company, 1961.

5. William C. Fels, "Modern College Usage or What Is The Public Relations Office Saying?," *Columbia University Forum,* Volume II, Number 3, Spring, 1959, pp. 39–41.

6. This condensation from the *Columbia University Forum* article appeared in *Time,* July 6, 1959, p. 58.

7. Fels, *op cit.,* p. 41.

8. *The New York Times,* June 7, 1959, p. 31.

9. See the comments on loyalty in Chapter 4.

10. Richard H. Shryock, *The University of Pennsylvania Faculty: A Study in American Higher Education,* Philadelphia: University of Pennsylvania Press, 1959.

11. *Time,* July 27, 1959, p. 41.

12. Edgar Z. Friedenberg, *The Vanishing Adolescent,* Boston: Beacon Press, 1959.

13. Fred M. Hechinger, "Teen-Age Tyranny Extends Its Empire," *The York Times Magazine,* March 19, 1961, pp. 21, 120–121.

14. Philip Jacob, *Changing Values in College,* New York: Harper & Row, 1957.

15. Lawrence W. Hyman, "Moral Values in Higher Education—A preliminary Report," *Journal of Higher Education,* Volume XXXII, Number 1, January 1961, pp. 36–39.

16. Theodore Caplow and Reece J. McGee, *The Academic Marketplace,* New York: Basic Books, 1958.

17. Helmut Thielicke, *Nihilism; Its Origin and Nature—With a Christian Answer,* New York: Harper & Row, 1961, p. 21.

18. Ordway Tead, *The Climate of Learning: A Constructive Attack on Complacency in Higher Education,* New York: Harper & Row, 1958, p. 20.

19. Richard Hofstadter, *op cit.,* pp. 185–186.

20. Karl Mannheim, *Man and Society in an Age of Reconstruction,* New York: Harcourt, Brace & World, 1951, p. 51 ff.

21. Robert K. Merton, "Bureaucratic Structure and Personality," *Social Forces,* Volume XVIII, Number 4, 1940, p. 560.

CHAPTER 9

1. Theodore Morrison, *The Stones of the House,* New York: Viking Press, 1953.

2. Ibid, *To Make a World,* New York: Viking Press, 1957.

3. Carlos H. Baker, *A Friend in Power*, New York: Chas. Scribner's Sons, 1958.

4. Charles Homer Haskins, *The Rise of Universities*, Ithaca: Cornell University Press, 1957, pp. 29–30.

5. David Riesman, *Constraint and Variety in American Education*, Lincoln, Nebraska: University of Nebraska Press, 1956, p. 94.

6. Robert B. Heilman, "Fashions in Melodrama," *AAUP Bulletin*, Volume XLV, Number 3, September, 1959, p. 360.

7. Carl Murchison, *A Handbook of Social Psychology*, Worcester, Mass.: Clark University Press, 1935, p. IX.

8. Philip Selznick, *TVA and the Grass Roots*, University of California Publications in Culture and Society, Berkeley: University of California Press, 1949, Volume III, pp. 250–259.

9. Reinhard Bendix, "Bureaucracy and the Problem of Power," *Public Administration Review*, Volume V, Number 3, 1945, pp. 194–195.

10. *Ibid*, pp. 194–209.

11. Ludwig von Mises, *Bureaucracy*, New Haven: Yale University Press, 1944.

12. Beardsley Ruml, *Tomorrow's Business*, New York: Farrar and Rinehart, 1945.

13. Robert K. Merton, "Bureaucratic Structure and Personality," *Social Forces*, Volume XVIII, Number 4, 1940, p. 560.

14. Chester I. Barnard, *The Functions of the Executive*, Cambridge: Harvard University Press, 1942, p. 163.

15. *Ibid*, p. 168.

16. Herbert A. Simon, "Decision-Making and Administrative Organization," *Public Administration Review*, Volume IV, Number 1, 1944, pp. 16–25.

17. Lyman Bryson, "Notes on a Theory of Advice," *Political Science Quarterly*, Volume LXVI, Number 3, 1951, pp. 321–339.

18. Benjamin M. Selekman, *A Moral Philosophy for Management*, New York: McGraw-Hill, 1959.

19. Hans H. Gerth, "The Nazi Party: Its Leadership and Composition," *The American Journal of Sociology*, Volume XLV, Number 4, 1940, pp. 517–541.

20. Max Weber, *The Theory of Social and Economic Organization*, translated by A. M. Henderson and Talcott Parsons, edited by Talcott Parsons, New York: Oxford University Press, 1947, p. 364.

21. *Ibid*, p. 367.

22. Chester I. Barnard, "Functions and Pathology of Status Systems in Formal Organizations," *Industry and Society*, edited by William F. Whyte, New York: McGraw-Hill, 1946, pp. 47–52.

23. *Ibid*, p. 81.

24. Ernest Earnest, *Academic Procession: An Informal History of the American College, 1636–1953*, New York: Bobbs-Merrill, 1953, p. 284.

25. *The New York Times*, April 23, 1961, p. 71.

26. *The New York Times*, February 19, 1961, p. 71.

27. Glendon Swarthout, *Where the Boys Are*, New York: Random House, 1960.

28. Earnest, *op cit.*, p. 187.

29. Several compilations of materials, in addition to a large quantity of

individual articles, reports, etc., have appeared regarding the Berkeley student revolt, providing one of the most extensive documentations of a particular series of events on a local campus that has become available in recent years. Among these compilations are: Hal Draper, *Berkeley: The New Student Revolt*, with an introduction by Mario Savio, New York: Grove Press, 1965; Michael V. Miller and Susan Gilmore, *Revolution at Berkeley: The Crisis in American Education*, with an introduction by Irving Howe, New York: Dell Publishing Company, 1965; Seymour Martin Lipset and Sheldon S. Wolin, *The Berkeley Student Revolt: Facts and Interpretations*, Garden City: Anchor Books, 1965.

CHAPTER 10

1. Ian Brook, *Jimmy Riddle*, New York: G. P. Putnam's Sons, 1961.
2. Max Weber, *The Theory of Social and Economic Organization*, translated by A. M. Henderson and Talcott Parsons, edited by Talcott Parsons, New York: Oxford University Press, 1947, p. 340.
3. Marshall E. Dimock, "Bureaucracy Self-Examined," *Public Administration Review*, Volume IV, Number 3, 1944, pp. 197–207.
4. Everett Knight, *The Objective Society*, New York: George Braziller, 1960.
5. Martin Buber, *I and Thou*, New York: Chas. Scribner's Sons, second edition, 1958.
6. Carl J. Friedrich, *Responsible Bureaucracy: A Study of the Swiss Civil Service*, Cambridge: Harvard University Press, 1932, p. 14.
7. Emerson Shuck, "Teacher's Role Book," *AAUP Bulletin*, Volume XLVI, Number 3, September, 1960, p. 270.
8. Albert Camus, *The Plague*, New York: Alfred A. Knopf, 1948.
9. Thorstein Veblen, *The Higher Learning in America: A Memorandum on the Conduct of Universities by Business Men*, New York: Sagamore Press, 1957, p. 5.
10. Irving Babbitt, *Literature and the American College*, Boston: Houghton Mifflin, 1908, p. 2.
11. Paul Nash, "Reading and the Professional Conscience," *AAUP Bulletin*, Volume XLVI, Number 4, December, 1960, p. 366.
12. *New York World-Telegram and Sun*, April 13, 1961, p. 35.
13. *The New York Times*, April 29, 1961, p. 25.
14. Richard Livingstone, *Some Thoughts on University Education*, New Haven: The Hazen Foundation, 1947, p. 12.
15. Jacques Barzun, *Teacher in America*, New York: Anchor Books, 1954, p. 25.
16. Ernest Earnest, *Academic Procession: An Informal History of the American College, 1636–1953*. New York: Bobbs-Merrill, 1953, p. 235.
17. Bruce R. Morris, "Faculty Salaries, Class Size, and Sound Education," *AAUP Bulletin*, Volume XLV, Number 2, June, 1959, p. 198.
18. Earnest, *op. cit.*, p. 157.
19. Mary McCarthy, *The Groves of Academe*, New York: Harcourt, Brace & World, 1952, p. 62.

Notes

20. Howard Mumford Jones, "The American Concept of Academic Freedom," *AAUP Bulletin*, Volume XLVI, Number 1, March, 1960, pp. 67–68.

21. Barzun, *op cit.*, pp. 187–188.

22. McCarthy, *op cit.*, p. 128.

23. Banesh Hoffmann, "The Tyranny of Multiple-Choice Tests," *Harper's Magazine*, Volume CCXXII, Number 1330, March, 1961, p. 37.

24. Charles Homer Haskins, *The Rise of Universities*, Ithaca: Cornell University, Press, 1957, p. 1.

25. Richard Hofstadter, *Academic Freedom in the Age of the College*, New York: Columbia University Press, 1961, p. 224.

26. George Boas, "The Three Magic Letters," *Pitt.* Volume XVI, Number 3, March, 1961, pp. 9–10.

27. *The New York Times*, April 29, 1961, p. 25.

28. *Ibid*, May 22, 1961, p. 33.

29. Granville Hicks, "Clarity, Clarity, Clarity," *Saturday Review*, Volume XLII, Number 32, August 1, 1959, p. 13. Also, James Reston on occasion has given concrete examples of the way in which the official language of the nations' leaders might be rewritten in plain English. *The New York Times*, July 27, 1958, p. 8E.

30. *Ibid*, January 9, 1961, p. 142.

31. McCarthy, *op. cit.*, p. 70.

32. Stephen Minot, "What a Seminar is Not," *AAUP Bulletin*, Volume XLIV, Number 4, December, 1958, p. 733.

33. Thus as Jacques Barzun says: "At a faculty meeting, a teacher asks the Director of Admissions why there seem to be more music students applying than before. The Director replies, 'Well, I should say that the forces undergirding the process are societal.' Or a Committee chairman wants to know what we do next. 'I think,' says the secretary, 'that we should go on to institute actual implementation.' " Barzun, *op. cit.*, p. 54. The usage here is not so much a special language as it is a stodgy formalistic expression in English.

34. Kingsley Amis, *Lucky Jim*, New York: Viking Press, 1953, p. 16.

35. Brooks Atkinson, "Critic at Large," *The New York Times*, September 1, 1961, p. 14.

36. Russell Kirk, "Is Social Science Scientific?" *The New York Times Magazine*, June 25, 1961, p. 11.

37. Robert K. Merton, "Now the Case for Sociology," *The New York Times Magazine*, July 16, 1961, p. 14.

38. C. P. Snow, *The Two Cultures, and the Scientific Revolution*, New York: Cambridge University Press, 1959.

39. Ernst Ekman, "The Program of a New University President of Three Hundred Years Ago," *AAUP Bulletin*, Volume XLVI, Number 4, December, 1960, p. 381.

40. Lloyd S. Woodburne, *Principles of College and University Administration*, Stanford: Stanford University Press, 1958, p. 67.

41. Robert Dubin, "Decision-Making by Management in Industrial Relations," *The American Journal of Sociology*, Volume LIV, Number 4, 1949, pp. 292–297.

42. Although the elimination of conflict is a primary objective of rules, it is not always the consequence. It has been shown that the post-Civil War

years were the most rebellious and undisciplined for students in colleges, yet never did the colleges have so many rules. *See:* Walter P. Metzger, *Academic Freedom in the Age of the University*, New York: Columbia University Press, p. 32.

43. Robert K. Merton, "Bureaucratic Structure and Personality," *Social Forces*, Volume XVIII, Number 4, 1940, p. 561.

44. Alvin W. Gouldner, "Discussion," *The American Sociological Review*, Volume XIII, Number 4, 1948, pp. 396–400.

45. Karl Mannheim, *Ideology and Utopia*, London: Routledge & Kegan Paul, 1948, p. 105.

46. Ralph H. Turner, "The Navy Disbursing Officer as a Bureaucrat," *The American Sociological Review*, Volume XII, Number 3, 1947, pp. 342–348.

CHAPTER 11

1. Max Weber, *The Theory of Social and Economic Organization*, translated by A. M. Henderson and Talcott Parsons, edited by Talcott Parsons, New York: Oxford University Press, 1947, p. 332.

2. C. Northcote Parkinson, "Parkinson's Law for Paper Work," *The New York Times Magazine*, July 26, 1959, p. 10.

3. *Ibid*, p. 10.

4. Geoffrey Murray, "Geneva," *The Christian Century*, Volume LXXVIII, Number 30, July 26, 1961, p. 913.

5. J. Donald Kingsley, "Executive Government," *Representative Bureaucracy*, Yellow Springs, Ohio: The Antioch Press, 1944, p. 265.

6. Ralph H. Turner, "The Navy Disbursing Officer as a Bureaucrat," *The American Sociological Review*, Volume XII, Number 3, 1947, pp. 342–348.

7. *The New York Times*, August 20, 1959, p. 5.

8. Thomas F. Tout, "The Emergence of a Bureaucracy," *The English Civil Service in the Fourteenth Century*, Manchester, England: University Press, 1916, Volume III, pp. 192–213.

9. *Ibid*, pp. 192–213.

10. Alvin W. Gouldner, "Red Tape as a Social Problem," in *Reader in Bureaucracy*, edited by Robert K. Merton, Ailsa P. Gray, Barbara Hockey, Hanan C. Selvin, New York: The Free Press, 1952, p. 410. I am deeply indebted to Professor Gouldner for a number of basic categories regarding red tape that are used in this chapter.

11. Edmund G. Love, *Arsenic and Red Tape*, New York: Harcourt, Brace & World, 1960.

12. J. M. Juran, *Bureaucracy: A Challenge to Better Management; a Constructive Analysis of Management Effectiveness in the Federal Government*, New York: Harper & Row, 1944, pp. 27–28.

13. Gouldner, *op cit.*, p. 418.

14. Peter M. Blau, *The Dynamics of Bureaucracy: A Study of Inter-Personal Relations in Two Government Agencies*, Chicago: University of Chicago Press, 1955, p. 206.

15. Carl J. Friedrich, "Some Observations on Weber's Analysis of Bu-

reaucracy," *Reader in Bureaucracy,* edited by Robert K. Merton, Ailsa P. Gray, Barbara Hockey, Hanan C. Seldon, New York: The Free Press, 1952, p. 29.

16. William J. Lederer, *A Nation of Sheep,* New York: W. W. Norton & Co., 1961, p. 110.

17. Robert H. Shaffer, "The Impact of Institutional Size and Complexity upon Student Personnel Services," Bloomington, Indiana: Indiana University, Mimeographed, p. 1.

18. Herbert A. Simon, "Decision-Making and Administrative Organization," *Public Administration Review,* Volume IV, Number 1, 1944, pp. 16–30.

19. H. E. Dale, *The Higher Civil Service of Great Britain,* New York: Oxford University Press, 1941, p. 30.

20. H. H. Gerth and C. Wright Mills, translators and editors, *From Max Weber: Essays in Sociology,* New York: Oxford University Press, 1946, p. 234.

21. Samuel A. Stouffer, Edward A. Suchman, Leland C. DeDinney, Shirley A. Star, and Robin M. Williams, Jr., *The American Soldier: Adjustment During Army Life,* Princeton: Princeton University Press, 1949, Volume I, pp. 291–401.

22. Chester I. Barnard, "Functions and Pathology of Status Systems in Formal Organizations," in *Industry and Society,* edited by William F. Whyte, New York: McGraw-Hill, 1946, pp. 64–68.

CHAPTER 12

1. Howard Nemerov, *The Homecoming Game,* New York: Simon and Schuster, 1957.

2. Frederic Morton, *Asphalt and Desire,* New York: Harcourt, Brace & World, 1952.

3. William Manchester, *The Long Gainer,* Boston: Little, Brown and Company, 1961.

4. Beardsley Ruml, *Memo to a College Trustee,* New York: McGraw-Hill, 1959.

5. John H. Crider, *The Bureaucrat,* Philadelphia: J. B. Lippincott Co., 1944, p. 39.

6. No special brief is held for the term "disabilities." Other terms quite properly might be used. One source, for example, refers to the "social pathologies of bureaucracy." *Reader in Bureaucracy,* edited by Robert K. Merton, Ailsa P. Gray, Barbara Hockey, Hanan C. Selvin, New York: The Free Press, 1952, pp. 396–397. Robert K. Merton speaks about the "dysfunctions" of bureaucracy. Robert K. Merton, "Bureaucratic Structure and Personality," *Social Forces,* Volume XVIII, Number 4, 1940, pp. 560–568. Chester I Barnard refers to "the pathological aspects of systems of status." Chester I. Barnard, "Functions and Pathology of Status Systems in Formal Organizations," in *Industry and Society,* edited by William F. Whyte, New York: McGraw-Hill, 1946, p. 71. Others use other terms. Particularly in the college is the failure to use available resources to study the problems of organization most apparent. Business, the military, and government have received by far the greatest amount of scientific as well as popular interest. Unfortu-

nately, the body of investigation on bureaucracies in general and their disabilities in particular is so scant that it would be unwise to be too dogmatic about terminology.

7. Walter Moberly in his classic statement, for example, includes a chapter on "Some Causes of our Present Discontent." Under this rubric he includes: shirking of fundamental issues, false neutrality, fragmentation, uncriticized presuppositions, and neglect of moral and spiritual factors. Walter Moberly, *The Crisis in the University*, London: SCM Press, 1949, pp. 50–70.

8. *Reader in Bureaucracy*, edited by Robert K. Merton, Ailsa P. Gray, Barbara Hockey, Hanan C. Selvin, New York: The Free Press, 1952, pp. 396–397.

9. Barnard, *op cit.*, p. 71.

10. Marshall E. Dimock, "Bureaucracy Self-Examined," *Public Administration Review*, Volume IV, Number 3, 1944, p. 198.

11. "Who Receives What and When?" *AAUP Bulletin*, Volume XLVI, Number 2, June, 1960, p. 232.

12. C. P. Snow, *The Two Cultures and the Scientific Revolution*, New York: Cambridge University Press, 1959.

13. Ibid, *The Affair*, New York: St. Martin's Press, 1960.

14. Edward H. Litchfield, "The University: A Congeries or an Organic Whole?" *AAUP Bulletin*, Volume XLV, Number 3, September, 1959, p. 375.

15. Mary McCarthy, *The Groves of Academe*, New York: Harcourt, Brace & World, 1952, pp. 66–67.

16. William Van O'Connor, *Campus on the River*, New York: Thomas Y. Crowell Co., 1959.

17. George Williams, *Some of My Best Friends are Professors: A Critical Commentary on Higher Education*, New York: Abelard-Schuman, 1958.

18. Irving Babbitt, *Literature and the American College*, Boston: Houghton Mifflin, 1908, p. 152.

19. Earl J. McGrath, *The Graduate School and the Decline of Liberal Education*, New York: Teachers College, Columbia University, Bureau of Publications, 1959.

20. Bernard Berelson, *Graduate Education in the United States*, New York: McGraw-Hill, 1960.

21. Philip Jacob, *Changing Values in College*, New York: Harper & Row, 1959.

22. Xenophon, *Memorabilia*, Book Four, Chapter Three, Translation by J. S. Watson, London: George Bell, 1891.

23. Herbert E. Hawkes and Anna L. R. Hawkes, *Through a Dean's Open Door*, New York: McGraw-Hill, 1945, pp. 190–191.

24. John W. Gardner, *Excellence: Can We Be Equal and Excellent Too?* New York: Harper & Row, 1961, p. 44.

25. A. Whitney Griswold, *Liberal Education and the Democratic Ideal and Other Essays*, New Haven: Yale University Press, 1959, p. 66.

26. Jackson Toby, "The American College Student: A Candidate for Socialization," *AAUP Bulletin*, Volume XLIII, Number 2, June, 1957, p. 321.

27. Ralph H. Turner, "The Navy Disbursing Officer as a Bureaucrat,"

Notes

The American Sociological Review, Volume XII, Number 3, 1947, pp. 342–348.

CHAPTER 13

1. May Sarton, *The Small Room,* New York: W. W. Norton, 1961.
2. *The New York Times,* August 3, 1961, p. 22.
3. Bernard I. Bell, *Crowd Culture: An Examination of the American Way of Life,* New York: Harper & Row, 1952.
4. George Derbner, "The Individual in a Mass Culture," *Saturday Review,* Volume XLIII, Number 25, June 18, 1960, p. 11.
5. Helmut Thielicke, *Nihilism: Its Origin and Nature—with a Christian Answer,* New York: Harper & Row, 1961, p. 18. Kafka's novels describe the lonely and frustrated individual in the grotesque world of uncaring organization. For example, Kafka, *The Trial,* translated by Willa and Andra Muir, New York: Alfred A. Knopf, 1937.
6. Hannah Arendt, *Between Past and Future: Six Exercises in Political Thought,* New York: The Viking Press, 1961.
7. Franz Neumann, *Behemoth: The Structure and Practice of National Socialism,* New York: Oxford University Press, 1942, pp 365–369.
8. Reinhard Bendix, "Bureaucracy and the Problem of Power," *Public Administration Review,* Volume V, Number 3, 1945, pp. 194–209.
9. Neumann, *op cit.;* Robert A. Brady, *Business as a System of Power,* New York: Columbia University Press, 1943.
10. Helmut Thielicke, *op cit.,* p. 45.
11. Peter M. Blau, *The Dynamics of Bureaucracy: A Study of Inter-Personal Relations in Two Government Agencies,* Chicago: The University of Chicago Press, 1955, p. 215.
12. Crawford H. Greenewalt, *The Uncommon Man: The Individual in the Organization,* New York: McGraw-Hill, 1959, p. 96.
13. *Anatomy of a Moral: The Political Essays of Milovan Djilas,* edited by Abraham Rothberg, with an introduction by Paul Willen, New York: Frederick A. Praeger, 1959.
14. Milovan Djilas, *The New Class,* New York: Frederick A. Praeger, 1957.
15. Hans H. Gerth, "The Nazi Party: Its Leadership and Composition," *The American Journal of Sociology,* Volume XLV, Number 4, 1940, pp. 517–541.
16. Carl J. Friedrich and Taylor Cole, *Responsible Bureaucracy: A Study of the Swiss Civil Service,* Cambridge: Harvard University Press, 1932, p. 28.
17. A. Whitney Griswold, *Liberal Education and the Democratic Ideal: And Other Essays,* New Haven: Yale University Press, 1959, p. 133.
18. "Report of the Committee on Professional Ethics," *AAUP Bulletin,* Volume XLIV, Number 4, December, 1958, p. 782.
19. Hans H. Gerth and C. Wright Mills, "A Marx for the Managers," *Ethics,* Volume LII, Number 2, Jauuary, 1942, p. 207.
20. Hans H. Gerth, *op cit.,* p. 517–541.
21. John H. Crider. *The Bureaucrat,* Philadelphia: J. B. Lippincott Co., 1944, p. 54.

22. Charles Homer Haskins, *The Rise of the Universities*, Ithaca: Cornell University Press, 1957, p. 24.

23. Beardsley Ruml, *Memo to a College Trustee*, New York: McGraw-Hill, 1959, p. 61.

24. Paul S. Lazarsfeld and Wagner Thielens, Jr., *The Academic Mind*, New York: The Free Press, 1958, p. 166.

25. Seymour Martin Lipset, *Agrarian Socialism*, Berkeley: University of California Press, 1950, p. 267.

26. Robert Michels, *Political Parties*, New York: The Free Press, 1949, p. 189.

27. Robert K. Merton, "The Unanticipated Consequences of Purposive Social Action," *American Sociological Review*, Volume I, Number 6, 1936, pp. 894–904.

28. *Ibid*, "Bureaucratic Structure and Personality." *Social Forces*, Volume XVIII, Number 4, 1940, p. 564.

29. Michels, *op cit.*, pp. 185–189.

30. Walter Lippmann, *Essays in The Public Philosophy*, Boston: Little, Brown, 1955.

31. Michael Young, *The Rise of the Meritocracy: 1870–2033: The New Elite of our Social Revolution*, New York: Random House, 1959.

32. Herbert A. Simon, *Administrative Behavior*, New York: Macmillan Co., 1945, pp. 110–119.

33. Ernst Troeltsch, *The Social Teaching of the Christian Churches*, New York: Macmillan Co., 1931, Volume I, p. 331.

34. Peter M. Blau, *op cit.*, pp. 201–202.

35. Marshall E. Dimock, "Bureaucracy Self-Examined," *Public Administration Review*, Volume IV, Number 3, 1944, p. 205.

Index

academic freedom, 110, 213–214
accrediting associations, 89–90
administration and administrators, 78–79; definition of, 103; power of, 79; *see also* dean of college; governing board; president of college
administrative tyranny, 13
admission procedures and impersonality, 151–152
advancement, *see* promotions
advantages of bureaucracy, 8–11, 18, 47–48
American Association of University Professors, 89; committee of, 48, 211, 224n, 236n
Army, and communication, restraints placed upon, 182; and higher education, influence upon, 37
authority, 124, 210; and bureaucratic aggressiveness, 131–132; definition of, 22, 130; in functional systems, 96–97, 98; hierarchy of, 21, 38; *see also* hierarchies of bureaucracies; limitations of, 21, 22; restraints upon, 21–22, in scalar system, 95–96, 97–98, 129–131; zone of indifference, 131; *see also* power

buck-passing, 103
bureaucracy, continuance of, 6–7; definition of, vii, 3, 12–14, 23; description of, 14–26; hugeness of, 4; and ideal-types, 23; improvement of, 6; objectives of, 16; origins of in college, 75–76; overextension of, 4
business, influenced by higher education, 37–38; influence upon higher education, 27–31, 33, 37; and paper work, 167; specialization of personnel, 28–29

ceremonialism, 136–144; and fads, 141–143; methods of, 137–141; reasons for, 136–137
chairman, department, 83, 210
change, possibilities for, 217–221
character building in higher education, 198–199
charisma, 105, 133–136; bureaucracy and, 133–134; definition of, 133; in higher education, 134, 135–136; rationalism and, 134–135
church, influence upon higher education, 33–35, 37; paper work, 167
church-sect analogy, 220
church-type college, 220
classroom, and impersonality, 152–156
college, *see* higher education
College Center of the Finger Lakes, 219
college officeholder, 41–55; and conservatism, 214–215; and generalism, 203; and goal displacement, 215–217; informally organized, 41; motivations of, 98–99; nature of office, 41–42; qualifications of, 42–51; questions for investigation, 53–55; salary of, 44; as a social type, 41, 47, 50–53; as source of disability, 195–197; and status, ways to increase, 60–63; *see also* promotions; style of life, 46–47; and success, 213; *see also* faculty member
communication, 98, 177–184; in college, 177–184; conditions for effectiveness of, 183–184; and red tape, 177; and technical language, 161
Communism, and bureaucracy, 5–6, 208–209
community, and bureaucratization, 206–208; and college relationships, 109–110, 203–205; as a force in